Teaching Cognates/*Cognados* Through Picture Books

Teaching Cognates/*Cognados* Through Picture Books

Resources for Fostering Spanish–English Vocabulary Connections

by

José A. Montelongo, Ph.D.
Anita Hernández, Ph.D.

and

Roberta J. Herter, Ph.D.

·P A U L·H·
BROOKES
PUBLISHING C?®

Baltimore • London • Sydney

Paul H. Brookes Publishing Co.
Post Office Box 10624
Baltimore, Maryland 21285-0624
USA

www.brookespublishing.com

Typeset by Progressive Publishing Services, York, Pennsylvania.
Manufactured in the United States of America by Integrated Books International, Inc., Dulles, Virginia.

The individuals described in this book are composites or real people whose situations are masked and are based on the authors' experiences. In all instances, names and identifying details have been changed to protect confidentiality.

Purchasers of *Teaching Cognates/Cognados Through Picture Books: Resources for Fostering Spanish–English Vocabulary Connections* are granted permission to access the online companion website titled the Cognate Companion for educational purposes. The website may not be used to generate revenue for any program or individual. See the Accessing the Cognate Companion Website page for details on how to access the site.

Cover photo by Javier Calderon/jaipixesphotography.

Library of Congress Cataloging-in-Publication Data

Names: Montelongo, José, 1974- author. | Hernandez, Anita, author. | Herter, Roberta J., author.
Title: Teaching cognates/cognados through picture books : resources for fostering Spanish—English vocabulary
     connections / by José A. Montelongo, Anita Hernández, and Roberta J. Herter.
Description: Baltimore : Paul H. Brookes Publishing Co., [2023] | Includes bibliographical references.
Identifiers: LCCN 2022036100 (print) | LCCN 2022036101 (ebook) | ISBN 9781934000458 (paperback) |
     ISBN 9781681256924 (epub) | ISBN 9781681256931 (pdf)
Subjects: LCSH: English language—Study and teaching (Elementary)—Spanish speakers. |
     Spanish language—Study and teaching (Elementary)—English speakers. | English language—Cognate words. |
     Spanish language—Cognate words. | Picture books for children—Educational aspects—United States. |
     Education, Bilingual—United States.
Classification: LCC PE1129.S8 M54 2023 (print) | LCC PE1129.S8 (ebook) | DDC 468.3/421—dc23/eng/20220909
LC record available at https://lccn.loc.gov/2022036100
LC ebook record available at https://lccn.loc.gov/2022036101

British Library Cataloguing in Publication data are available from the British Library.

2027   2026   2025   2024   2023

10   9   8   7   6   5   4   3   2   1

Contents

Accessing the Cognate Companion Website

The Cognate Companion website is an online resource to help teachers integrate cognate instruction into their regular content-area instruction. The Cognate Companion is a rich, searchable database of hundreds of award-winning picture books and the cognates found in these books. It also includes access to more than 300 brief cognate lesson plans than accompany the picture books, as well as with other useful downloads. The lesson plans are mentioned throughout this book in the Lesson Plan sidebars.

Purchasers of *Teaching Cognates/Cognados through Picture Books* are granted permission to access the Cognate Companion website for educational purposes.

To access the Cognate Companion:

1. Go to the Cognate Companion website https://brookespublishing.com/montelongo

2. Register to create an account and login.

3. Read the "How to Use the Cognate Companion Website" before getting started.

About the Authors

José A. Montelongo, Ph.D.

José A. Montelongo has taught reading and been a school librarian in El Paso for over 15 years prior to becoming a college librarian, teacher educator, and educational researcher. He has earned degrees in experimental psychology, education, and library science at University of Texas at El Paso, New Mexico State, and University of Texas at Austin, respectively. Dr. Montelongo's research and writing interests focus on Spanish–English cognate vocabulary, reading expository text, and school librarianship.

Anita Hernández, Ph.D.

Anita Hernández is Professor and the Don and Sarrah Kidd Endowed Chair in Literacy in the Department of Teacher Preparation and Administration and Leadership at New Mexico State University. She was a bilingual teacher for 14 years and has taught future teachers and classroom teachers for the past 24 years. She earned her Ph.D. in Language, Literacy, and Culture at Stanford University. She teaches and publishes in the areas of teacher education, biliteracy, and critical literacy. She is co-author of *Interactive Student Notebooks for English Learners, Text Sets: Scaffolding Core Literature for Secondary Students,* and *Viva Nuestro Caucus: Re-Writing the Forgotten Pages of our Caucus.*

Roberta J. Herter, Ph.D.

Roberta J. Herter taught English in Detroit Public Schools for 30 years, then went on to teach educators at Cal Poly, San Luis Obispo for 20 years. She earned her Ph.D. in English and Education at the University of Michigan. Her research and writing include literacy, writing, and second language learning.

Preface

Spanish–English cognates/*cognados* are words that possess identical or nearly identical spellings and meanings in both languages. For example, the English words, "person" and "transportation," are cognates of the Spanish words, *persona* and *transportación*, because of their respective Latinate origins. These words are among the more than 20,000 cognates in the English language, many of which are academic vocabulary words essential for reading and comprehending school texts. Systematic cognate instruction can strengthen the English and Spanish academic vocabulary of students from Spanish-speaking and bilingual homes, as well as that of students from English-speaking homes who are learning Spanish at school.

Not surprisingly, language educators have long been in favor of teaching Spanish–English cognates to bilingual learners—emergent and experienced—because of the ease with which the orthographically transparent words can be learned. To date, however, cognate instruction has generally been sporadic; rarely integrated coherently into content-area instruction. This book provides the first systematic and comprehensive guide to Spanish–English cognate instruction and assessment for bilingual teachers working in elementary classrooms, in bilingual (using two languages for instructional purposes) and in English-medium (primarily using English for instructional purpose) programs. A distinguishing feature of this book is that it is also for monolingual English-speaking teachers who work with diverse Spanish–English bilingual learners, and who see cognates as an important way to honor and enrich the oral and written Spanish language resources their students bring to the classroom.

This professional learning guide includes access to a companion website that we refer to as the *Cognate Companion*, a searchable database that is organized around the titles of more than 3,000 award-winning picture books. Teachers can search the Cognate Companion for picture books by title, author, subject, and reading-level to find appropriate picture books and all of their cognates, prefixes, roots, suffixes, reading levels, and subject areas. The Cognate Companion also includes access to "snap-on" cognate lesson plans that can easily be integrated into teachers' regular lesson plans, as well as a template with step-by-step directions for customizing instruction to address students' needs more precisely.

BENEFITS OF COGNATE INSTRUCTION

There are several benefits of cognate instruction and assessment for students. First, as students learn to recognize cognates and cognate parts, they can dramatically increase their academic vocabulary in both English and Spanish, which is an important part of academic biliteracy. Teaching emerging bilingual learners about Spanish–English cognates can also elevate the status of Spanish at school and help legitimize the Spanish language as a significant resource to be valued and learned, not only in bilingual classrooms but also in English-medium classrooms. Further, by using the book and its database, teachers can help their students unveil the morphological, orthographic, and semantic relationships between the English and Spanish languages, thereby providing them with a foundation for developing their metalinguistic awareness, knowledge, and skills.

There are also benefits of our approach to teaching cognates using picture books for teachers. This book and its Cognate Companion website work together as a professional learning guide and resource for teachers, instructional coaches, librarians, curriculum developers, consultants, and assessment and evaluation specialists who expect their bilingual students to develop strong academic vocabulary across content-areas in two languages. At least as important, college and university teacher educators can use this book and its Cognate Companion to introduce preservice teachers and graduate students to the use of Spanish–English cognates to develop academic vocabulary across two languages. Cognates can be an invaluable resource for creating rich instructional materials and lessons that will result in the advancement of schoolchildren's linguistic and meta-linguistic abilities.

THE AUTHORS

This book and its Cognate Companion arose from the authors' experiences as reading and writing teachers. As a reading teacher and school librarian who prided himself on developing his own materials and lessons, Dr. José Montelongo has introduced many elementary school students and their teachers to Spanish–English cognates through picture book read-alouds and vocabulary lessons to accompany the readings. Classically trained in the methods of cognitive psychology, he has also designed and conducted research studies on learning and memory for Spanish–English cognates and has written several articles on cognates.

Dr. Anita Hernández is a research professor of education with expertise in language, literacy, and culture. The principal investigator of several federal professional development grants, Dr. Hernández stresses the need for her preservice students and in-service teachers to incorporate Spanish–English cognates in both monolingual English and bilingual classrooms. She has also co-authored several articles and books on cognates and culturally relevant texts.

Dr. Roberta Herter—a professor, teacher educator, and high school English teacher who is monolingual in English—has been a strong advocate for incorporating cognate instruction with her secondary preservice students. She, too, has co-authored many articles on Spanish–English cognates.

In our experiences as classroom teachers and teacher educators, we have found that Spanish–English cognates have not received the attention they deserve in today's language classrooms. Language and content-area textbooks devote few, if any, lessons on cognates. As a result, the teachers we have encountered in college classrooms, schools, and educational conferences are often unfamiliar with cognates or their importance as academic vocabulary words or their language development potential for emergent bilingual learners.

As schoolteachers and teacher educators with degrees in bilingual education, literacy, English, library science, and psychology, we have endeavored to create a book and database as resources for elementary school classroom teachers and students learning in two languages. Our aim is to expand the teaching and learning of vocabulary by incorporating Spanish–English cognates through picture book instructional contexts, whether they are fluent in Spanish or not. We also want to expand the teaching of cognates from understanding them to identifying their morphological patterns and ways for all teachers to incorporate them in content-area units of study, with the goal of tapping into students' linguistic backgrounds and developing metalinguistic awareness about their two languages.

HOW TO USE THIS BOOK AND ITS COGNATE COMPANION WEBSITE

We wrote this book and its Cognate Companion so that the resources can be used by individual teachers as well as groups of teachers in professional learning communities. The chapters in the book are meant to provide individual teachers or groups with methods for teaching Spanish–English cognates. The first three chapters present strategies for introducing students to cognates and incorporating them in vocabulary lessons and activities to accompany picture book read-alouds. Chapters 4, 5, and 6 include methods for using concept induction to teach rules for converting cognate prefixes, root words, suffixes, and spelling patterns from Spanish to English and the converse. The final chapters, assist in planning cognate lessons and thematic units using picture books. Illustrative lesson plans and example content-area thematic units for various elementary grades are included. The final chapter presents an example cognate unit of instruction, which can be modified for different grade levels.

To facilitate the creation of cognate lesson plans, we searched through thousands of award-winning picture books and recorded every one of the Spanish–English cognates found in each selected book, and listed those on the Cognate Companion website. This resource will permit teachers to plan cognate lessons regardless of their own Spanish or English proficiency. And because the cognates are drawn from popular picture books, they represent a vocabulary pool of words that reflect current themes and content-area subjects appropriate for elementary school students.

In addition to the listing of the Spanish–English cognates from award-winning picture books that can readily be found in school and public libraries, the Cognate Companion also provides a breakdown of the Spanish–English cognates into their morphological elements. Because the great majority of Spanish–English cognates are Latinate or Greek in origin, teachers can use this feature of the database to plan lessons for essential prefixes, root words, and suffixes.

Teachers we work with notice the facilitative effects that teaching Spanish–English cognates has on spelling. They see an improvement in students' spelling because of the specific rules for converting English words to Spanish words. The Cognate Companion includes a field for selecting rule-governed cognates to assist in creating lesson plans.

As a time-saving measure, we created more than 300 ready-to-use lesson plans for Spanish, English, and/or bilingual picture books. The lesson plans include activities such as using context clues, creating flashcards, teaching morphology, making crossword puzzles, and engaging in sentence-completion exercises to help students expand their knowledge of cognates. Explore the Cognate Companion and its many curricular features. We pledge to add to the current list of award-winning picture books and the cognates they contain by including future award-winning books, more lesson plans, and further activities to promote the teaching and learning of Spanish–English cognates and the patterns that govern them. Watch the Cognate Companion website for these developments.

José A. Montelongo,
Anita Hernández,
Roberta J. Herter

For the Reader

A Guide to This Book's Formatting Conventions

This book uses particular formatting conventions to capture the Spanish and English languages, cognate rules, and components of language discussed throughout this text. To facilitate your reading experience, we have listed those formatting conventions below for your reference.

GLOSSARY TERMS

Bolded words in this book are terms that are defined in the Glossary. See the back matter of this book to find those definitions.

LANGUAGES: ENGLISH AND SPANISH

Throughout the book, English text and scripts are set in a Roman (plain) font. Spanish text and scripts are set in italic font.

BOOK TITLES

The titles of picture books are underlined to set them off. While book titles are typically italicized, we chose to underline in order to distinguish them from the italicized Spanish text.

COGNATE RULES

Similarly for cognate pairs, the English cognate will be set in Roman font, whereas the Spanish cognate will be in italics. Pairs are indicated by a slash between them (e.g., famous/*famoso*). Cognate parts use the same Roman and italics convention and are set in slashes (e.g., */des-/* for Spanish and /dis-/ for English).

COMPONENTS OF LANGUAGE

When letters (graphemes) are discussed, this book uses quotation marks around the letter in English, but angle brackets for the letter in Spanish (e.g., "c" as in "cat" vs. «*g*» in «*gato*»). The same convention is used for full words.

When phonemes (i.e., units of sound in language) are discussed, the book uses square brackets for phonetic transcription (e.g., [k] as in "cat").

Acknowledgments

Writing a book for educators is a collaborative endeavor. Many thanks to our editors and colleagues, Dr. Rebecca Field and Charles Field, whose nurturing guidance informed this work. We are also thankful to the editors at Brookes Publishing Co. and Caslon, Inc., especially Liz Gildea and Nicole Schmidl, for supporting us through this book and database project.

We would like to acknowledge the many colleagues, teachers, graduate students, librarians, and principals who helped make this work possible. We would especially like to acknowledge the faculties at Magoffin Middle School, Douglass Elementary School, and Deanna Davenport Elementary School in the El Paso, Texas area. Likewise, we would like to acknowledge the help of the many schools in the Hatch Valley School District (Michael Chávez), the Gadsden Independent School District (Travis Dempsey, María Hernández, Jorge Araújo), the Las Cruces Independent School District in New Mexico (Dr. Roberto Lozano, Carla Rodriguez Reagan, and Dr. Aine Garcia Post), and the Guadalupe Joint Union School District, Guadalupe, California for facilitating our work with teachers and students in their school district.

Graduate students are important for growing knowledge in the field. We would like to acknowledge the graduate students at New Mexico State University who contributed to new knowledge about Spanish–English cognates: Dr. Francisco Javier Serrano-Wall, Dr. Hillary Vozza, Dr. Yvonne Martínez, Dr. Paulo Oemig, as well as our current graduate students: Ignocencia Campos, Ida Madrid, Laura Urbina, Joseph Mata, Sylvia Nájera, Maricela Rincón, and Elisa Holguín.

We are especially grateful to the teachers: Pat Minjares, Rita Holguín, Rosa Delgado, Eliana Esquivel, and Sonia Chávez in New Mexico, as well as Jaime Cuello, Tino Alemán, Rosario Aronie, Julee Bauer, Rosie García, Martha García, María González, Camelia Ortiz-Álvarez, and Sal Reynoso in California.

We would also like to acknowledge the librarians and assistants at the various branches of the El Paso Public Library and the Thomas Branigan Library in Las Cruces for their assistance in the acquisition of the many award-winning picture books included in the Cognate Companion.

Thanks also to the following individuals:

- Mr. Carlos Montelongo for his expertise and help with computer technology throughout the years

- Our special colleagues: Dr. Kay Wijekumar, Dr. Richard Durán, Dr. Patricia Davidman, the late Dr. Leonard Davidman, Dr. Sue McBride, Dr. O.D. Hadfield, Dr. Suchint Sarangarm, Navjit Brar, Douglas Gates, Barbara Schaeder, Lynn Gamble, Laura Blanco, José Cabrales, John Wheatley, and the late Mike Payán

- The many authors of children's books for their creative genius in making this genre so pleasurable for children and grown-ups

Most importantly, this book is for the bilingual learners whose experiences, languages, and knowledge have for so long been relegated to the "back of the classroom."

In memory of my mentor, Dr. Edmund B. Coleman, psychologist, researcher,
and statistician par excellence, and of my father, Mr. José A. Montelongo, Sr. —JAM
For my children: Analicia, José Alejandro, Marco Antonio, and Juan Andrés, and for my
grandchildren: Madison Rose, Andrew Matthew, Joseph Noah, and Jude Alexander. —JAM

To Mrs. Sarrah Kidd, the Kidd Family, and in memory of Mr. Don Kidd for his contributions
to the Literacy programs at New Mexico State University and throughout the state. —ACH
To my mentors, Dr. Guadalupe Valdés and Dr. Kenji Hakuta. —ACH
For my family and all of their support and love: Rosa and Aurelio
Hernández, my brothers, nieces and nephews, and the Pindter family. —ACH

To Anne Ruggles Gere and the memory of Jay Luke Robinson, who
inspired a second career and the pleasure of lifelong literacy learning. —RJH

1

The Power of Cognates for Bilingual Learners

OBJECTIVES

☐ Define cognates and explain why they are an important category of words.

☐ Discuss how Spanish–English cognates became part of the English language.

☐ Describe how teachers can use picture books to teach Spanish–English cognates.

☐ Explain how teaching cognates can enhance the vocabulary development of bilingual learners.

Cognate Play

LESSON PLAN

Side by Side/*Lado a lado:* The Story of Dolores Huerta and César Chávez/*Lado a lado: La historia de Dolores Huerta y César Chávez*
(Brown, 2010)

As an introductory activity to the book, we ask that you read the English and Spanish texts below, taken from a page of the bilingual picture book, Side by Side/*Lado a lado:* The Story of Dolores Huerta and César Chávez/*La historia de Dolores Huerta y César Chávez* by Monica Brown:

"Dolores and Cesar drove from town to town, standing on the back of flatbed trucks and inviting farmworkers to join la causa, the cause for justice. Together they demanded better living working conditions for the farmworkers."

«*Dolores y César fueron de pueblo en pueblo. Se paraban en las plataformas de los camiones e invitaban a los campesinos a unirse a la causa a favor de la justicia. Juntos exigieron mejores condiciones de trabajo y de vida para los campesinos.*»

Now, reread the texts above and find the pairs of English and Spanish words that are the same or nearly the same in both spelling and meaning in the **bilingual** texts. Did you find inviting/*invitando*, cause/*causa*, justice/*justicia*, and conditions/*condiciones*? There is a special term for words that are similar in spelling and meaning in both Spanish and English—**cognates.**

As an English speaker reading a Spanish text or as a Spanish speaker reading an English text, you have probably noted the occurrences of cognates and treated them simply as random coincidences. You may be surprised to learn that there are more than 20,000 such Spanish–English cognates. And if you're like most of the teachers we've encountered in our work, you may even ask yourself the question, "Why was I never explicitly taught about these words in school, or in my teacher education program?"

This book is about teaching Spanish-English cognates in the elementary grades. Teaching them early and often. Not as a once-in-a-semester topic as is often the case in textbooks, but as an important component of the vocabulary lessons explicitly taught to students. Just the sheer number of cognates in the English language merits their inclusion in the vocabulary curriculum. But there is more to cognates than that. Teaching students, all students, about Spanish–English cognates enriches their vocabulary development because of their importance for academic literacy. Cognates comprise from one-third to one-half of an educated person's vocabulary. They also make up a sizable portion of the academic vocabulary found in the disciplines at all grade levels, from the early primary grades to the college years. And because they are ubiquitous throughout the academic curriculum teachers can begin cognate instruction as early as Grades K–5 through the medium of picture books.

Teaching Spanish–English cognates can be particularly advantageous to **bilingual learners**. This term includes students from Spanish-speaking homes who are learning English at school, students from English-speaking homes who are learning Spanish at school, as well as students who come from bilingual homes, can speak Spanish and English, but are mostly seen as English speakers at school. These diverse bilingual learners bring a wide range of expertise in oral and written English and Spanish that teachers can build on to dramatically expand their vocabulary. Because Spanish speakers learning English have developed a sizable Spanish vocabulary, they are able to recognize and acquire those English cognates that resemble the Spanish words they already know. Similarly, English speakers learning Spanish benefit from recognizing and learning cognates that are similar to the English words they know. Since cognates have so much potential for students learning English or Spanish as a new language, we believe that teaching them to bilingual learners can be a game changer for these students.

Teachers who use this book will learn strategies for integrating cognate instruction into their regular content-area instruction, in their bilingual and general education classrooms. To inform and enrich their work, we have created the Cognate Companion database. See the Accessing the Cognate Companion Website page in the front matter of the book for guidance on accessing the site.

The Cognate Companion is a rich resource that includes thousands of award-winning picture book titles and the cognates found in those books, and it is organized into three major components. We refer to the first component as the Find-a-Cognate database; teachers and students can use this feature to determine whether a word in English or Spanish is a cognate, and if so, to identify its cognate in English or Spanish. The second component of the Cognate Companion is the picture book directory, which allows teachers to search the database for picture books and the cognates they include, and select picture books that will be appropriate for their content-area instruction. The third component of the Cognate Companion includes cognate lesson plans for teaching cognate vocabulary that accompany more than 300 of the picture books in the database. We refer to each brief lesson plan as a **snap-on cognate lesson plan** because it can be integrated easily into content-area instruction. Every picture book discussed in this book has a lesson plan for it on the Cognate Companion; teachers will find **Lesson Plan** callouts throughout the book directing their attention to some of these lesson plans. Teachers can also use the Cognate Companion to create their own lessons. We include a brief cognate lesson planning template later in this book that teachers can use to create cognate lessons for their own classes.

Did you know?

There are more than 300 cognate lesson plans that accompany some of the picture books on the Cognate Companion. All of the picture books mentioned in this book have accompanying cognate lesson plans which teachers can adapt and use with their classes.

This chapter begins with a brief introduction to Spanish–English cognates, with attention to the history of the English and Spanish languages and how they relate to each other. Next, we explain how students who are learning English, Spanish, or both can benefit from the inclusion of cognates in the curriculum. We further suggest that all teachers, regardless of their English and Spanish proficiency, can use cognates as part of their interdisciplinary vocabulary instruction using the common literary practice of the picture book read-aloud and its associated activities. Finally, we look at Spanish–English cognates through the lens of the three-tier vocabulary system suggested by Beck et al. (2002; 2008), for selecting the words to include in their lessons.

WHAT ARE SPANISH–ENGLISH COGNATES?

Thus far, we have provided only a general idea of what cognates are. A more precise definition is that Spanish–English **cognates** are words that are spelled identically or similarly in both English and Spanish and possess the same or nearly the same meanings in both languages as a result of a shared **etymology**—the origin of a word and the historical development of its meaning. The following English and Spanish word pairs are examples of cognates: chocolate/*chocolate*, family/*familia*, mathematics/*matemáticas*, rapidly/*rápidamente*, and suspension/*suspensión*. Other languages share cognates (e.g., English-Italian, Spanish-French), but in this book we focus on word pairs that are similar in Spanish and English.

Spanish–English cognates possess varying degrees of similarity. Some are identical in the way they are spelled in both English and Spanish: actor/*actor*, horrible/*horrible*, and festival/*festival*. Others are spelled similarly: attract/*atraer*, button/*botón*, and normally/*normalmente*. Some cognates are so dissimilar it is difficult to believe they're cognates—as in the cases of autumn/*otoño* and flame/*llama*. Furthermore, cognates often differ in pronunciation, regardless of whether they are orthographically identical, similar, or different.

Some cognates are basic frequent words that need no instruction as to their meanings: elephant/*elefante*, family/*familia*, and tomato/*tomate*. Others are **academic vocabulary** words, which are traditionally used in scholarly dialogue and text and require explicit teacher-directed instruction such as congress/*congreso*, energy/*energía*, and triangle/*triángulo*. One important feature of this book is that it introduces teachers to rules for transforming Spanish words to their English cognates, as well as English words to their Spanish cognates.

When cognates are incorporated in instruction, students can develop both their **cognate recognition skills** and their **cognate generation skills.** That is, they can learn to guess the meanings of unfamiliar words and produce cognates in English or Spanish for increasing their understanding of texts. Furthermore, by learning rules for transforming words from one language to another, students will be able to correctly generate words in English or Spanish without explicit instruction, or at least offer an educated guess that may be understood by their listeners. The obvious similarities between Spanish–English cognates makes them natural vocabulary builders for all students wanting to learn English, Spanish, or both.

Using Cognates in the Classroom

We have been fortunate to work in diverse bilingual and **dual language classrooms** with bilingual and monolingual English-speaking teachers who provide their students with cognate instruction. This first vignette introduces two of these teachers, and the dialogue is illustrative of the types of interactions teachers have with their colleagues and their students.

In the vignette, we observe an experienced teacher mentoring a new colleague on the use of Spanish–English cognates at the beginning of the school term. Mrs. García teaches the Spanish language component of the first-grade dual language curriculum and Ms. Holcomb teaches the English language component. Mrs. García is bilingual and has more than 20 years of experience, while Ms. Holcomb is a monolingual English speaker with little experience working with students who are in early stages of English language development. Through the dialogue we learn one way that Mrs. García and Ms. Holcomb work together to improve instruction for bilingual learners whose home language is Spanish and who are just beginning to learn English at school:

Mrs. García: Are you all set for the little ones coming in on Monday?

Ms. Holcomb: I think so. I'm just a little worried about how to teach some of the students who don't speak much English. Do you have any suggestions?

Mrs. García: One of the things that works really well with my students is to introduce them to cognates. Do you know about cognates?

Ms. Holcomb: Are they the words that mean the same in Spanish and English?

Mrs. García: Exactly. They're great for helping kids learn vocabulary. I always point them out when I do a read-aloud of a picture book. The students like them because they are easy to learn. They also like the fact that their Spanish can help them.

The exchange between Mrs. García and Ms. Holcomb highlights an important point we have found in our work with teachers: those who have taught their students about Spanish–English cognates are often the best advocates for teaching these powerful vocabulary words.

The History of Spanish–English Cognates

Since cognates happen to be identical or similar in the English and Spanish languages, teachers and students might ask how these words came to be a part of the English language. To answer this question, we should first state that the most frequent English words have their roots in the Germanic languages spoken by the early English peoples. Spanish, like French and Italian, is a Latin-based language. Over the centuries, Latin-based words have entered into the English language as a result of the contact between the English people and their neighbors who spoke a Latinate language. Many of these words are the cognates we will introduce in this book. Important periods in the history of the English language are presented in Figure 1.1.

As we can see in Figure 1.1, English and Spanish originated in different branches of the Indo-European family of languages. English belongs to the Germanic branch of the Indo-European language family (via West Germanic and Old English) while Spanish is a member of the Italic—later Latin—branch of that same family.

Modern English (1700–Present)
Borrowings from Latin and Greek today were not present in the classical periods but are created from Latin and Greek prefixes, root words, and suffixes (Brinton & Arnovick, 2006).

Early Modern English (1500–1700 AD)
Latin and Greek words were the chief sources of new words during the Early Modern English period. Among them are the cognates "catalogue," "museum," and "orchestra" (Carver, 1991).

Middle English (1100–1500 AD)
The French-Speaking Normans conquered England in 1066 CE. As a result, over 10,000 Latinate words were introduced into the English Language (Baugh & Cable, 2012). Many of these words are the Spanish-English cognates we use today: "battle," "justice," and "romance."

Old English (450–1100 AD)
Approximately 450 Latinate words were introduced into England by Christian missionaries. Most prominent among these were words related to religion such as "altar," "mass," and "temple" (Carver, 1991).

(Before 450 AD)
Latinate words such as "mile," "plant," and "wine" were borrowed from the Romans, who shared a peaceful coexistence with the Celts (Brinton & Arnovick, 2006).

Figure 1.1.   Important periods in the history of the English language.

Prior to 450 A.D., the Romans and the Celts lived in close proximity to each other. Several Latin-based Spanish–English cognates became part of the English language and are still used today: mile/*milla*, plant/*planta*, and wine/*vino*.

Old English, which was spoken between 450 A.D. and 1100 A.D., evolved from the language brought to Britain by the Germanic tribes. The Old English of this time period was almost purely Germanic (e.g., "mile," "plant," "wine"). Latin words related to religion were introduced by Catholic missionaries in the seventh and eighth centuries, some of which are present-day Spanish–English cognates. Examples of these include altar/*altar*, disciple/*discípulo*, and mass/*misa*.

The Norman conquest of Britain in 1066 A.D. by William the Conqueror, brought a great influx of French words to English in the period now known as Middle English (1100 A.D. to 1500 A.D.). The Norman Vikings spoke French which, like Spanish, is a Latin-based language. It is estimated that over 10,000 French words entered into the English language during this period (Baugh & Cable, 2012), and approximately 75% of them are still used today (Carver, 1991). Among the Spanish–English cognates that entered into English during this period were calendar/*calendario*, dragon/*dragón*, and talent/*talento*.

The French words that entered English reflected the high status of the Norman conquerors, especially in the areas of government, law, the military, and church affairs (Baugh & Cable, 2012). Cognates such as battle/*batalla*, justice/*justicia*, sermon/*sermón*, and state/*estado* can be traced to the elevated positions held by the Normans in English life. Befitting their social status, the Normans lived well and the French words that entered into the English language reflect their lofty positions in society. Cognates such as feast/*festín*, lemon/*limón*, and pork/*puerco* are French in origin, as are castle/*castillo*, mansion/*mansión*, melody/*melodía*, and romance/*romance* (Brinton & Arnovick, 2006). During this period of French supremacy, Old English existed as a lower-class dialect spoken mostly by the peasants, artisans, and laborers (Brinton & Arnovick, 2006).

The Modern English Period (1700 A.D. to the present), is still influenced by Latin and Greek. However, many of these new words were created from the Latin and Greek prefixes, root words, and suffixes (Brinton & Arnovick, 2006). That is, they did not come directly from the Latin and Greek of the classical period. Furthermore, new English words are constantly being borrowed from other languages. Some of these, too, eventually become English–Spanish cognates as they are incorporated by these two languages.

THE IMPORTANCE OF TEACHING COGNATES

Today, the influence of history is still being felt, and it manifests itself everywhere in the vocabulary students learn in school, in the speech we use to communicate, and in the books we read. Due, in part, to the social structures of Norman-controlled England, the majority of the most frequent words in the English language (e.g., "book," "love," "woman") are of Germanic origin, while the preponderance of academic words (e.g., "analysis," "community," "symbol") are Latinate in origin, reinforcing the case for integrating cognate study into the curriculum today.

Accelerating Academic Vocabulary Development

Since Latin was the language of scholarship for much of the history of the Western world up until the 1800s, many of the Spanish–English cognates are academic vocabulary words (Hiebert & Lubliner, 2008). Cognates are the words teachers and students encounter in their content area textbooks. They are the words in boldface type that are often defined in textbook glossaries. Of the 570 words on the Coxhead (2000) Academic Word List, 82% or 465 are Spanish–English cognates. The importance of cognates also is evident at the library. An analysis of the Dewey Decimal System, by which books in school and public libraries are arranged, reveals that the majority of subject headings (e.g., mathematics/*matemáticas*, philosophy/ *filosofía*, religion/*religión*) are Spanish–English cognates (Montelongo, 2012).

   Cognate instruction allows students to strengthen connections between their home language and what they are learning in English across all content areas. We know that strong language and literacy skills—not only in English but in their home languages—are associated with increased academic achievement for diverse bilingual learners, including students from Spanish-speaking, English-speaking, and bilingual households. Given the size of the student population who either use Spanish at home, and/or are learning Spanish at school, and the fact that Latinos rarely reach academic parity with their White counterparts, cognate instruction can be a powerful tool for increasing student literacy levels, thereby enhancing overall academic achievement.

Facilitating Vocabulary Acquisition and Retention

Bilingual learners who have a working knowledge of cognates can use their expertise to decipher the meaning of unfamiliar words. For example, when a bilingual learner familiar with cognates encounters an unfamiliar English word such as "edifice" in the text, this student can almost instantly recognize that it as similar to the Spanish word, *«edificio»*, a word that is in the student's background knowledge. The student can then re-read the text this time substituting "edifice" for *«edificio»*. If the guess fits the context meaningfully, the student can make the connection that "edifice" is the cognate of *«edificio»*, thereby facilitating the formation of an association between the English word and its Spanish cognate. With repeated practice, a direct connection between the two cognates can be established in memory (DeGroot & Nas, 1991).

   Such is not the case with noncognates. Take, for example, the English word, "building", and *«edificio»*, its Spanish equivalent. "Building" does not possess the orthographic similarity to *«edificio»* that would make the bilingual learner recognize them as being equivalent. Explicit instruction or a visit to the dictionary is necessary for "building" and *«edificio»* to be seen as equivalents. As a result, it is more difficult for the bilingual learner to make a connection between "building" and *«edificio»*. It would also be more difficult to remember that "building" and *«edificio»* are synonyms than to recall that "edifice" and *«edificio»* share the same meaning. Since cognates are easier to learn than noncognates because of their similarity to Spanish words, their formation of memory associations are stronger (De Groot & Keijzer, 2008; Montelongo, 2002).

Meeting the Standards

Cognate instruction can be used to meet state reading and language standards because of the morphological correspondences between English and Spanish. As we will show in the chapters on cognate **morphology**, many of the cognate **prefixes**, **root words**, and **suffixes** that are used to form words in both English and Spanish are derived from the Greek and Latin languages. The Common Core standards often require the instruction of Latin and Greek morphological elements for particular grades. Some states such as California specifically mandate the explicit teaching of Spanish–English cognates for bilingual learners.

Taking Advantage of Background Knowledge

The students in bilingual classrooms come from diverse language backgrounds. Some come from homes where only Spanish is spoken, others come from homes where English and Spanish are spoken, while others come from English-speaking homes. Those who come from homes where Spanish is spoken have acquired the rule-governed phonological, syntactic, and semantic systems of Spanish. As a result of the many similarities between English and their home language Spanish, these students come to school with background knowledge that can be highly transferable for the learning of English essential to becoming bilingual and biliterate. School curricula that include cognate instruction take advantage of the background knowledge Spanish-speaking bilingual learners bring to the school setting.

Unfortunately, cognate instruction is rarely integrated into the school curriculum. Rather, the road to bilingualism is often fraught with obstacles, many of which are rooted in political biases that disadvantage the bilingual learner. Such is the case with the way languages and cultures are represented and evaluated. For example, English is afforded more status than Spanish in most U.S. contexts. The English spoken by monolingual English-speaking students and their mainstream American cultural practices are generally valued and promoted over the Spanish spoken by Spanish-speaking students and their home cultures. Bilingual learners, particularly those from low-income Spanish-speaking homes, are often made to hurdle insurmountable language barriers in a school system that rarely reflects or validates their linguistic and cultural backgrounds. With the exception of dual language bilingual programs, schools seldom encourage the continued acquisition and development of their students' home language and Spanish culture. Indeed, throughout the history of U.S. education, Mexican American and Latino students have often been labeled and treated as "deficient" or handicapped because they are new to English.

Another way in which political bias negatively impacts bilingual learners is in a lack of quality teaching these students receive. Some describe inequitable instruction as an **opportunity gap**, in that, unlike their monolingual peers, bilingual learners are often taught by teachers insufficiently prepared for this work. Fortunately, studies suggest that teachers who are **TESOL** (Teaching English to Speaker of Other Languages), or bilingually certified, or who are themselves bilingual, or bilingual in English and Spanish make the best teachers of bilingual students (Hopkins, 2012). The lack of adequate language acquisition training and certification requirements is evidence of the political bias among state and local leaders.

We believe that bilingual instruction for Spanish-speaking bilingual learners, or teaching the home language as a subject (e.g., Spanish for Spanish speakers) is socially right and just. Despite the lack of support for bilingual education, we feel that school curricula can and should be changed to support bilingual learners' academic achievement by teaching these students Spanish–English cognates.

> **Did you know?**
>
> Teachers can search the Cognate Companion for books with bilingual, multicultural, and social justice themes. For example, teachers can find picture books that focus on social justice themes in the Jane Addams Award Books.

The idea is neither novel nor new. For decades, educators have recommended teaching cognates to bilingual learners because of the similarities between the English words and their Spanish cognates (e.g., Corson, 1997; Johnson, 1941). Teaching cognates represents an "assets" approach in literacy instruction—one that builds on the knowledge that students already have—in contrast to a "deficit" approach, which assumes that Latino-English learners are deficient because they lack English (Valencia, 2010). Teaching cognates enables Spanish-speaking bilingual learners to engage with literacy more effectively than strategies that ignore or denigrate the linguistic knowledge these students bring to the classroom (Cummins, 2005). Lubliner and Hiebert (2011) correctly suggest that the effect of a Latinate background is to provide Latino bilingual learners with "funds of knowledge" (Moll et al., 1992) that give them an advantage over their English-only peers regarding acquisition of academic vocabulary.

In contrast to English-only policies, we believe that bilingual teachers should be urged to use all of their language abilities to model and promote bilingualism and **biliteracy** (the ability to read and write in two languages) for their bilingual learners and to provide them with the resources to do so.

> **LESSON PLAN**
>
> Teachers can search the Cognate Companion for children's books addressing bilingualism, including:
> - The Cow that Went Oink (Most, 2003)
> - Pepita Speaks Twice/ *Pepita habla dos veces* (Lachtman, 1995)
> - Speak English for us Marisol (English, 2005)

ALL TEACHERS CAN INCORPORATE COGNATES IN THEIR LESSONS

Students at all levels of English and Spanish proficiency can benefit from learning Spanish–English cognates. We find diverse bilingual learners in a wide range of contexts, including dual language and transitional bilingual programs, English-medium classes, and in Spanish classes for students new to Spanish as well as heritage Spanish speakers. Our experience working with teachers in different types of programs for bilingual learners has taught us that all teachers, regardless of their proficiency in English or Spanish, can provide effective cognate instruction as an integral part of their content-area teaching.

Bilingual teachers who work in dual language, transitional bilingual, world language, and heritage language classes can draw on their own bilingualism as a resource for cognate instruction. Monolingual English-speaking teachers working in dual language or general education programs can also teach cognates by drawing more on students' bilingualism. By teaching their students about cognates, they can help their students become better readers, writers, and communicators in both of their languages. In this book, we present strategies that we have found effective for teaching Spanish–English cognates through picture book read-alouds and related activities. As we discuss strategies, we will present examples observed in the classrooms of the following teachers:

Mrs. García, whom we met in the opening vignette, is a Spanish–English bilingual teacher who teaches the first-grade Spanish language component in a dual language classroom comprised of students from English-speaking, Spanish-speaking, and bilingual homes. Mrs. García is an experienced bilingual teacher who finds cognate strategies to be effective in her practice.

Ms. Holcomb, whom we also met in the opening vignette, is Mrs. García's teaching partner. She is an English monolingual who teaches the first-grade English language component in the dual language program. Ms. Holcomb is a new teacher who looks to her experienced partner teacher as a mentor and coach.

Ms. Smith teaches a second-grade general education class that includes many Spanish-speaking bilinguals who are officially designated as English learners, and she has a certification in TESOL. Ms. Smith is a monolingual English-speaking teacher who integrates cognate instruction into her content-area instruction, particularly English language arts.

Mr. Hampton is a Spanish teacher who teaches third grade in a Spanish immersion program, and all of his students are from monolingual English-speaking homes. Mr. Hampton uses cognate instruction to accelerate his students' academic vocabulary development in both Spanish and English.

Mrs. Martínez is a Spanish–English bilingual teacher in a third-grade transitional bilingual education classroom. Bilingual learners are generally exited from the bilingual program between second and fifth grades, depending on their English language proficiency. To date, the bilingual teachers have been using cognates as an integral part of the bilingual program. The school where she teaches has recently decided to engage all teachers in learning to teach cognates.

Mr. Cuello is a bilingual fourth-grade teacher in a bilingual classroom that includes Spanish speakers who are newcomers, English learners of intermediate proficiency, and those who have been reclassified from English learner to fully

English proficient. He raves about the results he has seen using cognate instruction with his heterogeneous group of students.

Ms. Williams is a monolingual English-speaking teacher who teaches English as a second language to fifth-grade students. Her newcomers are all Spanish speakers, some of whom can read and write in Spanish and others who have had their schooling interrupted and, therefore, have not yet developed strong literacy skills. Her bilingual learners who have been in the United States for more than one year are from many different parts of the world, and they speak many different languages, including Spanish. Most of these students have reached intermediate and advanced levels of English language proficiency.

We also include a few examples from other teachers that we have met through our work in schools.

Using Picture Books to Teach Cognate Vocabulary

Prioritizing the teaching of vocabulary in the early primary grades promotes the advancement of language learning for all students. To put this task in perspective, a broad range of academic vocabulary can be generated from about 4,000 root words, taught in the early grades (Biemiller, 2001).

In the primary grades, vocabulary teaching is embedded in reading instruction and is mostly limited to those words children already use in speech (Beck et al., 2002). These authors recommend that teachers look outside their basal readers for words to enrich the vocabularies of their primary grade students. They specifically encourage the practice of using the picture book read-aloud for vocabulary enrichment.

Teaching vocabulary to primary schoolchildren through storybook read-alouds has been an established practice for decades (Dickinson & Smith, 1994). Research has shown that elementary schoolchildren learn new vocabulary words through picture book read-alouds when they are followed by activities that provide elaborations of word meanings (Beck & McKeown, 2007). Also, Elley (1989) found that children learned the meanings of words in picture books when teachers explained what the new words meant as they read. Kindle (2009) observed teachers using successful vocabulary-building strategies during picture book read-alouds that included definitions, examples, imagery, and morphemic analysis among other strategies. Finally, in a review of read-aloud studies, Biemiller and Boote (2006) concluded that explanations and elaborations of word meanings during read-alouds led to significant vocabulary gains, thus establishing further justification for read-alouds as vehicles for teaching vocabulary.

Storybook read-alouds can be effective vehicles for teaching students new vocabulary because of the engaging interactions teachers can have with their students (Morgan, 2009). In our work with primary school bilingual learners, we, too, have found that picture book read-alouds are excellent for introducing bilingual learners to cognates and enriching vocabulary. Children at all grade levels enjoy the read-alouds of picture books such as Martha Speaks (Meddaugh, 1997).

> **LESSON PLAN**
>
> Martha Speaks
> (Meddaugh, 1997;
> translated by
> Alejandra López
> Varela)

Teachers need high-quality picture books for their read-alouds (Fisher et al, 2004). As defined by Fisher et al. (2004), "high-quality picture books" are those that have won an award or have been recommended by a literacy organization such as the *International Literacy Association*. Teachers can use picture books to design lessons that teach cognates and nurture the development of bilingualism and biliteracy.

The Picture Books in the Cognate Companion

The Cognate Companion is a comprehensive tool and resource that includes the listing of every cognate in each of over 3,000 award-winning picture books. It also includes over 300 lesson plans, including lesson plans for all the picture books referred to in this book. The awards, such as the *Caldecott Medal Award,* which was first given in 1937, are well-established on a national level, while others, such as the *New Mexico-Arizona Book Award,* are more recent and regional in scope. Some awards such as the *Caldecott Medal Award,* celebrate the illustrations and artwork in picture books. Other picture-book awards honor works that have social or cultural themes. Picture books that have earned the *Jane Addams Children's Book Award,* for example, are especially noteworthy because they are intended to promote peace and social justice (Friess, 2014; Montelongo et al., 2015).

> **Did you know?**
>
> Teachers can search the Cognate Companion database for picture books, snap-on lesson plans, and cognate vocabulary to use in their content-area instruction.

One award that is particularly relevant to speakers of Spanish who are learning English is the *Américas Book Award* because of the multicultural picture books that authentically portray Latinos in the United States and Latin America (Montelongo et al., 2018). It is sponsored by the *Consortium of Latin American Studies Programs* (CLASP). The *Association for Library Service to Children* (ALSC) also publishes the *Pura Belpré Award* for writers and illustrators who portray and celebrate Latino culture (Montelongo et al., 2014). The majority of picture books found in the Cognate Companion have earned one or more of the awards in Table 1.1.

The Cognate Companion also includes hundreds of picture books listed by professional organizations such as the *National Science Teachers Association of America* (NSTA) and the *International Literacy Association* (ILA). Such organizations publish their own lists of exemplary trade books intended for children in preschool through high school. Books such as those found in the *Texas 2x2 Reading List,* are selected by committees of educators from the Texas Library Association (Montelongo et al., 2014). Those in the ILA's *Teachers' Choices Reading List* are the result of a voting survey of teachers (Montelongo et al., 2014), while the *Children's Choices Book List* is compiled from the votes of the children who have read the book (Hernández et al., 2016). Many of the picture books included in the Cognate Companion were drawn from the book lists in Table 1.2.

Table 1.1.   List of book awards included in the Cognate Companion

Book Awards	Subject Matter	Age Group	Description of Picture Books
Américas Book Award	Multi-cultural	Children	Multicultural picture books that authentically portray Latinos in Latin America and the United States
Caldecott Medal	Open	Children	Award to the artist for the most distinguished picture book in the United States
California Young Reader Medal	Open	Grades K–3	State award for picture books originally nominated, read, and voted for by young children
Geisel Award	Open	Beginning readers	Award given to the author(s) and illustrator(s) of the most distinguished American book for beginning readers
Jane Addams Children's Book Award	Social justice	4–8 years old	Award given to the children's books that promote peace, social justice, and the equality of the sexes and all races
Monarch Award	Open	Children	Illinois state award given to picture books that have been read and voted on by K–3 students
New Mexico-Arizona Book Awards	Open	Children	Regional reading award given to outstanding picture books, commonly those having a Southwestern flavor
Notable Children's Book Award	Open	Children	Books of fiction, information, and poetry that reflect and encourage children's interests in exemplary ways
Pura Belpré Award	Multi-cultural	Children	Award given to Latinx writer and illustrator whose work portrays and celebrates the Latino cultural experience
Charlotte Zolotow Award	Open	2–7 years old	Award given to outstanding picture books for children (birth through age 7)

Table 1.2. Book lists included in the Cognate Companion

Book Lists	Subject Matter	Age Group	Description of Picture Books
Children's Choices Book List	Open	Grades K–5	List of picture books voted for by children and recommended by teachers and librarians
National Science Teachers Association Outstanding Trade Books	Science	Grades K–5	List of outstanding science trade books nominated by a panel selected by *National Science Teachers Association*
Notable Social Studies Trade Books for Young People	Social Studies	Grades K–5	List of books evaluated and selected by a committee appointed by the *National Council for the Social Studies*
Teachers' Choices Reading List	Open	Grades K–5	List of classroom-tested children's trade books that are reviewed and voted on by teachers across the country
Texas 2x2 Reading List	Open	2–7 years	State list of recommended books for children age 2 to second grade
Tejas Star Reading List	Multi-cultural	5–12 years	State list of recommended multicultural books to discover the benefits of bilingualism and multilingualism

Picture books are rich sources of Spanish–English cognates for educators wishing to design and teach a cognate-rich vocabulary curriculum (Montelongo et al., 2013). Our analysis of thousands of quality picture books empirically supports the idea that they are a treasure trove of cognates large enough to create a rich cognate vocabulary curriculum.

The number of cognates in a picture book varies from book to book. Some picture books have only a few cognates while others have more than 100. For example, winners of the *Theodore S. Geisel Award* include titles that have as few as two cognates in a book while others contain more than 80 cognates (Montelongo, 2013). For the more than 140 *Teachers' Choices* books we surveyed, the average number is approximately 62 cognates per book (Montelongo & Hernández, 2013). In general, the number of Spanish–English cognates in a picture book written in English is approximately 20 cognates per book, while the number of cognates in a book written in Spanish averaged about 25 (Montelongo et al., 2013).

Using the Three-Tiered System to Select Cognates for Instruction

In their two influential books on vocabulary instruction, Beck et al. (2002; 2008) presented a three-tiered system for selecting the words from picture books to teach as enriched vocabulary. In the system, words range from those that need no formal instruction to others that require extensive instruction. **Tier One** words are high-frequency words such as "book," "red," and "apple" that rarely require teacher instruction as to their meanings. The majority of these most frequent words are Germanic in origin and are, therefore, usually not English-Spanish cognates.

Tier Two words are those vocabulary words that (a) are not ordinarily used or heard in everyday language; (b) appear across a variety of content areas; (c) are important for understanding content-area textbooks; and (d) allow for rich representations and connections to other words (Kucan, 2012). Tier Two words may also be thought of as "sophisticated adult words." Most of these words are cognates borrowed from Latin. The words, "diligent," "profession," and "tolerate" are examples of Tier Two words. Beck et al. (2002) suggest that teachers dedicate the majority of their vocabulary instructional time to Tier Two words, many of which are synonyms of basic vocabulary words. **Tier Three** words are defined as academic vocabulary words that are specific to particular topics in specific disciplines: "oligarchy" (social studies), "pollen" (biology), and "rhomboid" (geometry). As Tier Three words do not usually appear across a variety of texts, their definitions can be explicitly taught when their meanings are necessary for understanding a particular discipline-specific text. Most Tier Three words are also overwhelmingly Spanish–English cognates.

Tier One cognates. Tier One cognates are the most common cognate words in picture books meant for young readers in the early primary grades. These words are important because

Table 1.3. Examples of Tier One cognates

air/*aire*	escape/*escapar*	lion/*león*	princess/*princesa*
animal/*animal*	explore/*explorar*	machine/*máquina*	promise/*promesa*
attack/*atacar*	family/*familia*	mama/*mamá*	round/*redondo*
baby/*bebé*	famous/*famoso*	minute/*minuto*	salt/*sal*
bottle/*botella*	favorite/*favorito*	monster/*monstruo*	school/*escuela*
carry/*cargar*	flower/*flor*	mountain/*montaña*	secret/*secreto*
castle/*castillo*	for/*por*	music/*música*	sound/*sonido*
cereal/*cereal*	fresh/*fresco*	my/*mi*	space/*espacio*
check/*chequear*	fruit/*fruta*	new/*nuevo*	stomach/*estómago*
chocolate/*chocolate*	garage/*garaje*	pair/*par*	sweater/*suéter*
class/*clase*	garden/*jardín*	papa/*papá*	telephone/*teléfono*
color/*color*	giant/*gigante*	paper/*papel*	television/*televisión*
count/*contar*	group/*grupo*	part/*parte*	three/*tres*
cream/*crema*	hour/*hora*	pass/*pasar*	tiger/*tigre*
decorate/*decorar*	important/*importante*	pear/*pera*	tomato/*tomate*
defend/*defender*	in/*en*	perfect/*perfecto*	train/*tren*
delicious/*delicioso*	insect/*insecto*	plant/*planta*	truck/*troca*
different/*diferente*	is/*es*	plate/*plato*	use/*usar*
difficult/*difícil*	letter/*letra*	popular/*popular*	visit/*visitar*
elephant/*elefante*	line/*línea*	practice/*practicar*	voice/*voz*

they can be used to teach bilingual learners about cognates in the early stages of cognate instruction. Examples of Tier One cognates are presented in Table 1.3. Readers will note that many of the words refer to persons and items around the house, things to eat, and animals—mom/*mamá*, bottle/*botella*, family/*familia*, and elephant/*elefante*—all of them familiar to even the youngest of schoolchildren.

Tier Two cognates. Students benefit from direct instruction of Tier Two cognates. As part of the analysis of picture books that led to the formulation of their three-tiered vocabulary system, Beck et al., (2002; 2008) provided lists of suggested Tier Two target vocabulary words for each of the picture books they sampled. An analysis of Tier Two vocabulary in both of the Beck et al., (2002; 2008) books revealed that more than half (53%) of the words they listed were Spanish–English cognates (Montelongo et al., 2016). The results of this study suggest that literacy experts and teachers examine Tier Two words with a cognate/noncognate classificatory lens. Doing so permits teachers the opportunity to design rich cognate lessons that provide bilingual students with easier and wider access to the academic curriculum.

Examples of Tier Two cognates found in the award-winning picture books included in this book and in the Cognate Companion website are presented in Table 1.4. Readers can observe that many of these words are Latinate in origin and are synonyms for Tier One words, which have Old English roots. For example, distant/*distante* means the same as the English noncognate Tier One word, "far." Similarly, mend/*remendar* is a synonym for "fix." Humorous/*humorístico* is another way of saying that someone or something is "funny." Such cases remind us that Tier Two words are often conceptually no more difficult than Tier One words and, therefore, are well within a bilingual learner's capacity to learn. The difficulty lies in the fact that the bilingual learner does not typically form associations between cognate vocabulary words in their two languages without direct instruction. Teachers can design strategically focused lessons to help their students make these kinds of connections. Teachers can find model lesson plans for each of the picture books mentioned in the Cognate Companion.

Some Tier Two words, however, are less frequent in spoken language and written text and are more abstract than Tier One words. Cognates such as code/*código*, enthusiasm/*entusiasmo*, and misery/*miseria* have no easy Tier One synonyms and may be conceptually more complicated

Table 1.4. Examples of Tier Two words in award-winning picture books

Picture Book	Examples of Tier Two Cognate Words
Abuela's Weave	commercial/*comercial*; elaborate/*elaborado*; intricate/*intrincado*; rumor/*rumor*
Arrowhawk	distant/*distante*; firm/*firme*; gradually/*gradualmente*; mend/*remendar*; remote/*remoto*; signal/*señalar*
Braids	flow/*fluir*; guide/*guía*; pause/*pausar*; prefer/*preferir*; spicy/*especiado*; suppose/*suponer*
George Washington's Teeth	battle/*batalla*; fierce/*feroz*; invade/*invadir*; secure/*seguro*; sentinel/*centinela*
In My Family	briefly/*brevemente*; constant/*constante*; culture/*cultura*; offering/*ofrenda*; phase/*fase*
Journey of the Nightly Jaguar	ebony/*ébano*; glorious/*glorioso*; legend/*leyenda*; refuge/*refugio*; species/*especie*
Honeybees	code/*código*; colony/*colonia*; flexible/*flexible*; intruder/*intruso*; pattern/*patrón*
Me, Frida	admire/*admirar*; annual/*anual*; contain/*contener*; elite/*élite*; entire/*entero*; ornate/*ornamentado*
Prietita and the Ghost Woman	cure/*curar*; examine/*examinar*; ingredient/*ingrediente*; intently/*atentamente*; lagoon/*laguna*
Roadrunner's Dance	admit/*admitir*; agile/*ágil*; convinced/*convencido*; inhibit/*inhibir*; sacred/*sagrado*; timid/*tímido*
The Santero's Miracle: A Bilingual Story	aroma/*aroma*; assure/*asegurar*; intone/*entonar*; pale/*pálido*; pigment/*pigmento*; pure/*puro*
A Season for Mangoes	ancestor/*ancestro*; concentrate/*concentrar*; humorous/*humorístico*; traditional/*tradicional*
Sit-in: How Four Friends Stood Up . . .	accuse/*acusar*; committee/*comité*; conviction/*convicción*; dignity/*dignidad*
Uncle Rain Cloud	alert/*alerto*; anxious/*ancioso*; effect/*efecto*; furious/*furioso*; innocent/*inocente*; insist/*insistir*

for many bilingual learners in the early primary grades. Such Tier Two words require direct instruction that is connected to the content-area concept.

Tier Three cognates. Many Tier Three words are Spanish–English cognates. This fact is not surprising given that Latin was the language of the academic disciplines. Examples of Tier Three words are shown in Table 1.5. Most of the Tier Three words on the list, such as "cumulus,"

Table 1.5. Examples of Tier Three cognates in award-winning picture books

Picture Book	Tier Three Word(s)	Picture Book	Tier Three Word(s)
Gregor Mendel: The Friar . . .	recessive/*recesivo*; stamen/*estambre*	Wolfsnail: A Backyard . . .	radula/*rádula*; tentacle/*tentáculo*
Neo Leo: The Ageless Ideas . . .	helical/*helicoidal*; kinetoscope/*kinetoscopio*	Yucky Worms	clitellum/*clitelo*; mucus/*mucosidad*
Animal Eyes	phylum/*filo*; tapetum/*tapete*	Zin! Zin! Zin! A Violin	nonet/*noneto*; octet/*octeto*; septet/*septeto*
Bones	cranium/*cráneo*; metacarpal/*metacarpeano*	A Fine, Fine School	cubism/*cubismo*; impressionism/*impresionismo*
Global Warning	dioxide/*dióxido*; methane/*metano*	Are Trees Alive?	fungus/*hongo*; stomata/*estomas*
Redwoods	hyperion/*hiperión*; stratosphere/*estratósfera*	Dancing in the Wind	adagio/*adagio*; troglodite/*troglodita*
Life in the Boreal Forest	coniferous/*conífera*; taiga/*taiga*	What's for Dinner? . . .	omnivore/*omnívoro*; phalarope/*falaropo*
Raptor Rescue!	epoxy/*epóxido*; scalpel/*escalpelo*	Monet Paints a Day	cadmium/*cadmio*; impressionist/*impresionista*
Arctic Lights, Arctic Nights	cirrus/*cirro*; cumulus/*cúmulo*	Pablo	carapace/*caparazón*; coleopteron/*coleóptero*
No Monkeys, No Chocolate	aphid/*áfido*; hyphae/*hifa*; pollinate/*polinizar*	Tan to Tamarind . . .	masala/*masala*; mica/*mica*; sambar/*sambar*
Meadowlands: A Wetlands . . .	chromium/*cromo*; zooplankton/*zooplancton*	Togo	antitoxin/*antitoxina*; diphtheria/*difteria*

"igneous," and "recessive," were culled from trade books in the sciences—although there are also examples of cognates taken from nonscience books: "cubism," "nonet," and "troglodyte." Not surprisingly, the majority of Tier Three words are most often found in picture books for the upper primary students.

Teachers can use the three-tiered system for categorizing vocabulary proposed by Beck et al., (2002; 2008) as a guide for selecting cognate words from picture books. Tier One words can be used in the primary grades to build young bilingual learners' conception of cognates, while also building a cognate vocabulary base that will be used throughout their school years. Teachers can devote most of their instruction to Tier Two cognates, while reserving instruction for Tier Three cognates to those instances where the meaning of the word(s) is essential for understanding the text.

Parent Education: Awareness of Cognates

Teaching parents about cognates is important because it can help the family maintain Spanish, while also reinforcing home-school connections. At many of the schools we visit, Spanish-speaking parents are told by school administrators, counselors, and teachers, that their children should speak only English at school. Because parents want to do what is best for their children, they sometimes restrict or stop speaking Spanish with their children at home. There is no research-based evidence for this recommendation. Rather, educators who work with bilingual learners need to understand the research demonstrating that students who maintain and strengthen their home languages develop stronger academic language and literacies in English, and demonstrate higher academic achievement in English (Wright, 2019). A focus on cognates can support their student's/child's vocabulary development in their two languages.

Including Spanish–English cognates as a topic during family literacy nights is an important step in convincing parents and grandparents of the importance of their children maintaining and strengthening their Spanish as they acquire English. By demonstrating the similarities between the English and Spanish languages, teachers can do their part to encourage bilingualism for students who already possess such a strong foundation in Spanish, even when the teacher doesn't speak Spanish. Teachers also can encourage parents to read bilingual books that include cognates to strengthen their students' metalinguistic understanding of these words.

SUMMARY

Spanish–English cognates are an especially powerful category of words that can be introduced and taught in kindergarten through sixth grade for students at all levels of English and Spanish proficiency. These cognates entered into the English language as a result of the complex historical interactions between the peoples who spoke Latinate languages and the peoples who spoke Germanic languages. Today's English language is comprised of a high-frequency Germanic component and Latin-based academic vocabulary.

Teachers at all literacy levels in English and Spanish can provide their bilingual learners with access to academic language across all grades and disciplines through cognates. The rich cognate vocabulary found in award-winning picture books can be utilized to teach cognates through picture book read-alouds and associated vocabulary activities. Moreover, having parents become aware of the usefulness of Spanish–English cognates will encourage student learning and the retention of the speakers' home language.

The Cognate Companion that accompanies this book catalogs the thousands of Spanish–English cognates found in thousands of award-winning picture books. It also provides lesson plans and ideas that teachers can use as part of their suite of read-aloud activities.

REFLECTION AND ACTION

1   What are the benefits of cognate study for Spanish–English bilingual students?

2   In what ways do cognates facilitate the acquisition of bilingual fluency?

3   How can cognate study enhance the vocabulary development of the bilingual learners in your class?

4   Use the Cognate Companion to find award-winning picture books appropriate for your grade level. How might you incorporate the teaching of cognates into your lesson plans using these books?

2

Introducing
Students
to Cognates

OBJECTIVES

- [ ] Introduce the concept of cognates to students.

- [ ] Use concept induction to teach students about cognates.

- [ ] Show students how to use cognates as context clues to determine the meaning of words.

Cognate Play

Examine the lists of English and Spanish word pairs. What is special about the pairs on these lists?

English	Spanish
edifice	*edificio*
terrible	*terrible*
puerile	*pueril*
absolve	*absolver*
repeat	*repetir*
pharaoh	*faraón*

See the footnote on the next page for the answer.

T his chapter looks more closely at the importance of teaching cognates, and shares instructional ideas for introducing bilingual learners to cognates, and for preparing these students for ongoing cognate instruction—throughout the year and across grade levels. We discuss strategies and activities that teachers can use to teach and reinforce the concepts and rules pertaining to cognates. We end the chapter with **context clues strategies** for teaching students how to guess the meanings of unfamiliar words using information from the text itself.

THE IMPORTANCE OF TEACHING COGNATES AS A LANGUAGE CATEGORY

The vignette below introduces the importance of teaching cognates explicitly. In it, a Mexican-American grandfather (Grampa) has a conversation with his granddaughter (Mi'ja), a third-grader, when she returned from school:

Grampa: Mi'ja, come and tell Grampa what you learned today at school.

Mi'ja: Grampa, Miss Fernández taught us about cognates!

Grampa: Cognates? What's that, Mi'ja?

Mi'ja: Don't you know? They're words that are the same in English and Spanish. They're spelled the same and they have the same meaning!

Grampa: Oh! I know there are some Spanish words that are the same in English. Like «*chocolate*» and «*animal*». But no one ever told me they were called cognates.

Mi'ja: Yeah, and Miss Fernández says there are more than 20,000 of them. That's a lot! And you know what, Grampa? Many cognates are important for school learning.

Grampa: Wow, Mi'ja, that's great! I remember when teachers didn't let us use our Spanish in school, not even the teachers who knew Spanish.

Mi'ja: Well, I'm happy they let us use our Spanish at school!

Grampa: Yeah, Mi'ja! I just wonder how much different it would have been for me and my friends who weren't allowed to use our Spanish. Maybe, we would've read more books and learned a lot more—and even had better lives.

Mi'ja: I'm going to look around the house for things that are cognates as part of my homework assignment.

Grampa: Let me help you, Mi'ja. I want to learn, too. I think it'll be fun to learn about these "cognates."

In the recent past, Spanish-speaking students like Grampa in the vignette would often come across an English word that looked and sometimes sounded like a Spanish word. Not having been taught that such words had a special term for them, they probably noted the coincidence and left it at that. Such moments remained private because, like Grampa, no one ever taught them a term for such words. And since the Spanish language was not usually a part of the curriculum, teachers and students rarely discussed these Spanish words, if at all. As a result, bilingual learners never viewed their Spanish language as a resource for comprehending text, writing an essay, or giving a speech (Ruiz, 1984).

Teaching students about these words termed "cognates" creates a place in memory where the words can be stored and accessed, thus bestowing upon them a legitimacy in the curriculum that permits classroom study and discussion. Giving students a term for this category of words expands their **metalinguistic awareness**, or the ability to think about patterns in language use (Bialystok, 2001). Cognate instruction provides them with a means of communicating their thoughts about language with their teachers and with their fellow students.

Answer: Each word pair is similar or identical orthographically. Each word pair shares the same meaning. Each word is derived from the same root word.

GETTING STARTED WITH TEACHING STRATEGIES FOR COGNATES

An important strategy for teaching students about cognates is **concept induction** as demonstrated in the study of the English and Spanish cognate pairs in the Cognate Play activity at the beginning of this chapter. Concept induction, a form of discovery learning, is a pedagogical approach that encourages students to uncover linguistic patterns through observation, comparison, and contrast. Because of the time and effort students put into concept induction, it frequently leads to significantly more durable long-term learning. More importantly, it provides students with a model for learning cognate concepts and rules on their own.

In this vignette, Mr. Hampton introduces his students to the notion of cognates. Recall that Mr. Hampton teaches the third-grade Spanish component in a Spanish immersion program, and that all of his students are from monolingual English-speaking homes. Let us look at an English translation of the class discussion. He starts by writing three words on the board in Spanish:

> **LESSON PLAN**
>
> anniversary/
> *aniversario—Going Down
> Home with Daddy*
> (Lyons, 2019)
> important/*importante—
> Man on the Moon: A Day
> in the Life of Bob*
> (Bartram, 2002)
> select/*seleccionar—
> Uncle Rain Cloud*
> (Johnston, 2001)

Mr. Hampton: Class, look at the three words on the board: «*aniversario,*» «*importante,*» and «*seleccionar*». What do they have in common?

Paul: They're not synonyms. They're not antonyms. Are they all verbs? Nouns?

Mr. Hampton: No, but they do have something in common. They're all from a category of words. Can anyone guess what it is? (No student responds). Let's see if you can figure it out. Maybe, we can make up a category. Let's see. Hmmm! What is «*aniversario*» in English?

Luisa: "Anniversary."

Mr. Hampton: That's right, "anniversary"! Now, what are «*importante*» and «*seleccionar*» in English?

Osvaldo: «*Importante*» is "important," and «*seleccionar*» is "select."

Mr. Hampton: Correct, Osvaldo! Using these hints, can anyone come up with a category?

Chelsea: They're words that are the same or almost the same in English and Spanish.

Mr. Hampton: Exactly! These words are known as «*cognados,*» words that are spelled the same or nearly the same in one language and that also mean about the same thing. Has anyone else, a teacher maybe, talked to you about «*cognados*»?

Assorted voices: No!

Alicia: What are «*cognados*» called in English?

Mr. Hampton: They're called "cognates." What's great about «*cognados*» or "cognates" is that they're just as useful to those of you learning Spanish as they are to students learning English. There are over 20,000 of them, and most of them are important for understanding the books you will need to read in high school and college! Now that you know what cognates are, be on the lookout for them! They're everywhere!

> *Did you know?*
>
> Teachers can search for books that include specific cognates on the Cognate Companion, and then select the cognates their students would respond to.

Cognates can be used in a variety of classroom settings. In Mr. Hampton's bilingual classroom, cognates are used to help facilitate the acquisition of Spanish by home-language English students.

Likewise, cognates can be used in general education (English-medium) classrooms to facilitate the acquisition of English by home-language Spanish students. In dual language classrooms, students from English-speaking, Spanish-speaking, and bilingual homes can broaden their vocabulary in English and Spanish through cognate study.

Using the Concept Induction Strategy to Teach Cognates in a First-Grade Class

How might Mr. Hampton's lesson on cognates be given in a first-grade classroom? For that we turn to Ms. Holcomb's first-grade dual language classroom (Ms. Holcomb teaches the English component) as she introduces English-Spanish cognates to her students using the concept induction strategy. Follow along as Ms. Holcomb uses guided questions with contrastive analysis to introduce the concept of cognates to her first graders and ends the lesson with reinforcing and demonstrating learning.

| Ms. Holcomb: | Class, let's look at these two lists. We'll call the lists "Cognates," and we will see why in a minute. The list on the left contains English words, the one on the right contains Spanish words. Let's study these lists and try to figure out what cognates are. Let's start by reading them out loud together. Ready? (She points to an English word first and then a Spanish word.) |

Cognates

English words	Spanish words
lion	*león*
chocolate	*chocolate*
idea	*idea*
precious	*precioso*

Ms. Holcomb:	What is the same or different about the English and Spanish words?
Rosario:	"Chocolate"! «*Chocolate*» is the same in English and Spanish.
Ms. Holcomb:	In what ways, Rosario?
Rosario:	They're spelled the same in English and Spanish.
Ms. Holcomb:	That's true, but what else?
David:	They also mean the same in English and Spanish.
Ms. Holcomb:	What about the other words?
Assorted voices:	They are all spelled almost the same, and they mean the same thing.
Ms. Holcomb:	Yes, all of you are correct! They're spelled the same or almost the same, and they mean the same thing in English and Spanish. So what do you think cognates are?

Ms. Holcomb then has her students work with partners to generate a definition of cognates in English, although pairs are free to use English, Spanish, or both as they work out their definitions. After this activity, the class comes together, and they jointly construct the following definition: "Cognates are words in English that are spelled the same or almost the same in Spanish and they have the same meaning."

The concept induction strategy Ms. Holcomb uses to help generate the definition of a key vocabulary word includes several different steps. Ms. Holcomb uses a series of guided questions to invite students to notice similarities and differences in spellings and meanings of the

Spanish–English pairs on the four cognate pairs presented in the lesson. She had pairs of students generate their own definitions using whatever language(s) they needed as a group to complete the task. The contrastive analysis that students engage in also supports their development of metalinguistic awareness (Beeman & Urow, 2013; Escamilla et al., 2014). Because the language for instruction is English in Ms. Holcomb's class, they completed their definitions in English.

Reinforcing and Demonstrating Learning

Once students have generated their shared definition of cognates, Ms. Holcomb encourages her students to become language detectives, always keeping their eyes open for cognates. Equipped with this definition, students are invited to search their classrooms, schools, and homes for cognates.

Ms. Holcomb: Can you look around the room to see if there are any other cognates?

Griselda: Is "paper" a cognate? It is «*papel*» in Spanish.

Ms. Holcomb: Yes, that's right, Griselda! "Paper" and «*papel*» are cognates. They are spelled almost the same and they mean the same thing. Can anyone else find another example of a cognate?

María: How about "computer" and «*computadora*»?

Ms. Holcomb: Yes, María, they are cognates! Boy, you all are really understanding cognates! Let's see who can find the most cognates around your homes. So, for homework, write down all the cognates you can see or think of around your homes.

Searching for cognates in and around their homes is an excellent way to get other family members involved in learning about cognates. One teacher provided her students with a piece of butcher paper and asked her students to write down the names of items around the house that were cognates. Some of the students came back with the butcher paper completely filled with the English words and the Spanish words side by side. One student returned the next day asking for more pieces of butcher paper. She was especially excited about cognates because she was going to teach her Spanish-speaking mother English, while her mother taught her Spanish. Figure 2.1 shows fourth-grade students with the butcher paper lists of cognates they made.

Other teachers in the school can employ the same lesson in their classrooms with some variation. Upper-grade teachers, for example, can reinforce this activity in their classrooms by having their students comb through their Spanish texts for words that look like English words. Mr. Hampton, who teaches a Spanish immersion third grade, has his students look for cognates among the signage in the library. Almost all of the subject terms in the library are cognates (Montelongo, 2012). Mr. Cuello, the fourth-grade teacher, has his students identify

Figure 2.1.   A cognate **home–school connection** with two fourth-grade bilingual students.

the cognates in documents such as the *Preamble to the Constitution* in his social studies class, and box them as shown below:

We the People of the |United States|, |in order| to |form| a more |perfect| |Union|, |establish| |Justice|, ensure |domestic| |Tranquility|, |provide| for the |common| |defense|, |promote| the |general| Welfare, and |secure| the Blessings of |Liberty| to ourselves and our |Posterity|, do |ordain| and |establish| this |Constitution| for the |United States of America|.

Students can use the Find-a-Cognate database on the Cognate Companion to check their work and generate the Spanish cognates for these terms as needed (e.g., United States/*Estados Unidos*; to form/*formar*; perfect/*perfecto*). Teachers can also structure activities where students can discuss their observations and questions.

Distinguishing Cognates From Translations

In the early phases of teaching students about cognates, teachers will sometimes find that some students don't completely grasp the concept of a cognate. A common problem that teachers face in introducing cognates is that students sometimes overgeneralize the concept of a cognate to include translations. That is, they confuse translations with cognates. Typically, this happens when a teacher asks the students to offer their own examples of cognates, as we see in the following dialogue. The teacher is Mrs. García, a first-grade teacher in a dual language classroom who is herself a Spanish–English bilingual and who is Ms. Holcomb's teaching partner. After introducing students to the concept of cognates, she assigned them the task of finding examples of cognates in and around their homes. The dialogue takes place primarily in Spanish after the students have returned to school one day after the initial introduction of cognates:

Mrs. García: For homework, you all went home and looked around for examples of cognates. Does anyone want to share their examples? Remember that cognates mean the same and are spelled identically or similarly.

Graciela: I found "refrigerator." The Spanish word for refrigerator is *«refrigerador.»*

Mrs. García: That's a good example, Graciela! Other examples?

Roberto: How about "sun" and *«sol»*?

Mrs. García: Roberto, "sun" and *«sol»* mean the same thing. But they are not spelled the same or almost the same. *«Sol»* is a translation of the word "sun." Translations are not the same as cognates. Remember, cognates are words that mean the same thing and are spelled the same or nearly the same. Think about the spelling! Like the words "lion" and *«león,»* or "idea" and *«idea.»*

Andrés: How about "shoe" and *«zapato»*?

Mrs. García: Andy, good try! But "shoe" and *«zapato»* are translations. They mean the same, but remember, they have to be spelled the same or nearly the same. For example, *«elefante»* and "elephant," or *«familia»* and "family."

In the dialogue, Roberto and Andrés offered examples of translations, not cognates. To help students distinguish cognates from translations, Mrs. García provided explanations and examples about the importance of similarity in spelling. Mrs. García also created an anchor chart of common cognates that her first graders could identify easily.

Another point needs to be made about translations. When students offer English translations for Spanish cognates, they may be doing so because the English translation is more common than the English cognate itself. For example, suppose a teacher asks her students for an English word that means the same as its Spanish cognate, *«rápido.»* Most bilingual learners will answer with the word, "fast," not with the English cognate, "rapid." This is because the language learners have heard the word "fast" more frequently in English and have learned its meaning. In cases where a frequent non-cognate English word is more strongly associated with a Spanish word than its English cognate, we suggest that teachers acknowledge that the more frequent word is a translation of the Spanish word and seize the moment to teach students that the less common English cognate, "rapid," is one that they may eventually encounter and use. In our classroom lessons, we often tell the students that less frequent cognates such as "rapid" are $100-dollar words, or that they are words that "people in college" use. Such comments make learning these less-frequent cognates educational and motivating.

Activities for Reinforcing the Concept of a Cognate

Once students understand what cognates are, it's a good idea to provide other activities to reinforce their learning. As we have seen, one useful and diagnostic homework activity for reinforcing the concept of a cognate is to have the students look for and write down the cognates they find in their homes or neighborhoods and present them during class time. The teacher can then evaluate the students' work and identify those who understand the concept of a cognate and those who will require additional practice. Teachers can use the following types of activities to reinforce the concept of a cognate and assess student learning.

Cognate Word Sorts

Word sorts are concept-building activities that are a staple in the K-3 classroom. In the typical word sort, teachers provide students with cards or flashcards with one word typed on each card. Students then review the words and sort them into categorized piles. To create a cognate word sort, teachers can type out a set of common cognates in English and a matched set of words in Spanish. As we see in Figure 2.2, the students' task is to match the English words with their Spanish cognates and learn them through association (Hernández & Montelongo, 2018).

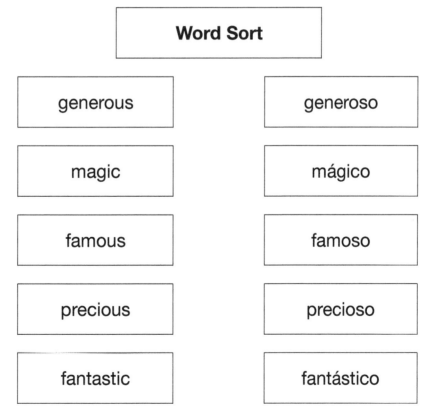

Figure 2.2. Word sort.

Cognate Word Searches

Word searches are popular puzzles found in daily newspapers and activity books in almost all K-12 classrooms. In their common form, students are asked to find and circle the hidden words listed in a word bank in what seems to be a word soup. The words to search for can be read left to right, right to left, up-down, and down-up. Teachers often organize word searches thematically, in connection with their content-area instruction. These kinds of word searches can also help students strengthen their spelling. An example of a cognate word search is presented in Figure 2.3. In it, students are to locate the Spanish cognates of the English words drawn from four different categories. Cognate word searches, however, are different and more challenging, because they require searching for words in the word soup that are of a different language than those in the text box.

Cognate Word Walls

A word wall is an instructional tool for supporting vocabulary learning. Word walls often contain vocabulary words that students have studied in the past or are currently studying. The words can be found on classroom bulletin boards located around the classroom. The purpose of a word wall is to reinforce learning of the vocabulary words.

In teaching students about words that are variations of the base word such as "complete," "completely," and "completeness," Templeton (2010) suggests stacking the words in order for students to see the similarities and differences in spelling, as in:

differ

different

difference

Following Templeton (2010), we recommend stacking the cognates so that the differences between the English cognate and the Spanish cognate are more obvious.

Teachers can create a cognate word wall including Spanish and English cognates on any classroom bulletin board or whiteboard. They often use different colors to easily contrast Spanish and English on their cognate word walls. The word wall in Figure 2.4 presents the English words above the Spanish words, using different colors, making it easy for students to see the spelling differences between the words. Some teachers prefer to place the Spanish on top of the English to symbolically elevate the status of Spanish relative to English.

Cognate Anchor Charts

In later chapters, you will learn that there are rules for converting Spanish words into English words and the converse. To reinforce the learning of cognate conversion rules, teachers can have their students create anchor charts containing the English words and the Spanish cognates that exemplify the rule. This allows students to strengthen their understanding of how to use cognate rules to generate new vocabulary. As in the case of word walls, teachers and students can use different colors to contrast the English and Spanish cognates. The anchor chart might also include the explicit conversion rule, or alternatively, contain only the example cognates side by side for the students to regenerate the rule.

Directions: Find the English words in the puzzle that are cognates of the Spanish words below (answers are provided).

Cognate Categories

```
G G N U A M M J W A T D T F
B A B O O N Y L I U Z I V F
B L O U S E U Z C O Y O T E
H E P J Y C A M E L A H R R
A S A N D W I C H G J O Y X
P C A V E L S Y S A L A D B
S W E A T E R Y B T Z A A V
J A G U A R G N P A M S T T
B I O R K E X E J S O U P Z
V A L L E Y R I V M D T O V
M O U N T A I N N W L T R O
Y O G S J R E C E R E A L T
W C L I P A N T S B O O T S
Y F L A K E U L J I E O W V
```

Foods		**Landforms**	
cereal _____		cueva _____	
ensalada _____		lago _____	
sándwich _____		montaña _____	
sopa _____		valle _____	

Clothing		**Animals**	
blusa _____		babuino _____	
botas _____		camello _____	
pantalones _____		coyote _____	
suéter _____		jaguar _____	

Figure 2.3. Word search for cognate categories.

COGNATES AS CONTEXT CLUES

Bilingual learners often encounter words or phrases that are unfamiliar to them when they are reading. The inability to understand the unknown words or phrases affects their comprehension and may be frustrating. In some cases, students can ask a classmate or teacher for the meanings of troublesome words or phrases. However, there are times when no one is available to help. Furthermore, searching for the meanings of words or phrases in dictionaries takes time and attention away from reading the text, thereby affecting fluency. For situations such as these, bilingual learners can be taught to use cognates as **context clues** to help them guess the meanings of unfamiliar words or phrases.

Figure 2.4. A word wall from a third-grade classroom.

State language arts standards in reading require students to learn various skills that may be subsumed under the context clues umbrella. Such strategies encourage students to use familiar words near the unknown words as clues to the meaning of the unknown word or phrase. Context clue strategies can include synonyms and antonyms, personal experiences, definitions of terms mediated by the different forms of the verb "to be" ("is," "was," "were"...). Context clues might also be punctuation clues (parentheses) or **boldface type** that provide hints about the meaning of an unknown word. Appositive words or phrases are also considered context clues.

Teaching bilingual learners (and indeed all learners) to use Spanish–English cognates as context clues for guessing the meanings of unfamiliar words, cognates and noncognates alike, is an important meaning-making skill (Montelongo et al., 2011). We encourage teachers to show students how to substitute cognates for unfamiliar words or phrases until they can make sense of the words or sentences.

Deciphering the Meaning of Unfamiliar Words in Texts

Once they understand what cognates are, students can be taught to use cognates to decipher the meanings of unknown words. One way to figure out the meaning of an unfamiliar word is to transform the unknown English word into Spanish (or Spanish to English) and see if it makes sense in that particular context. Since Spanish cognates are most often Tier Two and Tier Three words, it is a good strategy to convert the unfamiliar word from one language to the other, as shown in the following dialogue, in which Mr. Cuello shows his fourth-grade students how to use cognates to make sense of challenging sentences.

Mr. Cuello: Students, today we are going to learn how to figure out the meanings of unfamiliar words and phrases. Let's read the following sentence together [writes on board]: Many valuable articles were lost inside the burning "edifice."

How can we guess what the word "edifice" means without having to ask other people or look in a dictionary?

Marcelo: Look on the Internet!

Mr. Cuello: I guess you could do that, but that would take you away from what you're reading. We've talked about Spanish–English cognates, right? Well, it turns out that one way of guessing at the meanings of unknown words like "edifice" is to try to convert them to cognates. What do you think the word "edifice" is in Spanish?

Alicia: I think it might be «*edificio*.»

Mr. Cuello: Wonderful guess, Alicia. Yes, "edifice" in Spanish is «*edificio*.» But you have to check to see if it fits in that context. What is an «*edificio*»?

Guillermo: It's a building.

Mr. Cuello: You're right, Guillermo! Now, does it make sense in the sentence? Let's try it by substituting "building" for "edifice." "Many valuable articles were lost inside the burning 'building.'" It does work! Does everyone see that?

Assorted voices affirm Mr. Cuello's question.

Mr. Cuello: Let's see if we can come up with a rule. Take a few minutes and we'll see what you come up with.

Marcelo: How about: "Whenever you come to an unknown word in English, try to make it a Spanish word and then check the context to see if it works."

Mr. Cuello: That's really good, Marcelo! It really is. But, can we change just one word to make it even more precise?

Diana: I know! "Whenever you come to an unknown word in English, try to make it a Spanish cognate and then check the context to see if it works."

Mr. Cuello: That's it, Diana! Make it a Spanish cognate. Great!

Mr. Cuello's lesson is an important one for students because it legitimizes cognates as a resource that students can use to help them understand what they are reading. This important lesson need not be delayed until Mr. Cuello's fourth-grade class. Ms. Holcomb and her partner in the first-grade dual language program, Mrs. García, can start laying the foundations for legitimizing the use of cognates in the early grades. Teachers in grades two and three can bolster the use of cognates as context clues by highlighting this strategy whenever a teachable moment arises.

Using cognates as context clues is also important for the students. Not only do they learn a way of deciphering the meanings of unknown words in context, but they are using their home language to do so. A piece of anecdotal evidence may serve to make this point. Several years ago, the authors were teaching fourth-grade students how to use cognates as context clues in a classroom that included English monolinguals and bilingual learners. One of the authors suggested that the students who knew Spanish try to convert the unknown English words to familiar Spanish words. Upon seeing some of the successes the bilingual learners were having, one English monolingual student lamented, "I wish I knew Spanish."

Cognate Synonyms as Context Clues

Sometimes readers find that synonyms of unfamiliar words in later sentences provide clues to the meanings of the unfamiliar word. One strategy that bilingual learners can use to find the meaning of an unfamiliar word is to look for cognates in context that may be synonyms of the word. The following dialogue is intended to teach students how to search for potential cognate synonyms. Here, Mrs. Martínez, an experienced English–Spanish bilingual English as a second language (**ESL**) teacher, directs her third-grade students in a transitional bilingual classroom to look for cognate context clues that are synonymous with the phrasal verb—"look forward to."

Mrs. Martínez: Today, we are going to learn a way to figure out the meanings of words and phrases without having to ask other people or look in a dictionary or thesaurus. Let's read the following sentence together [writes sentence on board]:
"Billy was looking forward to riding on the train. He anticipated having a wonderful experience." What do you think the phrase "looking forward to" means? Let's look at the other words in the two sentences and see if there are any clues telling us what "looking forward to" means. Let's start by asking the following question: Is the phrase "looking forward to" a person, place, or thing? Is it an action? Is it a description of something?

Penelope: It's an action!

Mrs. Martínez:	Yes, Penny! Ok, so . . . is there another action word or phrase in the sentences besides "looking forward to"?
Geraldo:	"Anticipate"! It's the same in Spanish «*anticipar*.» It means to expect, like in the future. I think it means "to look forward to."
Mrs. Martínez:	Exactly! "Look forward to" means to "anticipate," in this case a wonderful experience. You can substitute the word «*anticipar*» for the phrase "looking forward to," and you get an idea of what the sentences mean. Do you all see what Geraldo did? He searched around the word or phrase for a word that is used in the same way as the unfamiliar phrase without consulting a dictionary or asking anyone else. So, can we think of a rule for using synonyms as context clues? Talk to your partners. Then, we'll see what you come up with.
Tomás:	Lila and I came up with one: "Whenever you come to a word or phrase you don't know, look around in other sentences for cognate words or phrases that may be used as synonyms of the unfamiliar word or phrase."
Mrs. Martínez:	Very good, Lila and Tomás! I'll write their definition on the board and all of you write it down in your Language Arts notebooks.

In this excerpt, we see that Geraldo used his Spanish background knowledge to guess that the English word "anticipate" is nearly the same as its Spanish cognate, «*anticipar*,» which he knows. In the case of cognate synonyms, students not only learn the connection between the English and Spanish cognates, but also a connection between the cognate pair and other words or phrases. In the dialogue, Geraldo guessed that the phrasal verb "look forward to" is probably synonymous with «*anticipar*.»

Cognate Antonyms as Context Clues

This next dialogue illustrates how teachers can teach students to use cognates that are antonyms or opposites of unfamiliar words or phrases as context clues. As was true of cognate synonyms discussed above, teaching students to recognize cognate antonyms is a powerful strategy. Like synonyms, the ability to figure out the meanings of unfamiliar words or phrases often requires much time and practice to develop. Fortunately, this strategy can be taught with the cognate vocabulary words taken from award-winning picture books. In this dialogue, we see how Ms. Williams, a monolingual English-speaking fifth-grade ESL teacher, shows her bilingual learners how to use antonyms to decipher the meanings of unfamiliar words.

Ms. Williams begins by writing the following sentences on the board: "The three coyotes 'raided' the corral in hopes of capturing a young calf. However, the valiant cows defended all of their calves."

Ms. Williams:	Let's read the sentence together. What does the word "raided" mean?
Alma:	Does it mean "to enter"?
Ms. Williams:	In a way, yes, but it means a little more. What kind of word is "raided"? I mean, is it a person, place, or thing? An action? A description? Look around the word for clues.
Grace:	It ends in /-ed/. So, maybe it's a verb.
Ms. Williams:	Good thinking, Gracie. You're right, the /-ed/ helped you identify it as a verb. What else?
Jorge:	Coyotes like to eat cows. So, maybe "raided" means "to eat the calves."
Ms. Williams:	You're so close, Jorge. What does the word "however" tell us?

Guadalupe:	It tells us here comes the opposite.
Ms. Williams:	Good, Lupe! The signal word, "however," means that the opposite is coming. So, we know that "raided" is a verb and that the second sentence is telling us that something different is coming. Is there a verb in the second sentence?
Arturo:	"Defended?"
Ms. Williams:	Excellent, Arturo. How do you say "defended" in Spanish?
Arturo:	*«Defender»*! It's a cognate, too!
Ms. Williams:	Good job! Now, here is the important part: What verb is the opposite of "defend?"
Anita:	"Attack!" The opposite of "attack" is "defend"! The cognate for "attack" is *«atacar»*!
Ms. Williams:	Wow . . . good job everybody! Let's see if it gives meaning to the sentence. [Ms. Williams erases "raided" and substitutes "attacked."] Let's read it together. "The three coyotes 'attacked' the corral in hopes of capturing a young calf. However, the valiant cows defended all of their calves."
Ms. Williams:	"Attacked" fits perfectly. Do you all see what we did? We figured out the meaning of a word we didn't know by looking at the clues around the unfamiliar word. For the word "raided" we looked for words that meant the opposite. We found the word "defended," which is a cognate. We then substituted the cognate, "attack," which is the English word for *«atacar,»* which is the opposite or antonym of *«defender,»* or "defend" in English.
Ms. Williams:	So, class, what's a rule for figuring out the meaning of an unknown word using antonyms? Can anyone think of one?
David:	How about: "Whenever you come to a word or phrase you don't know, look around in nearby sentences for cognates that may be used as antonyms or opposites of the unknown word or phrase?"
Ms. Williams:	Very good! I'll write it on the board and you all write it in your cognate notebook!

Teaching students to look for cognates that are antonyms of the unknown word to figure out word meaning is more complicated than looking for a word synonymous with the unknown word. This is because students must go beyond looking for a word that means the same to looking for one that is the opposite in meaning. As we observed in the dialogue, it often means that students need to take an extra step to guess the antonym cognate. Therefore, teachers may wait until students have had sufficient practice using synonyms as context clues before they teach them to use cognate antonyms as context clues.

In the dialogue, we also observed that Ms. Williams taught her students to use the signal word, "however," to help them anticipate something that was opposite to what went before. Signal words, such as "but" and "however" can also be used to facilitate student recognition of cognate antonyms.

Parenthetical Cognates as Context Clues

There are times when there are no cognate synonyms or antonyms near the unfamiliar word to use as clues to the word's meaning. However, authors occasionally use parentheses to provide a definition context clue to the meaning of the unfamiliar word. When the parenthetical term is a cognate, it can be used to understand the meaning. An example is provided in the following dialogue between Mrs. Martínez and her third-grade transitional bilingual class:

Mrs. Martínez: I want to give you all another clue for guessing at the meanings of unknown words or phrases. Let's look at this sentence:
"The scientist revealed his thoughts (ideas) on the subject in his diaries."
Looking at the sentence, what do you think the word "thoughts" means?

Patricia: It means "ideas."

Mrs. Martínez: You're right! How did you figure it out?

Patricia: The parentheses! They tell us that the word in parentheses is the same as the word that comes before it. If you substitute the cognate "ideas" for the word, "thoughts," you get a sentence that makes a lot of sense.

Mrs. Martínez: Yes, good job, Patricia! Many times, a writer will put a clue to the meaning of an unfamiliar word in parentheses, so you can guess the meaning of an unknown word without having to ask anyone else or consulting a dictionary. Can anyone think of a rule for parentheses and guessing the meanings of words?

Mateo: How about something like, "Whenever you come to a word or phrase you don't know, look for a word in between parentheses to tell you its meaning."

Mrs. Martínez: Mateo, you nailed it! I'm going to write this down and I want you to write it in your cognate notebook.

Teachers can tell students that sometimes authors use other punctuation clues, such as boldface type or dashes to provide the meaning of the unfamiliar word. They can reinforce this knowledge by creating sentences in which boldface type or dashes take the place of parentheses.

Cognate Appositive Words and Phrases as Context Clues

A context clue similar to a parenthetical cognate is when a word or phrase acts as an appositive for the unknown word. An appositive is a word or phrase that renames the word or phrase preceding it. Most appositives are set between commas instead of parentheses or brackets. Here again, students who have been taught to use cognates have an advantage when the words or phrases in apposition are cognates. The following dialogue illustrates how Mr. Cuello teaches his bilingual fourth-graders about an appositive context clue that is a cognate:

Mr. Cuello: Let's look at this sentence and read it out loud:
"Each Native American pueblo had adobe houses situated around a town square, or plaza." Without looking in a dictionary or the Internet, what do you think a "town square" is?

José: I think "plaza" means the same as "town square," because the words after the comma tell us what a "plaza" is the same as.

Mr. Cuello: Yes, that's right, José! Class, do you all see that the comma is there to tell the reader that what follows is another way of saying the word or phrase before the comma? What kind of word is "plaza"?

Dolores: It's a cognate!

Mr. Cuello: Exactly, Dolores, it is a cognate! Do you see that knowing that "plaza" is a cognate can tell you what the phrase "town square" means?

Mr. Cuello: Can you think of a rule for using an appositive word or phrase as context to figure out what a word means?

Xochitl:	I think this will work: "Whenever you come to a word or phrase you don't know, look for a cognate following the comma to tell you its meaning."
Mr. Cuello:	Absolutely correct! Class, write this down as Xochitl dictates it to you.

Cognate Examples as Context Clues

Another common type of context clue also relies on the use of students' background knowledge. In this case, student learners can be taught to use cognate examples around the unknown word to infer that word's meaning. The dialogue that follows illustrates how Ms. Galván teaches this critical skill in her third-grade class:

Ms. Galván:	Class, we have learned that we can substitute cognate synonyms and sometimes the antonyms of cognates whenever you come to a word you don't know. Sometimes, the cognates are in other sentences. So, you have to look around the word for the cognates to substitute. Let's first read this sentence: "Many 'crops' grow in the fields of California. Among them are 'broccoli,' 'spinach,' and 'tomatoes.'" Can anyone figure out what the word "crops" means? Let's start with the first sentence that states that "crops" grow in fields. What grows in fields?
Magdalena:	Fruits and vegetables!
Ms. Galván:	Exactly! Fruits and vegetables! Let's see if the examples in the next sentence help us understand that "crops" are fruits and vegetables. It says that among them are "broccoli, spinach, and tomatoes."
Victoria:	Broccoli, spinach, and tomatoes are vegetables! So, crops are fruits and vegetables.
Ms. Galván:	Excellent, Victoria! But, a tomato is a fruit. So, it seems that crops are both fruits and vegetables. What is special about the fruits and vegetables in the second sentence?
Mariá:	They're cognates! "Broccoli" is «*brócoli*» and «tomato» is «*tomate*»! "Spinach" is «*espinacas*»!
Ms. Galván:	Very good! The three words are cognates. So, in this case, you were able to figure out that crops are fruits and vegetables because the examples "broccoli," "spinach," and "tomatoes" are cognates. Ms. Galván now points out that the students can use examples around the word or in nearby sentences to understand its meanings, especially if they're cognates. She writes the new rule they've induced and asks them to repeat what she's written.
Ms. Galván:	Can any of you state a rule for using cognate examples to guess the meanings of unfamiliar words? Take a few minutes to think about it.
Rosario:	"Whenever you come to a word or phrase you don't know, look for examples of cognates that may give you hints about the unknown word's meaning."
Ms. Galván:	Good job, Rosario! I'm going to dictate this to you while you write it down.

Teaching students how to use cognate context clues to comprehend words is an important skill they will need as the texts they encounter include more academic vocabulary. We have found that teaching context clues, with or without cognates, can be difficult. Students cannot learn to use context clues to increase comprehension in one lesson. To improve students' abilities to use cognates as context clues, teachers are encouraged to regularly include cognate context clues activities within and across grade levels throughout elementary school and beyond. To this end, we have included context clues activities in many of the lesson plans in the Cognate Companion as a way of making meaning out of problematic vocabulary.

Reflecting on Cognate Strategies

The following vignette presents a conversation among four primary school teachers from the same school seated at a table following their district's professional development workshop about Spanish–English cognates strategies. The four are Ann Merriman, the literacy coach; María Madrid, a second-grade teacher who teaches the Spanish component of the dual language program; her partner, Sheila Graham, who teaches the English component of the dual language program; and Olivia Salgado, a second-grade teacher in a general education classroom.

Ann: I think that was a pretty good workshop. I never gave cognates much thought. But these kids come with a language they can use to decipher words they don't know. Seems like a powerful resource to have, I can see why it is important to give cognates a name so that we can discuss them as a class as a whole or on a one-to-one basis when we encounter them in our readings. What do you think, Olivia?

Olivia: I like that idea of teaching cognates, too. I've forgotten most of my Spanish. I wish I hadn't lost my Spanish. These kids shouldn't either.

María: I liked the idea of creating concept induction exercises to teach cognates. I think it will stimulate students to discover the cognate concepts we want to teach them. It will also model for them a way to learn on their own. I think that's really important.

Sheila: I liked the way the presenters used word searches. I think most word searches are a big waste of time, but the cognate word searches showed us that they have a real purpose. I especially loved the word walls and the anchor charts. I can get really creative with those.

Ann: I especially loved the context clues exercises. Talk about preparing students to become good readers, these are skills every reader should have. We just don't do enough teaching about context clues. I'm going to look at the lesson plans in the Cognate Companion for ideas on the picture books I can use to teach context clues.

SUMMARY

Spanish–English cognates constitute an important language category, especially for students learning Spanish or English as an additional language. Therefore, they require a term of their own, so that language learners, their peers, and their teachers can discuss them with each other. Attention to cognates also contributes to metalinguistic awareness.

Concept induction is an important strategy for teaching cognates. Also known as discovery learning, concept induction allows teachers to provide models for students to discover linguistic patterns on their own through observation and comparison. Concept induction often leads to durable learning because of the engagement students devote to it.

Cognates can be used as important context clues for skillfully guessing the meanings of unfamiliar words in a text, which may have cognate synonyms, antonyms, appositive words or phrases, and examples around them to help the reader guess their meanings. Other cognate-related context clues include forms of the verb "to be," boldface type, and parentheses. When students use context clues to guess the meanings of unknown words, they don't lose their train of thought in searching through dictionaries or asking others for help.

REFLECTION AND ACTION

1   Discuss your plans for introducing cognates to your students.

2   Review the dialogues on context clues. Select vocabulary words from your read-alouds to illustrate each of the context clues: synonyms, antonyms, appositive words or phrases, examples, definitions suggested by the forms of the verb "to be," as well as punctuation clues. Use the sentence models in the chapter for your implementation of this activity.

3   Select a picture book that you can use to teach students how to use cognates as context clues. Try it out with students in your class. Share what happened with a colleague.

3

Using Picture Book Read-Alouds to Teach Cognates

OBJECTIVES

☐ Learn how to use the Read-Aloud framework to organize cognate instruction.

☐ Develop visuals and practice activities to reinforce cognate vocabulary.

☐ Select a picture book and identify cognates to teach in your content-area instruction.

Cognate Play

The Merriam-Webster Thesaurus (https://www.merriam-webster.com/thesaurus) is an excellent source for finding synonyms, many of which are Spanish–English cognates. For example, the following set of words are given as synonyms for the frequent word, "huge." How many of these words are cognates? Circle the cognates:

astronomical, Brobdingnagian, bumper, colossal, cosmic, cyclopean, elephantine, enormous, galactic, gargantuan, giant, gigantesque, gigantic, grand, herculean, heroic, Himalayan, humongous, immense, jumbo, king-size, leviathan, mammoth, massive, mega, mighty, monster, monstrous, monumental, mountainous, oceanic, pharaonic, planetary, prodigious, super, super-duper, supersize, supersized, titanic, tremendous, vast, walloping, whacking, whopping.

We'll return to this activity later in the chapter.

An important goal of this book is for teachers to be able to use picture book read-alouds to promote cognate instruction in their literacy curriculum, as well as in any content-area instruction. Because there is no one definitive way for teaching cognate vocabulary to students through picture book read-alouds, teachers are encouraged to find ways that work best for them and their students. After several years of teaching cognates with picture books, we have adopted an instructional read-aloud framework that has worked well for us and the teachers and students we work with. The framework consists of three parts: 1) pre-reading activities; 2) the read-aloud; and 3) post-reading activities. We discuss each of these in greater detail in the following sections.

ENGAGING BILINGUAL LEARNERS WITH COGNATES IN PICTURE BOOKS

Although basal readers for the early grades focus on sight words, picture books provide language-rich, opportunities for teaching vocabulary to elementary school children (Dickinson & Smith, 1994). Picture books are veritable treasure troves for Spanish–English cognates (Montelongo et al., 2013). The over 3,000 picture books in the Cognate Companion include over 13,000 different Spanish–English cognate words, with more being added yearly.

> **Did you know?**
>
> There are more than 3,000 award-winning picture books, with more than 13,000 Spanish–English cognates on the Cognate Companion. Teachers can search for picture books by content area and cognates to integrate into their lessons.

Using Spanish–English Cognate Activities to Accompany Picture Book Read-Alouds

Ms. García, a second-grade bilingual teacher, had a recent conversation with a first-year teacher, Mrs. Pérez, who was preparing to teach her second grade dual language literacy block at the start of the school year. Mrs. Pérez needed some guidance on teaching vocabulary to her second-grade Spanish-speaking English learners.

Mrs. Pérez: I am a little worried about how to teach vocabulary to my students. Most of them are English learners who are at early stages of English language development. Do you have any tips that might help?

Ms. García: Well, one of the things I do from the very beginning is teach the students about Spanish–English cognates. Are you familiar with cognates?

Mrs. Pérez: I learned a little bit about cognates in my teacher prep program. The professors there taught us about these words, but they never showed us how to teach them or when to teach them or even where to look for them.

Ms. García: Well, they probably taught you that cognates are words that have the same meaning and the same, or almost the same, spelling in English and Spanish. This makes them ideal vocabulary words to teach students learning English because the students may recognize some of these words as being similar to Spanish words they know. So, it's a good way for them to use their Spanish to learn English and it helps them maintain and develop their home language.

Mrs. Pérez: Those are great points!

Ms. García: Yes, and did you know that there are more than 20,000 cognates? And it's easy to find cognates in picture books.

Mrs. Pérez: I knew that there were a lot of cognates. I didn't realize that there were that many. I had never thought about looking for cognates in picture books. So, when do you teach your cognate lessons?

Mrs. García: Every time I do a picture book read-aloud, I use the cognates from the picture books I'm going to read that day. I front-load them before the read-aloud, and then I create activities with them for after the read-aloud.

Mrs. Pérez: What kind of cognate activities do you make?

Mrs. García: One of the things I do is develop cognate mini-lessons on cognate morphology or cognate spelling. Sometimes, I make up lessons on how to use cognate context clues and other times I create vocabulary fill-in-the-blank activities. I also make cognate flashcards, word walls, and anchor charts to reinforce what I've taught.

Mrs. Pérez: Yeah! These would be easy and worthwhile activities to create, and engaging as well!

In the dialogue, Mrs. Pérez learns that cognates can be used often as part of her read-aloud activities. She also takes note of all the cognate activities she can create and sees that it's reasonable timewise to prepare cognate activities for her read-alouds.

SEQUENCING COGNATE ACTIVITIES FOR READ-ALOUDS

Teaching students about cognate vocabulary words through picture book read-alouds is just like teaching regular vocabulary words, except that you are using two languages rather than one. In this section, we describe some of the different cognate reading activities we use and the sequence we follow when we work with teachers and their students. The Read-Aloud framework for the sequencing of the pre-reading and post-reading activities is presented in Figure 3.1.

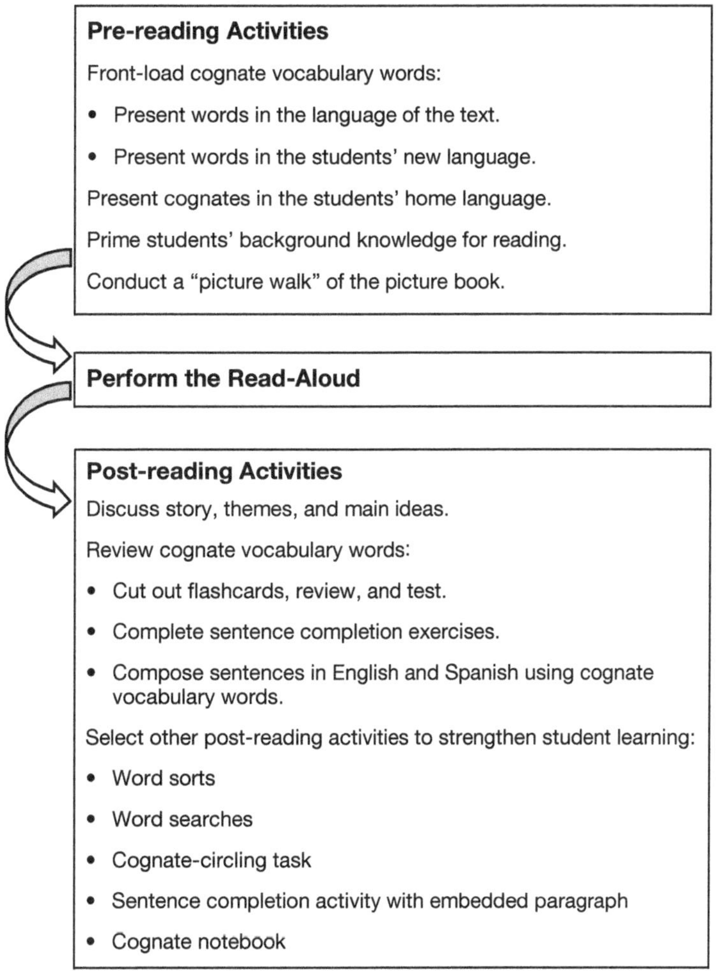

Pre-reading Activities

Front-load cognate vocabulary words:

- Present words in the language of the text.
- Present words in the students' new language.

Present cognates in the students' home language.

Prime students' background knowledge for reading.

Conduct a "picture walk" of the picture book.

Perform the Read-Aloud

Post-reading Activities

Discuss story, themes, and main ideas.

Review cognate vocabulary words:

- Cut out flashcards, review, and test.
- Complete sentence completion exercises.
- Compose sentences in English and Spanish using cognate vocabulary words.

Select other post-reading activities to strengthen student learning:

- Word sorts
- Word searches
- Cognate-circling task
- Sentence completion activity with embedded paragraph
- Cognate notebook

Figure 3.1. The Read-Aloud framework with cognate activities.

Pre-reading Activities to Build Interest in the Read-Aloud

The pre-reading activities we describe here are intended to engage students in learning the cognate vocabulary words in both English and Spanish, as well as to build interest in the read-aloud of the picture book. We typically begin by introducing four to nine cognates from the book that are essential for understanding the text and that will enrich students' vocabularies. We also choose cognates that can be used to create mini-lessons to follow the read-aloud.

Frontloading the Cognate Vocabulary

In the following paragraphs, we present an example of how to introduce the cognate vocabulary words from a picture book prior to reading the story. This is often referred to as front-loading (Dutro & Moran, 2002). By introducing the vocabulary words first, students are better able to comprehend the story. Front-loading also permits teachers a quick-and-easy formative assessment of students' knowledge of the cognate vocabulary words, thus allowing them to provide clarifications and elaborations for the words students don't seem to understand.

To prepare for the pre-reading activities of the read-aloud, we print each of the cognate vocabulary words we want to introduce on cardstock with the English and Spanish cognates printed on opposite sides of the card. These presentation cards should be large enough for all students to see and should fit on a pocket chart for display purposes throughout the entire read-aloud activity.

Once the presentation cards have been created and the students are seated in anticipation of the read-aloud, we present each cognate pair with the words in the language of the text first and ask the students to provide the cognate of the presented word. Thus, if a text is in English, we present the English side of the cards first because they are the words that will actually appear in the text, and we ask the students to provide the Spanish cognate. After the students have offered a response for all of the target words in English, we proceed with the presentation of the Spanish words and have the students answer with the respective English cognates. To ensure that the cognate associations have been learned, we then present the cards displaying the English words again and have the students tell us their Spanish cognates. For Spanish texts, we follow the same sequence except that we begin with the presentation of the Spanish words first and end with the English.

After each of the cognate cards has been presented in both languages, we place the cognate cards on a pocket chart. The cognate cards corresponding to the language of the text should be displayed outwardly on the pocket chart. Thus, if the text is in English, the English side of the card should be shown on the pocket chart. Conversely, if the text is in Spanish, the Spanish side should be displayed.

Let's follow Mr. Cuello as he conducts a read-aloud of the Américas and Jane Addams award-winning book, The Composition (Skármeta, 2003), a provocative story of a nine-year-old boy, Pedro, living in a country run by an oppressive dictator. In the story, the government is conducting a contest in the local schools with a prize to be awarded to the student writer of the best composition on the topic, "What My Family Does at Night." The true reason for the competition is that the government wants to find out what families are engaged in activities against the dictatorship in order to arrest them. In the story, Pedro witnessed one of his friends' fathers being arrested and taken away by soldiers. The man has never returned. Pedro knows that his parents listen to antigovernmental propaganda on the radio every night and are against the dictatorship. The central question of the book is, "Will Pedro unknowingly betray his parents in his composition?"

Mr. Cuello begins by presenting the cognate vocabulary word pairs he wants his students to learn—arrest/*arrestar*, colleague/*colega*, dictator/*dictador*, military/*militar*, obedience/*obediencia*, patriot/*patriota*, protest/*protestar*, and resistance/*resistencia*. He selects these words from the Cognate Companion because he believes they are crucial to the understanding of the story and

| LESSON PLAN |
| The Composition (Skármeta, 2003) |

because they will enrich his student's vocabularies. Mr. Cuello printed out the different pairs of cognates on individual sheets of cardstock, with the English word on one side and its Spanish cognate on the other side. Since the text is written in English, Mr. Cuello begins the lesson by presenting the individual cardstock flashcards displaying the English side first and asking the students to read and pronounce the words as they are shown:

> ### Did you know?
> Teachers can use the Cognate Companion to identify all of the cognates in any picture book included on the database.

Mr. Cuello:	(Showing the flashcard containing the word, "patriot") Class, what's this word? What does it mean?
Martín:	"Patriot"! It's someone who fights for their country. Soldiers are patriots.
Mr. Cuello:	Students, how do you say patriot in Spanish? What does it mean?
Adriana:	«*Patriota*». It means someone who fights for their country.
Mr. Cuello:	Yes, the Spanish word for "patriot" is «*patriota*». [Mr. Cuello turns over the cardstock flashcard to display the Spanish word, «*patriota.*»] Does everybody see that the English word, "patriot," and the Spanish word, «*patriota*», are spelled nearly the same? And they mean the same thing. Does everyone see this? What do we call words that mean the same and are spelled the same or nearly the same?
Students:	Cognates!
Mr. Cuello:	Yes, cognates! Now, look at the word "colleague." What is it in Spanish? (There is no response). Class, the Spanish word for "colleague" is «*colega*». Has anyone heard the word, «*colega*»? (Again, no response.)
Olivia and other students:	What does it mean, Mr. Cuello?
Mr. Cuello:	Well, "colleague" and «*colega*» are cognates that mean someone who works with you, like a co-worker. For example, your music teacher, Mr. Peterson, and I are colleagues. Does that help? (Mr. Cuello then continues his lesson by showing the rest of the selected cognates from *The Composition* in the same manner before starting the introduction to the picture book.)

Notice that Mr. Cuello presented the English words first because the picture book is in English and he wanted to determine how much instruction he needed to provide for the students to learn the meaning of each word. Since many of the students correctly identified "patriot," Mr. Cuello confidently moved to the next cognate vocabulary words. However, when none of the students gave the correct response to the word "colleague," Mr. Cuello provided them with a clear example of a person who is a co-worker. After the presentation of the cognate vocabulary words in both English and Spanish and once he was satisfied that his students had a working understanding of the cognate vocabulary words, Mr. Cuello shifted the focus of the lesson from vocabulary to the reading and understanding of the story and its themes.

Previewing the Picture Book

As part of the pre-reading activities, we like to build interest in the story by taking students on a "picture walk" through the book, encouraging them to comment on the illustrations or photos, and asking them to predict what the book is about. We also introduce the selected vocabulary as it appears in the picture walk and emphasize any recurring words or phrases. Whenever possible, we invite students to relate their personal experiences to the topic(s) in the picture book. We also try to provide some biographical information about the author and the illustrator, especially if students are familiar with some of their other books.

In the following dialogue, we continue with Mr. Cuello and follow him as he builds student interest in the picture book, <u>The Composition</u>:

Mr. Cuello:	Students, today I will be reading you the book, *The Composition*, a book written by Antonio Skármeta, and illustrated by Alfonso Ruano. Mr. Skármeta is from Chile and lived there when it was run by a dictator. One of our vocabulary words is "dictator," which is a cognate of the Spanish word, «*dictador*». Do any of you think you know what it might be like to live in a country ruled by a dictator?
Raúl:	I've heard that Hitler was a dictator. Is that true?
Mr. Cuello:	Yes, he was a dictator.
Patricia:	My grandfather says Hitler did a lot of bad things and killed a lot of people!
Roberto:	I've heard about the story of Anne Frank and her family. Was Hitler the dictator that punished people like her?
Laura and other students:	Yeah! I've heard of Anne Frank, too. So sad! Didn't they have to live in an apartment and never go out?
Mr. Cuello:	Yes, all the things you've said are true. So, can we agree that living under a dictatorship is probably pretty bad. (Students nod in agreement.) Now, let's look at some of the pictures to get an idea of what the book is about. Can you all see the book cover?
Sylvia:	There's a young boy reading a piece of paper and there are soldiers behind him.
Nina:	Oooh! That's scary! The soldiers are carrying rifles. Are they going to shoot him?
Mr. Cuello:	Let's look at some of the other pictures.
Yarelli:	In that picture, he's playing soccer with his friends. Looks like he's having fun!
Pablo:	Why is there a soldier in the classroom? I'd be scared if there was a soldier in this classroom!
Mr. Cuello:	You guys are pretty observant! Let's read the story to find out the answers to your questions.

Through the picture walk, Mr. Cuello was able to activate the students' interest in <u>The Composition</u>. The students made a connection between the word "dictator" and Adolph Hitler, as well as one between Anne Frank and living under a dictator. The pictures from the book grabbed the student's attention, making them want to listen to the story.

Reading the Picture Book

An important reason for reading picture books aloud to students is to model the reading and comprehension skills good readers use, as well as to demonstrate the fun and pleasure that comes from reading. To make reading fun and interesting, teachers can assume the personas of the various characters in the story, changing their emotions and their voices as the parts demand. In other words, they should "ham it up" and enjoy what they're doing! The students will appreciate their read-alouds so much more.

To ensure that the read-aloud is educational and pleasurable, teachers need to prepare for the read-aloud by reading the book themselves several times before reading it to the class. Previewing makes for a more fluid and interesting reading of the story. It also gives the teacher ideas as to what specific reading skills to teach or model, as well as what questions to ask. The picture book preview also allows a teacher to envision and prepare for some of the different student responses to the reading of the story.

Post-reading Activities

After reading the picture book aloud, we encourage students to review the details of the story, discuss the important illustrations, and talk about the themes presented by the author. We discuss the setting, characters, plot, and moral(s) of the story with the students, who share the feelings they experienced during the reading of the story. This post-reading period is a time when students can ask for clarification about things they didn't understand. It is a time to deepen student learning about the theme, the meaning of the character's intended actions, social justice issues, or the language used in the text. We use the post-reading activities as assessments of their students' comprehension.

When a class has finished its discussion of the story and its themes, we return to the study of the cognate vocabulary words. We begin by reviewing the meanings of the cognate vocabulary words as they occurred in the story. We sometimes do this by rereading the portion of the story containing the vocabulary words. As each of the cognates are reread in context, we can assess student knowledge of the words by calling on different students to provide the meanings of the cognate vocabulary words, as well as their cognate equivalents. The rereading of the cognate words in context deepens the learning of the words, while having the students recall the cognate equivalent in the other language strengthens associations between the English and the Spanish cognates.

Teachers can assess and reinforce the learning of the cognate word pairs through post-reading activities like the following:

Flashcards and Word Sorts

We typically prepare flashcards for each student in the class to reinforce the learning of the vocabulary words. The flashcards should be printed on letter-sized cardstock sheets containing the words in one language on one side and their cognate pairs on the other side. The students cut out the flashcards and review them. After reviewing the cognate pairs on the flashcards, the students test themselves and each other. While students are reviewing the flashcards and testing themselves, teachers can walk around the room to ensure that students are learning the cognate pairs. They can also resolve any questions students have about particular word meanings.

Words may be categorized in a variety of ways. Using the flashcards from their cognate word banks, teachers can create different word sort activities for their class. To do the word sorts, teachers would have to show their students how to sort the words into the various categories: semantic, syntactic, and morphological, among others (Hernández & Montelongo, 2018).

A first-grade dual language teacher, for example, might have bilingual learners arrange the cognate words in alphabetical order. A second-grade teacher could instruct the bilingual learners in the class to organize the cognates by parts of speech. Upper primary grade teachers can have their students classify words by semantic categories. Suffice to say, word sorts can be fun and challenging for bilingual learners in the primary grades.

Dictionary and Etymology Exercises

Dictionary exercises are a common activity in the elementary school. There are sets of dictionaries in almost every classroom library. Teachers can have students find the meanings of the cognate vocabulary words in the dictionary as part of their post read-aloud activities. A dictionary definition provides students with a more precise meaning of the cognate word than just its synonym. Moreover, many dictionaries provide example sentences that help students grasp the meanings of the words and improve their verbal repertoire.

Dictionaries that contain word etymologies (histories) make engaging exercises featuring Spanish–English cognates possible. Since word etymology is important to the study of cognates, dictionary exercises that require students to search for the origin of a cognate word can help build their understanding of how languages have developed through history. Furthermore, the study of a word's etymology can often lead to the discovery of interesting facts that might stimulate students' imaginations, as illustrated in the following vignette. Mr. Cuello, the fourth grade bilingual teacher, is teaching his students how to use the dictionary to locate word etymologies.

Mr. Cuello: Class, did you know that the English language is made up of words that come from other languages. In fact, many of the cognates we have learned have come to us from the Latin and Greek languages, and often through the French spoken by the Normans, which itself came from Latin. You can sometimes find out where a word comes from by using the dictionary. Most dictionaries give you the pronunciation of a word and its meaning while some dictionaries also give you the language from which the word came from, as well as how it was originally used.

Pablo: Why do we have to do that? Can't we just look for a word's meaning?

Mr. Cuello: One of the things I've seen is that finding out where a word comes from will often tell you whether the word is a cognate. Let's use the dictionary to look up the etymology of the word "coward." Let's find out what language it came from, and what this information tells us. So, look for the word, "coward," in your dictionaries.

Georgina: I found it! It says that "coward" comes to English from the Old French word, «couie». meaning "tail," and it is related to the Latin word, «cauda».

Mr. Cuello: Good! Did everybody find the etymology for the word "coward"? What does the fact that it is related to Latin suggest about a possible Spanish word for "coward"?

Marisela: It tells us that maybe "coward" may have a cognate in Spanish.

Mr. Cuello: Absolutely! Now, can anyone think of a Spanish word that is spelled the same or nearly the same as "coward" and has the same meaning?

Lionel: Oh, yeah! «Cobarde» means "coward" and it's spelled almost the same.

Mr. Cuello: Good, Lionel! Does everyone see how using the etymology of a word might suggest a Spanish–English cognate?

Most Students: Yes, Mr. Cuello! We get that!

The etymology exercise in the vignette not only reinforced what the students had previously learned about the origin of many cognates, but also served to make language study more interesting. The vignette continues with another benefit of etymological study.

Mr. Cuello: Class, studying a word's etymology also helps you learn a word's meaning by telling you what the word meant when it was first used. Look again at the etymology for "coward." What does the dictionary say about its original meaning?

Belinda: It says that "coward" came from the Old French word «cuard», which means the same as the word «couie,» which means "tail," which came from the Latin word, «cauda».

Mr. Cuello: OK, so what does being a coward have to do with the word "tail?"

Edison: The dictionary says that the word probably came from the idea of a scared animal running away with its tail between its legs.

Mario: I've seen a dog run away like that. That makes a lot of sense! Now, every time I think of the word, "coward," I'll see a dog running away with its tail between its legs.

Mr. Cuello: Now, do you all see how learning about a word's etymology can be interesting!

Bilingual Dictionary Exercises

Some classroom libraries also have sets of Spanish–English dictionaries for their bilingual learners. Bilingual learners love to use their bilingual dictionaries because they provide students with translations for the words they are studying. Moreover, many of the translations are cognates. For students in the upper elementary grades, online Spanish–English dictionaries such as wordreference.com (https://www.wordreference.com) are excellent references. Because of their usefulness and popularity, teachers can create exercises using Spanish–English dictionaries, not only in bilingual or world language classes, but also in general education classes.

Spanish–English dictionaries are also a source for finding interesting and fun facts in a serendipitous way. For example, a Spanish-speaking bilingual student may not know there is an English word that is a cognate of the Spanish word, «edificio». While perusing the English portion of the Spanish–English dictionary, the student might come across the word, "edifice," and discover that "edifice" means the same as «edificio». Because of situations like this, teachers might make discovering cognates in a bilingual dictionary a frequent activity in their classrooms.

Thesaurus Exercises

Students in the upper primary grades also can be taught to use a thesaurus to find synonyms and antonyms of their cognate vocabulary words.

The word "thesaurus" is derived from the Greek word for treasury, and a treasury of words is what a thesaurus is. Earlier, we learned a way of categorizing academic vocabulary into three tiers (Beck et al., 2002; 2008). Recall that Tier One words are defined as basic vocabulary words such as "bottle," "lion," and "mother" that do not require explicit instruction by a teacher. Students know these words from their everyday life experiences. Tier Two words are general vocabulary commonly found in books such as "fragile," "inspire," and "valiant" that may be found across disciplines. Tier Two words often require a teacher's explanation because they are sophisticated words found in textbooks and are used less frequently in everyday conversation. Since many of the words in a thesaurus are Tier Two academic vocabulary words, exercises involving the consultation of a thesaurus can lead to the discovery of other cognate synonyms and cognate antonyms. Finally, Tier Three words are those specific to a discipline and almost always require instruction: "idiom," "oligarchy," and "rhomboid."

Most of the frequent words used in the English language are Germanic in origin. These tend to be Tier One words that are comprised of one or two syllables. Tier Two words are usually less frequent and are most often derived from the Latin or Greek. They often have two or more syllables, like the cognates "contradistinctively" and "interdisciplinary."

To have students discover this for themselves, teachers can give their students a list of Tier One noncognates and instruct them to find synonyms and antonyms of these words. Teachers can then have their students change the various English synonyms and antonyms to words in Spanish. Students will often find that many of the synonyms and antonyms of the Tier One noncognates are Spanish cognates.

Recall that we had you examine the synonyms of the common Anglo-Saxon Tier One word, "huge" in the Cognate Play activity that opened the chapter. The online version of the Merriam-Webster Thesaurus (https://www.merriam-webster.com/thesaurus/huge) listed the following synonyms for the word "huge." Below, we have italicized the Spanish–English cognates.

astronomical, Brobdingnagian, bumper, *colossal, cosmic, cyclopean, elephantine, enormous, galactic, gargantuan, giant, gigantesque, gigantic, grand, herculean, heroic, Himalayan,* humongous, *immense, jumbo,* king-size, *leviathan, mammoth, massive, mega,* mighty, *monster, monstrous, monumental, mountainous, oceanic, pharaonic, planetary, prodigious, super,* super-duper, supersize, supersized, *titanic, tremendous, vast,* walloping, whacking, whopping.

As you can see, most of the synonyms for "huge" are Tier Two words. More importantly, of the forty-four words on the list, thirty-three italicized words (75%) are Spanish–English cognates. In other words, three-fourths of the words on the list have a Spanish cognate! Although this might not always be the case, such exercises drive home the point that learning cognates is important for academic vocabulary development in both English and Spanish.

Sentence Completion Exercises

A common activity in elementary school classrooms is the sentence completion activity. In its typical form, the sentence completion activity sheet consists of a word bank that includes the vocabulary words the students are studying. The rest, or body, of the worksheet is comprised of incomplete sentences, which the students are to use complete with a word from the word bank to render a logical sentence.

Teachers employ the sentence completion activity to reinforce and formatively assess student understanding and use of the vocabulary words they have been taught. They can also use the sentence completion activity sheet as a summative assessment of the many different cognate vocabulary words they have taught through the picture book read-alouds and their assorted activities. Teachers can develop sentence completion activity sheets using their own sentences and administer them as needed. Moreover, they can generate English and Spanish versions of the sentence completion task to assess students' biliteracy growth.

The sentence completion activity can be used in other ways, too. An important Common Core standard in the elementary grades is finding the main idea and the supporting details that prove or explain it. This skill is invaluable for learning how to summarize, especially for students in the third grade and beyond. We bring up this discussion of main ideas in a vocabulary book because the sentence completion activity can be modified to reinforce main idea instruction (Montelongo & Hernández, 2007).

To make sentence completion exercises that can be used to strengthen main idea instruction, we first compose a paragraph comprised of sentences containing some of the Spanish–English cognates we want our students to learn. Then, we create sentences using the remaining cognates from the list of words we are teaching. These sentences are unrelated to each other and unrelated to the sentences that form the complete paragraph. Then, we mix the related sentences from the embedded paragraph with the unrelated sentences.

The student's task is to complete the unfinished sentences with one of the vocabulary words in the textbox. Next, the students cut up all the sentences into strips. Once this is done, students should separate the sentences that comprise the paragraph from those that are unrelated. Having isolated the related sentences, the students must then decide upon the order of the related sentences using the main idea sentence as the first sentence.

LESSON PLAN

Sit-in: How Four Friends Stood Up by Sitting Down (Pinkney, 2010)

Through these sentence completion exercises, students not only practice their use of cognate vocabulary words, but also practice separating the main idea from supporting details and arranging sentences logically to create a paragraph, thus reinforcing their writing skills as well. An example of such a sentence completion activity intended for fourth grade students is presented in Figure 3.2. The example activity consists of a cognate word bank from vocabulary drawn from the Jane Addams Award honor book, Sit-in: How Four Friends Stood Up by Sitting Down (Pinkney, 2010). In the activity sheet, the six sentences that make up the embedded paragraph are mixed with four other unrelated sentences. To successfully complete the activity, students first finish the sentences with the appropriate cognates from the textbox, then cut out the sentences into strips, and lastly separate the related sentence strips from those that are not part of the embedded paragraph. Next, they decide upon the main idea and supporting details, and arrange them in a logical order as shown in Figure 3.2.

Teachers can vary the difficulty of the task by making the nonrelated sentences similar in subject matter to those that form the embedded paragraph, as we have done in the activity presented in Figure 3.2. They can also extend the activity by having their students rewrite the paragraph in their own words or by asking their students to substitute the cognate vocabulary with noncognate synonyms, or both.

In our interactions with students, we have found that students enjoy the hands-on processes involved: cutting out the sentences, separating the related sentences from the unrelated ones,

---

Directions: Fill in the blanks with the appropriate word. Then, sequence the sentences to reveal the hidden paragraph.

| accused | arrest | cause | integrated | justice |
| patrons | protest | resisted | segregated | treatment |

1. Martin Luther King led the _____ for equal rights for all people in the 1960s.

2. To _____ these unfair practices, four African American college students sat down and waited to be served in a "whites only" lunch counter.

3. The next day, other people went to the restaurant to support the students' fight for _____.

4. African Americans could not eat in the same restaurants as white _____.

5. The woman in the restaurant _____ the temptation to eat the high-calorie cheesecake.

6. The police could not _____ them because the students did not do anything violent.

7. In the early 1960s, many public places in the southern states were _____.

8. The students _____ of cheating on the test were expelled from the school.

9. As a result of the students' actions, many public places in the South were _____.

10. The accident victim refused the medical _____ offered to him at the hospital.

Here are the six sentences that comprise the hidden paragraph:

(7) In the early 1960s, many public places in the southern states were <u>segregated</u>. (4) African Americans could not eat in the same restaurants as white <u>patrons</u>. (2) To <u>protest</u> these unfair practices, four African American college students sat down and waited to be served in a "whites only" lunch counter. (3) The next day, other people went to the restaurant to support the student's fight for <u>justice</u>. (6) The police could not <u>arrest</u> them because the students did not do anything violent. (9) As a result of the students' actions, many public places in the South were <u>integrated</u>.

Directions: On a separate paper, use the sentences in the embedded paragraph to compose a paragraph in your own words.

Figure 3.2. A sentence completion activity containing an embedded paragraph.

locating the main idea, and then rewriting the sentences in their own words. Students especially enjoy the activity if it is in a word document on a computer, and they are free to manipulate the sentences by cutting and pasting them. Students who have access to the Internet can enjoy the activity even more when they can embellish their work by importing online pictures related to the topic of their writing.

Cognate-Circling Task

A quick and easy way to assess a students' understanding of cognates is to have them circle all of the cognates in a piece of text. This activity is known as the cognate-circling task. The text for a cognate-circling task can be drawn from a picture book, random sentences, or clusters of related sentences for the activity. In the following examples, Mr. Cuello asked his students to circle all the cognates in the texts.

There are many ways of scoring student performance for cognate understanding. Take the two examples of English and Spanish cognate-circling tasks presented in Figure 3.3a and Figure 3.3b. One way of scoring these examples is to tally the number of correct answers and divide this number by the total number of cognates in the text plus the number of noncognates circled to provide an adequate measure of student cognate understanding. The higher the percentage, the better the performance. For example, a student who correctly circles sixteen of the eighteen different cognates (the cognate "protein," appears several times in the text, but should only be counted once) in the English version of "The Proteins" text while erroneously circling

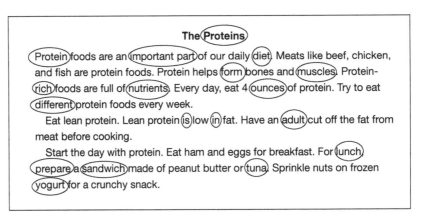

Figure 3.3a. A cognate-circling task for English text, with cognates circled.

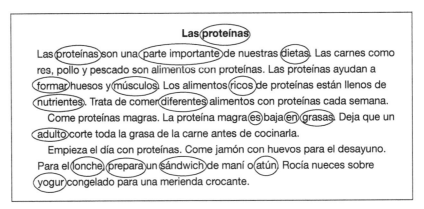

Figure 3.3b. A cognate-circling task for Spanish text.

only three noncognates earns a score of 16/21 (76%), which is a good score. A student who correctly circles only five of the eighteen cognates and erroneously circles ten noncognates earns a score of 5/28 (18%). Such a student probably needs a re-teaching of the concept of a cognate.

SUMMARY

Picture books are an excellent source for Spanish–English cognates. Teachers can use the cognate vocabulary in picture books to create read-alouds that enhance the learning of cognates in context. In this chapter, we have presented a literacy framework with pre-reading and post-reading activities that can be used not only to teach and reinforce content area reading, but also to enhance important cognate vocabulary learning.

Pre-reading activities are designed to front-load important cognate vocabulary essential to the comprehension of the picture book being read aloud, as well as to spark student interest in the story content. Teachers can use the pre-reading activities to make connections between the book and what the students already know about the topic and want to explore more. Post-reading activities provide teachers with opportunities to assess student understanding of a story's content, and to teach students valuable vocabulary lessons about Spanish–English cognates. We described examples of a wide range of activities (e.g., flashcards; bilingual dictionary, thesaurus, and etymology exercises; sentence completion tasks, words sorts, and cognate-circling tasks) that teachers can adapt and use in their classrooms.

REFLECTION AND ACTION

1   Review the read-aloud framework, Figure 3.1. How does the sequencing of the activities in this framework compare to what you are already doing?

2   Which of the pre-reading and post-reading activities listed in the read-aloud framework, Figure 3.1, do you already incorporate with your read-alouds? What might you like to add to your practice?

3   Design a post-reading cognate activity to use with your students. Implement the activity in your classroom and reflect on your practice.

4   Use the pre-reading, reading, and post-reading framework with a picture book of your choice to create a cognate vocabulary lesson plan for your students. Implement the lesson and reflect on your practice and on the students' learning.

4

Teaching Cognate Prefixes and Root Words

Cognate Play

A wonderful resource for all teachers is the WordReference.com online language dictionaries (https://www.wordreference.com). A family of bilingual dictionaries for most of the Romance languages, it contains a Spanish–English dictionary that not only provides language equivalents for English and Spanish words, but also the etymology and morphology of the English word. With respect to morphology, WordReference.com is ideal for finding English words that have a particular root word. Since many of the English words have either a Latin or Greek root, most of the words derived from them will be Spanish–English cognates.

The WordReference.com online Spanish–English dictionary lists the following English words for the Latin root, /-voc-/, which means "to call." Review the list below and circle or highlight all words that are Spanish–English cognates:

advocate, avocation, convocation, convoke, equivocal, evocative, evoke, invocation, invoke, irrevocable, provocation, provocative, provoke, revoke, unequivocal, vocabulary, vocal, vocation, and vociferous

(The answer is on the bottom of the next page.) This type of activity is good not only for teaching word roots, but also for teaching students about the influence prefixes such as /ad-/, /con-/, and /e-/ have on the meanings of words.

T he study of the internal structure of words and word forms is known as morphology. In this chapter, we focus on morphology, specifically cognate prefixes and root words, especially those derived from Latin and Greek. Prefixes and root words are fundamental for recognizing cognates and making sense of texts, as well as for generating new words. Learning to recognize prefixes and root words is an important meaning-making strategy, which we refer to as a cognate recognition strategy. When students are faced with an unfamiliar word, they can often deconstruct the word into its component parts and make a reasonable guess at the word's meaning from the word parts. As we will see in this chapter, teaching bilingual learners about cognate prefixes and root words provides opportunities for students to use what they know in one of their languages to acquire vocabulary in the other language. Through such an assets-driven approach, teachers demonstrate that they respect and value the home languages students bring with them to school. In the case of Spanish-speaking English learners, failing to teach these students the many cross-linguistic connections deprives them of valuable vocabulary strategies that can help them become bilingual and biliterate.

PREFIXES, ROOT WORDS, AND THE GENERATIVE NATURE OF LANGUAGE

The ability to combine prefixes and root words is just as useful for generating new words as it is for deciphering the meanings of unfamiliar words. Spanish-speaking bilingual learners can learn to use their knowledge of cognate prefixes and root words to create words that look and sound like English words that can be understood by English speakers. Similarly, English-speaking bilingual learners can use their knowledge of morphology to generate Spanish-like words that can be comprehended by a Spanish speaker.

Learning about the ways prefixes and root words interact to affect meaning can play a significant role in building new language vocabulary. At the basis of our discussion of prefixes and root words is the morpheme, the smallest unit of language that carries meaning. The word "cat" is a morpheme, as is the prefix, /re-/. However, there is an important distinction between the two. "Cat" can stand alone as a word in English, whereas /re-/ is a bound morpheme—a part of a word, such as a prefix or suffix, that has meaning but cannot stand alone. The idea that morphemes can be joined to generate new words reflects the generative nature of language. We saw the generative power of combining prefixes, root words, and suffixes in the list of words having the root word, /-voc-/. Once bilingual students understand cognate morphology, they will be able to use prefixes and root words as conduits to metalinguistic awareness—the ability to compare and contrast languages and discuss their features.

Cognates derived from Latin tend to be morphologically complex. Most cognates are multi-syllabic words comprised of one or more affixes (prefixes or suffixes) and a root word, as in the following examples: distraction/*distracción,* incredulous/*incrédulo,* and progression/*progresión.* Each of these examples consists of a prefix, a root word, and a suffix.

The meanings of many Latin-based words, a large percentage of which are Spanish-English cognates, can be predicted by deconstructing them into their component parts. Examine the following set of cognate words with the same root word, /-tract-/: contract/*contraer,* distract/*distraer,* and extract/*extraer.* The English root word, /-tract-/ and its Spanish cognate root, /-traer-/ are derived from the Latin root word, {trahere}, meaning "to draw" or "to pull." The changes in whether something is drawn or pulled depend on the meaning of the prefixes; /con-/ means "together," /dis-/ signifies "a reversal," and /ex-/ means "out," resulting in the following changes in meaning:

contract/*contraer*   to draw together

distract/*distraer*   to draw away

extract/*extraer*   to draw out

Answer: They are all Spanish–English cognates except for "avocation."

When bilingual learners understand that the changes in meaning result from the interactions between prefixes, root words, and suffixes, they can begin to understand how to derive the meanings of unfamiliar words. Learning this strategy is made even easier when the prefixes and root words are cognates.

Using Cognate Prefixes and Root Words Students Know in their Home Language

In the following dialogue, Mrs. Martínez explains to her colleague Mr. Davis how she teaches students about cognate prefixes and root words. Mrs. Martínez teaches third grade and Mr. Davis teaches fifth grade in a transitional bilingual program:

Mr. Davis: Mrs. Martínez, I've been trying to teach my students about using prefixes and root words to make sense of words they don't know. I spend a lot of time using different examples and exercises, but they don't seem to get it.

Mrs. Martínez: Maybe all you need are some examples that your students can relate to. I always try to use the cognates that they already know in Spanish. This way, they don't have to worry about the meaning of the words that result from combining prefixes, root words, and suffixes because they'll already know what the word means.

Mr. Davis: Cognates? Aren't those words that are the same in English and Spanish? Can you give me an example of how that works?

Mrs. Martínez: Let's say you wanted to teach the root word, /-port-/, which means "to carry." You can use the prefixes /ex-/, /im-/, and /trans-/, which mean "out," "in," and "across" to form the cognates export/*exportar*, import/*importar*, and transport/*transportar*. Since the students already know the meaning of the Spanish words *exportar*, *importar*, and *transportar*, they can just concentrate on the meanings of the prefixes and the root words as word parts.

Mr. Davis: Yeah, that makes a lot of sense. I think I'll try it. Thanks!

Mrs. Martínez's advice to Mr. Davis is another example of how useful the Spanish language is for learning English. Using cognates to teach bilingual learners about morphology can make it easier to learn the meanings of prefixes and root words.

Finding Cognate Prefixes and Root Words in Picture Books

Picture books are rich sources of Spanish–English cognates, and they contain many words composed of cognate prefixes and cognate root words that, in combination, result in the formation of new cognates. While working in classrooms, we like to teach bilingual learners how to recognize prefixes and root words to decipher the meanings of unknown words. We most often do this with the prefixes and root words we find in picture books.

> **Did you know?**
>
> The Cognate Companion can be used to find particular prefixes and root words to teach through picture book read-alouds.

Elementary school teachers have the advantage of being able to use picture book read-alouds across the various school subjects throughout a school day. This makes read-alouds ideal for teaching bilingual learners the meanings of many common prefixes and root words that occur across the disciplines. For example, Mr. Cuello designed a lesson to show students that the English prefix, /dis-/ means the same as the Spanish prefix, /des-/. During the read-aloud of the picture book, <u>Fry Bread: A Native American Family Story</u> (Maillard, 2019) in his social studies class, he introduced the Tier Two cognates discover/*descubrir*. Later that day, Mr. Cuello reinforced the lesson on the prefix rule, /dis-/ = /des-/ with the cognates disappear/*desaparecer* using the picture book, <u>The World of Whales: Get to Know</u>

the Giants of the Ocean (Dobell, 2020) during science class. As these examples demonstrate, Mr. Cuello taught and reinforced the cognate prefix rule, /dis-/ = /des-/, in combination with different words at different points in the school day.

Searching for specific prefixes and root words in different picture books to create a cognate morphology lesson can be time-consuming. A teacher might spend hours looking through many picture books for a specific prefix or a particular root word. You can search the Cognate Companion to find picture books that contain particular prefixes or root words. This handy feature frees up the time for a teacher to concentrate on the process of creating lessons. This is illustrated in the following example.

> **Did you know?**
>
> Many of the lesson plans in the Cognate Companion contain exercises for teaching cognate prefixes and root words as part of a picture book's read-aloud activities.

Ms. Williams, one of our expert teachers, wanted to find picture books that contain the cognate root, /-clud-/, for creating a multidisciplinary morphology lesson for bilingual learners in her fifth grade English-as-a-second-language (ESL) class. To do this, she conducted a search through the Cognate Companion for words with the root, /-clud-/ by typing /-clud-/ in the text box. Voilà! Lists of words that include /-clud-/ appeared on the computer screen along with the picture books that contained that root. Ms. Williams selected three award-winning picture books and the cognates she needed for her lesson in a relatively short period of time. She taught the cognate pair, exclude/*excluir*, from the picture book,

> **Did you know?**
>
> Teachers can search the Cognate Companion for books in specific content areas that include particular cognates.

Poems to Dream Together (Alarcón, 2011) during her language arts class. For her science class, Ms. Williams read Grow: Secrets of Our DNA (Davies, 2020) and introduced the word, "include" and its cognate, «*incluir*». In her social studies class, she used No Truth Without Ruth: The Life of Ruth Bader Ginsburg (Krull, 2021) as her read-aloud and presented a lesson on the cognates, conclude/*concluir*. Ms. Williams selected the cognates she would need for her lessons in a relatively short period of time from three different picture book awards: International Literacy Association (ILA) Children's Choices, National Science Teaching Association (NSTA), and ILA Teachers' Choices. The examples of Mr. Cuello and Ms. Williams illustrate the versatility of the Cognate Companion. Whether searching for a particular cognate word or morphological element, such as a prefix or a root word, teachers can use the Cognate Companion to find what they need to create cognate morphology lessons.

> **LESSON PLAN**
>
> Poems to Dream Together
> (Alarcón, 2011)
> Grow: Secrets of Our DNA
> (Davies, 2020)
> No Truth Without Ruth:
> The Life of Ruth Bader
> Ginsburg
> (Krull, 2021)

Teaching Students to Decipher Words Using Prefixes and Root Words

The following dialogue shows how Ms. Smith, who teaches a second-grade general education class, uses the concept-induction teaching strategy in a lesson on deciphering the meaning of words using the cognate prefixes, /tri-/, /bi-/, and /uni-/ and the root word, /-cycle-/. The vocabulary lesson was created to accompany the read-aloud of the picture book, Pedal Power: How One Community Became the Bicycle Capital of the World (Drummond, 2017).

After discussing the themes in Pedal Power, Ms. Smith began a lesson on the concepts of prefixes and root words using the word "bicycle." First, she had her second grade students direct their attention to the Spanish–English cognates written on the board, along with their definitions:

> **LESSON PLAN**
>
> Pedal Power: How One Community Became the Bicycle Capital of the World
> (Drummond, 2017)

tricycle/*triciclo*   a cycle with three wheels

bicycle/*bicicleta*   a cycle with two wheels

unicycle/*uniciclo*   a cycle with one wheel

Ms. Smith:	Students, let's look at the words and their definitions on the board and read them aloud. What do they have in common?
Simona:	All the words are about cycles.
Ms. Smith:	Yes, that's true! Is there anything else?
Larry:	The English words and the Spanish words have prefixes that are the same. The English words have /-cycle-/ and the Spanish words have c-i-c-l, which is like the English word, /-cycle/.
Ms. Smith:	Yes, Larry, that's right! The English and Spanish prefixes are the same and the root word, /-cycle-/, means "wheel." It is the same as the Spanish root, /-ciclo-/. What makes the cycles different?
Rosalba:	The prefixes tell us the number of wheels the cycles have. The tricycle has three wheels, the bicycle has two, and the unicycle has one.
Ms. Smith:	Yes, that's right! So, what do you think the prefix, /tri-/, means?
Class:	Three!
Ms. Smith:	How about /bi-/ and /uni-/?
Class:	Two and one!
Ms. Smith:	Yes, that's right! Do you all see how you can figure out how different words are related to each other by studying prefixes and root words?
Assorted Students:	Yes, Ms. Smith!

In the vignette, Ms. Smith used concept induction to get the students to guess at the roles prefixes and root words play in determining meaning—prefixes modify the meaning of the root word. Most important, the second-grade students learned that deconstructing words into prefixes and root words can help them unveil the semantic relationships among words they hadn't previously known.

The Cognate Companion can be used to find picture books to extend Ms. Smith's lesson on the prefixes, /uni-/, /bi-/, and /tri-/, and the root word, /-cycle-/, in her classes throughout the school day. During story time, Ms. Smith read Clothesline Clues to the First Day of School (Heling, 2019), a picture book that includes an example of the /uni-/ prefix in the cognate pair, uniform/*uniforme*. For her math class, she read The Crayon Counting Book (Muñoz Ryan, 1996), which contains the /bi-/ word, binary/*binario*. In science class, Ms. Smith did a read-aloud of Bugs Are Insects (Rockwell, 2015), which contains the cognate, triangle/*triángulo*. To extend the lesson to a different prefix but the same root word, Ms. Smith also read the picture book, Tiny Creatures: The World of Microbes (Davies, 2016) during science class. This book contains the cognate, recycle/*reciclar*, consisting of the prefix, /re-/, and the root word, /-cycle-/. The ability of Ms. Smith to use different picture books to reinforce the learning of particular prefixes illustrates one of the useful features of the Cognate Companion.

In the next vignette, Mrs. Martínez, a third grade Spanish–English bilingual teacher in a transitional bilingual education classroom, uses concept induction to show her bilingual learners how the prefix, /pro-/, can be used to guess the meaning of an unfamiliar word such as *"provoke"* found in the picture book titled, When Marian Sang: The True Recital of Marian Anderson (Muñoz Ryan, 2002). To begin her

---

LESSON PLAN

Clothesline Clues to the First Day of School
(Heling, 2019)

The Crayon Counting Book
(Muñoz Ryan, 1996)

Bugs Are Insects
(Rockwell, 2015)

Tiny Creatures: The World of Microbes
(Davies, 2016)

LESSON PLAN

When Marian Sang: The True Recital of Marian Anderson
(Muñoz Ryan, 2002)

lesson Mrs. Martínez presents the following lists of English and Spanish cognate pairs and their meanings, which she has written on the board:

List 1	List 2	Meaning
proceed	*proceder*	to move forward
project	*proyectar*	to throw forward
provoke	*provocar*	to call forward

Mrs. Martínez: Class, look over the words in List 1 and List 2. What do they have in have in common?

Teresa: The Spanish words in List 2 all begin with the prefix, /pro-/, just like the English words in List 1.

Mrs. Martínez: Yes, /pro-/, is a cognate prefix in English and Spanish. They are spelled the same and mean the same thing. What can we say about the root words?

Pablo: The Spanish root words are cognates of the English root words. For example, /-ceed-/ is the same as */-ceder-/*, /-ject-/ is the same as */-yect-/*, and /-voc-/ is */-voc-/* in Spanish.

Mrs. Martínez: Excellent! Now, let's look at how the prefix, /pro-/, changes these words.

Lorenzo: The prefix, /pro-/, tells us that the root word is going forward.

Mrs. Martínez: That's correct, Beto! The prefix, /pro-/, usually tells us about something going forward. Can anyone else think of other cognates paired with /pro-/?

Maribel: How about promise/*promesa*?

Mrs. Martínez: That's right, Maribel. "Promise" is the combination of the prefix, /pro-/ and the root word, /-mis-/, meaning to send. Combining both of them means to send something forward. Any others?

Leo: How about "provide"?

Mrs. Martínez: Good, Leo. The root word, /-vide-/, means "see." Combining /pro-/ and /-vide-/ means moving "seeing forward," in the sense of looking ahead.

In the dialogue, Mrs. Martínez, like Ms. Smith in the preceding vignette, encouraged the students to compare the list of English words with the list of Spanish words. This led the students to recognize that both sets of words began with the same cognate prefix, /pro-/. Her students realized the English and Spanish words were cognates. Mrs. Martínez' students made the connection that words beginning with the prefix, /pro-/, has to do with moving forward and she strengthened the learning by providing them with the elaboration of the words, "promise" and "provide."

To reinforce the learning, Mrs. Martínez consulted the Cognate Companion to find other picture books containing the prefix, /pro-/ used with other root words. There, she found the word, "propose," meaning "to put forward," in the picture book titled: The Youngest Marcher: The Story of Audrey Faye Hendricks, a Young Civil Rights Activist (Levinson, 2017), which she read in her social studies class. For her language arts class, she retaught the word, "promote," while reading poems from Woke: A Young Poet's Call to Justice (Browne, 2020). In science class, she pointed out the word "progress," in her read-aloud of Pollen: Darwin's 130-Year Prediction (Pattison, 2019).

LESSON PLAN

The Youngest Marcher: The Story of Audrey Faye Hendricks, a Young Civil Rights Activist
(Levinson, 2017)

Woke: A Young Poet's Call to Justice
(Browne, 2020)

Pollen: Darwin's 130-Year Prediction
(Pattison, 2019)

TEACHING BILINGUAL LEARNERS ABOUT PREFIXES

Now that we've reviewed how prefixes and root words work together, let's take a look at techniques for teaching specific prefixes. In our work with teachers and students, we use four strategies for teaching prefixes in the context of cognate instruction: 1) teach Latin and Greek prefixes which have both English and Spanish cognates, 2) have students generate cognates that use prefixes, 3) explicitly teach cognate prefixes that are not identical, and 4) teach Germanic prefixes that are not Spanish–English cognates. The following sections discuss each of these strategies in detail.

Common Latin and Greek Cognate Prefixes

Bilingual learners can grow their vocabularies using the large number of Latin and Greek prefixes and root words shared by English and Spanish. These prefixes often carry meanings related to important semantic concepts such as number: /bi-/, /mono-/; location: /dia-/, /trans-/; sameness: /sym-/, /syn-/; or negation: /il-/, /im-/, /in-/, to name just a few. By teaching bilingual learners how English and Spanish cognate prefixes are related, teachers can help students build strategies for either recognizing unfamiliar words as cognates, or for generating new words to express their ideas. Some common Latin prefixes and examples of Spanish–English cognates possessing those prefixes are presented in Table 4.1. Similarly, common Greek prefixes and examples of Spanish–English cognates possessing those prefixes are presented in Table 4.2.

The tables include only those cognates that appear at least once in one of the picture books listed in the Cognate Companion. Note that some prefixes (e.g., /il-/, /im-/, /in-/) are grouped together. Even though they are derived from the same prefix, /in-/, their spellings differ to ease the pronunciation of the words they help form. And while each table provides only a few examples, it is easy to find other words having the same prefixes using the Find-A-Cognate database, an important component of the Cognate Companion that provides a listing of over 18,000 Spanish–English cognates.

> **Did you know?**
>
> You can use the Find-a-Cognate database to check if either English/ Spanish words having the same prefix, root, or suffix have a cognate (either Spanish or English).

Table 4.1. Common Latin cognate prefixes

Latin prefixes	Meaning	Example cognates
/bene-/	good	benediction/*bendición*, benefactor/*benefactor*, benefit/*beneficio*, benevolence/*benevolencia*
/bi-/	two, twice	biceps/*bíceps*, bicuspid/*bicúspide*, bicycle/*bicicleta*, bilingual/*bilingüe*, binoculars/*binoculares*
/ex-/, /e-/	out	educate/*educar*, emerge/*emerger*, emigrate/*emigrar*, eminent/*eminente*, emulsify/*emulsionar*, enormous/*enorme*
/extra-/	outside	extra/*extra*, extraordinary/*extraordinario*, extraterrestrial/*extraterrestre*, extravagant/*extravagante*
/in-/, /im-/, /il-/	not	immediate/*inmediato*, immense/*inmenso*, immortal/*inmortal*, immunity/*inmunidad*, impossible/*imposible*
		incredible/*increíble*, indignant/*indignado*, indomitable/*indomable*, inevitable/*inevitable*
/inter-/	between, among	intercept/*interceptar*, interfere/*interferir*, intermittent/*intermitente*, interrogate/*interrogar*
/pre-/	before	precede/*preceder*, predict/*predecir*, prefix/*prefijo*, preoccupy/*preocupar*, prevent/*prevenir*
/pro-/	forward	proceed/*proceder*, proclaim/*proclamar*, produce/*producir*, progress/*progresar*, promote/*promover*
/re-/	again	reappear/*reaparecer*, refresh/*refrescar*, reiterate/*reiterar*, renew/*renovar*, report/*reportar*, retract/*retractarse*
/tri-/	three	triangle/*triángulo*, triceps/*tríceps*, tricycle/*triciclo*, trilobite/*trilobites*, trio/*trío*, triple/*triple*
/trans-/	across	transfer/*transferir*, transform/*transformar*, translucent/*translúcido*, transmit/*transmitir*
/uni-/	one	unicorn/*unicornio*, unicycle/*uniciclo*, uniform/*uniforme*, unite/*unir*, universe/*universo*, university/*universidad*

Table 4.2.   Common Greek prefixes

Greek prefixes	Meaning	Example cognates
/ana-/	up, back, against	anagram/*anagrama*, analogy/*analogía*, analysis/*análisis*, anatomy/*anatomía*
/auto-/, /aut-/	self	autism/*autismo*, autobiography/*autobiografía*, autograph/*autógrafo*, automatic/*automático*
/cata-/	down, against	cataclysm/*cataclismo*, catalog/*catálogo*, catapult/*catapultar*, catastrophe/*catástrofe*
/dia-/	through, across	diabetes/*diabetes*, diagnose/*diagnosticar*, diagonal/*diagonal*, diagram/*diagrama*
/di-/	two, double	digraph/*dígrafo*, dilemma/*dilemma*, dioxide/*dióxido*, diphthong/*diptongo*
/epi-/	upon, over	epidemic/*epidemia*, epidermis/*epidermis*, epilepsy/*epilepsia*, epilogue/*epílogo*, episode/*episodio*
/micro-/	small, millionth	microbe/*microbio*, microorganism/*microorganismo*, microphone/*micrófono*, microscope/*microscopio*
/mono-/	one, single	monocular/*monocular*, monopoly/*monopolio*, monoxide/*monóxido*, monotonous/*monótono*
/peri-/	around	perimeter/*perímetro*, periodic/*periódico*, peripheral/*periférico*, peristalsis/*peristalsis*
/proto-/	primitive	protagonist/*protagonista*, proton/*protón*, prototype/*prototipo*, protozoan/*protozoo*
/syn-/, /sym-/	together, same	synapse/*sinapsis*, syncopate/*sincopar*, synonym/*sinónimo*, syntax/*sintaxis*, synthesize/*sintetizar*
		symbol/*símbolo*, symmetry/*simetría*, symphony/*sinfonía*, symptom/*síntoma*

Teaching the Meanings of Prefixes

Teachers can develop rich vocabulary lessons featuring prefixes to accompany picture book read-alouds. In the classes we teach, we give students the meaning of a few prefixes and then teach them about the rich cognate morphology and the relationships between English words and their Spanish cognates. We then encourage students to generate additional cognates on their own. We have students practice generating new words made up of cognate prefixes and root words to grow their productive vocabulary in English and Spanish.

> **LESSON PLAN**
>
> Bug Shots: The Good, the Bad, and the Bugly
> (Siy, 2011)

Ms. Williams, a fifth-grade ESL teacher, wanted to teach her students the meaning of the cognate prefix, /trans-/, which means "across and beyond," using a science picture book. She consulted the Cognate Companion and found an NSTA science book Bug Shots: The Good, the Bad, and the Bugly (Siy, 2011). This picture book presents its readers with a close look at different types of bugs. Among the many cognates in the book are two cognate verbs having the prefix, /trans-/: transmit/*transmitir* and transfer/*transferir*. In her lesson, Ms. Williams teaches her students the meaning of the prefix, /trans-/. The short dialogue below presents a portion of Ms. Williams' lesson.

Ms. Williams: Class, two of the words we encountered in Bug Shots contained the prefix /trans-/: "transmit" and "transfer." In the book, the author tells us that, "Flies spread germs and 'transmit' disease," and also that, "Insects are pollinators; they 'transfer' pollen grains." What do you think the words, "transmit" and "transfer," mean?

René: They both have to do with moving something.

Ms. Williams: That's right, René! So, what do you think the prefix /trans-/ means?

Laura: Does it mean to move something from one place to another?

Ms. Williams: Exactly, Laura! Now, what else is special about these words?

Paco: I think they're cognates! "Transmit" is «*transmitir*» in Spanish and "transfer" means the same as «*transferir*». They have the same prefix in English and Spanish.

Ms. Williams: Wow, Paco! Are there any others you can think of?

Guadalupe: "Transcontinental" and «*transcontinental*». It means to move "across a continent."

Ms. Williams: Very good, Guadalupe! Any others?

Jaime: How about "transoceanic" and «*transoceánico*»? It means "across the ocean."

Ms. Williams: Excellent, Jaime!

In the dialogue, we see that Ms. Williams used the sentences containing the cognates directly from the book to have the students infer the meaning of the cognate prefix. Then, she checked for understanding by asking the students to generate their own examples.

Explicitly Teaching Cognate Prefixes That Are Not Identical

Not all cognate prefixes are identical. Therefore, teachers must make time to show students those prefixes that are not identical when transforming an English word to its Spanish cognate and the converse. Learning about such cognate prefixes will help students not only to recognize cognates, but also to generate new words that will help them express their thoughts. For example, when students know that the English prefix, /dis-/, is the same as the Spanish prefix, /des-/, they can use this rule to recognize that "disobey" and «*desobedecer*» are cognates. In addition, students will be able to use the rule to generate a word that at least approximates the English or Spanish cognate they want to communicate as shown in the following vignette. In the following dialogue, Ms. Williams uses explicit instruction to demonstrate cognate prefix rules to her ESL fourth, fifth, and sixth grade students, most of whom are Spanish speakers who are either newcomers or bilingual learners of intermediate and advanced levels of English language development.

Ms. Williams: Students, we've learned that English words often have prefixes that are the same as their Spanish cognates. Sometimes, however, the prefix for English words are different from their Spanish cognates. For example, English words having the prefix, /dis-/, are often the cognates of Spanish words having the prefix, /des-/. Examine the following list of cognates:

List 1	List 2
disconnect	*desconectar*
dishonor	*deshonrar*
disinfect	*desinfectar*
disobey	*desobedecer*

As you can see, the prefixes are spelled slightly differently. After the students see that the English prefix and the Spanish prefix are different, Ms. Williams continues the lesson:

Ms. Williams: Today, I'm going to show you a way for testing to see if two words are cognates of each other. Take the words, "disappear" and «*desaparecer*». Are they cognates? Let's see! First, let's change the English prefix, /dis-/ to /des-/. This gives us «*desappear*». Next, let's change "appear" to its Spanish cognate, «*aparecer*». Put these together and what do you get? «*Desaparecer*»! So, the English word, "disappear," and the Spanish word, «*desaparecer*», are cognates. Do you see how useful that strategy is? Now, let's use the same strategy to see if there is a Spanish cognate for the word "discover".

Brisa: If you change the /dis-/ to /des-/, you get «*descover*». Then, if you change "cover" to «*cubrir*», you get «*descubrir*»!

Ms. Williams: Very good, Brisa! Yes, the Spanish cognate for "discover" is «*descubrir*». Students, do you see how we can generate new words by knowing that some prefixes are the same or nearly the same in English and Spanish? What would the cognate for "disembark" be?

León: I think it would be «*desembarcar*», because /dis-/ equals /*des-*/ and "embark" is «*embarcar*»!

Ms. Williams: Excellent, León! Did everyone see how León transformed the English word "embark" to its Spanish cognate, «*embarcar*»?

Assorted Voices: Yes, Ms. Williams!

In the dialogue, Ms. Williams uses explicit instruction to teach students a strategy for testing to see if two words are cognates even though their prefixes are slightly different. Then, Ms. Williams showed her students the same strategy to generate new words for those cases in which the English and Spanish prefixes are not the same. To ensure the students learn the prefix rule, Ms. Williams creates an anchor chart. She also asks her students to look for other examples of the rule /dis-/ → /des-/ and has them create their own personal anchor charts using the cognates they find.

Teaching Germanic Cognate Prefixes

As was discussed in an earlier chapter, modern-day English is generally composed of words derived from Germanic languages and words that are Latin-based. Much of what is sometimes called everyday language is derived from Germanic languages, while much of what is often called academic language is derived from Latinate languages like Spanish. Germanic words are typically not Spanish–English cognates. Therefore, learning to discriminate between Germanic prefixes (e.g., /fore-/, meaning "before" or "front," and /over-/, meaning "too" or "excessively") and Latin-based prefixes will help students recognize Spanish–English cognates. A list of some of the more common Germanic cognate prefixes, their meanings, and examples of English words derived from Germanic languages is presented in Table 4.3.

In the following dialogue, Ms. Williams uses the concept-induction strategy to teach her fifth-grade ESL students that Germanic prefixes signal the presence of words that are not Spanish–English cognates. To begin the lesson, Ms. Williams writes the following words and synonyms on the board.

/fore-/

forecast—predict in advance

forerunner—someone who came before

foreshadow—gives warning of what may come

/pre-/

predict—forecast in advance

predecessor—someone who came before

presage—gives warning of what may come next

Table 4.3. Common Germanic prefixes and their meanings

Germanic prefix	Meaning(s)	Non-cognates
/fore-/	before, front	forearm, foreshadow
/mis-/	bad, badly	misbehave, misread
/out-/	beyond, more than	outnumber, outspend
/over-/	too, excessively	overdone, overachieve
/un-/	do the opposite of	undo, unlock
/under-/	beneath, lower than	underfed, underground

Ms. Williams: Class, today let's compare the prefixes, /fore-/ and /pre-/ and some of the words that can be formed from them. What do you notice about the two sets of words?

Students: Some of the words have the same meaning.

Ms. Williams: Exactly! The words formed from the prefix, /fore-/, are synonyms of the words formed from the prefix, /pre-/. Now, class, let's look at these English words and their meanings in Spanish.

[**Ms. Williams** writes on board.]

forecast—*predecir*   predict—*predecir*

forerunner—*predecessor*   predecessor—*predecesor*

foreshadow—*presagiar*   presage—*presagiar*

Vianey: Teacher, the words formed from the prefix, /pre-/, are cognates. The words formed with the prefix, /fore-/, are synonyms, but not Spanish–English cognates.

Ms. Williams: You're right! This is because prefixes, such as /fore-/ come from a Germanic language, Old English. Most of these words are not Spanish–English cognates. Words that have prefixes that come from Latin and Greek are often Spanish–English cognates. This is important because whenever you come to an unfamiliar word that begins with a Germanic prefix, such as /fore-/, don't try to think of a Spanish cognate word that has that prefix. It probably won't work.

In the dialogue, we observe Ms. Williams contrasting lists of words having Germanic prefixes and Latin prefixes. This permits the students to see that the words formed from Germanic and Latin and Greek prefixes had similar meanings, but only the words formed from Latin and Greek prefixes are cognates. To extend this lesson, teachers can have their students look through the dictionary for words beginning with the Germanic prefixes listed in Table 4.3 to see if they resemble any Spanish words.

FOCUSING ON ROOT WORDS

As was the case with prefixes, cognates can be learned through the study of Latin and Greek root words and can lead to the acquisition of other words possessing the same root. Furthermore, just as Latin and Greek prefixes are likely to be similar in English and Spanish, the same can be said for root words derived from the Latin and the Greek. Many cognates possessing common Latin and Greek roots can be found in the Cognate Companion. Some were presented earlier in the chapter. We learned the root word, /-traer-/, means "to draw or pull," /-port-/ signifies "to carry," and /-cycle-/ means "circle or cycle." A listing of some common Latin and Greek root words are presented in Table 4.4 and Table 4.5, respectively.

> **LESSON PLAN**
>
> *I, Galileo*
> (Christensen, 2012)

In the following dialogue, Mr. Cuello uses concept induction to establish the relationship between root words and Spanish–English cognates through the cognate vocabulary culled from the picture book, I, Galileo (Christensen, 2012), a biography of the great 17th-century astronomer Galileo Galilei (1564–1642). Specifically, Mr. Cuello uses the cognates contradict/*contradecir* and predict/*predecir* to teach the meaning of the Latin root, /-dict-/, meaning "to say." To start, Mr. Cuello writes down the words "contradict" and "predict" on the board.

Mr. Cuello: Class, look at the words I've written on the board. How are these words, "contradict" and "predict," alike?

Students: They both have the letters "d-i-c-t."

Table 4.4. Common cognate Latin roots

Latin Root	Meaning	Example cognates
/aqua-/	water	aquamarine/*aquamarina*, aquarium/*acuario*, aquatic/*acuático*, aqueous/*acuoso*
/-cede/	to yield	cede/*ceder*, exceed/*exceder*, precede/*preceder*, proceed/*proceder*, recede/*retroceder*
/-corp-/	body	corporation/*corporación*, corpse/*cuerpo*, incorporate/*incorporar*, incorporeal/*incórporeo*
/-dict-/, /-dic-/	to say	benediction/*bendición*, contradict/*contradecir*, dictator/*dictador*, dictionary/*diccionario*
/-duct-/	to lead	aqueduct/*acueducto*, conductor/*conductor*, introduction/*introducción*, productive/*productivo*
/-equ-/	equal	equal/*igual*, equality/*igualdad*, equator/*ecuador*, equilibrium/*equilibrio*, equivalent/*equivalente*
/-ject-/	to throw	eject/*eyectar*, injection/*inyección*, objective/*objetivo*, projector/*proyector*
/magni-/	great	magnification/*magnificación*, magnificent/*magnífico*, magnify/*magnificar*, magnitude/*magnitud*
/-port-/	to carry	airport/*aeropuerto*, deport/*deportar*, import/*importar*, portable/*portátil*, transportation/*transportación*
/-script-/	to write	description/*descripción*, inscription/*inscripción*, manuscript/*manuscrito*, prescription/*prescripción*
/-spec-/	to see	inspect/*inspeccionar*, perspective/*perspectiva*, prospector/*prospector*, spectator/*espectador*
/-spir-/	to breathe	conspiracy/*conspiración*, inspiration/*inspiración*, respire/*respirar*, spiritual/*espiritual*
/-tract-/	draw, pull	attract/*atraer*, distract/*distraer*, extract/*extraer*, subtract/*sustraer*, tractor/*tractor*
/-viv-/	to live	revive/*revivir*, survive/*sobrevivir*, vivacious/*vivaz*, vivid/*vívido*, viviparous/*vivíparo*

Mr. Cuello:	Yes. And what are "contradict" and "predict" in Spanish?
Penelope:	"Contradict" is «*contradecir*», and "predict" is «*predecir*». They're cognates.
Mr. Cuello:	That's right! They are cognates. What does it mean to "contradict" someone?
Juan:	It means to say the opposite of what someone else said.
Mr. Cuello:	You're right, "to say the opposite." So, what does "predict" mean?
Alma:	It means to say that something will happen before it happens.
Mr. Cuello:	Yes! So, what do "contradict" and "predict' have in common?

Table 4.5. Common cognate Greek roots

Greek root	Meaning	Example cognates
/-aster-/, /-astro-/	star	asterisk/*asterisco*, astronaut/*astronauta*, astronomer/*astrónomo*, disastrous/*desastroso*
/-bio-/	life	biochemical/*bioquímico*, biography/*biografía*, biology/*biología*, bioluminescent/*bioluminescente*
/-chrono-/	time	chronic/*crónico*, chronicle/*crónica*, chronology/*cronología*, chronometer/*cronómetro*
/-cycle-/	circle	bicycle/*bicicleta*, encyclopedia/*enciclopedia*, recycle/*reciclar*, tricycle/*triciclo*, unicycle/*uniciclo*
/-gon-/	angle	diagonal/*diagonal*, hexagonal/*hexagonal*, octagon/*octágono*, polygon/*polígono*
/-graph-/	writing, recording	autograph/*autografo*, calligraphy/*caligrafía*, paragraph/*párrafo*, phonograph/*fonógrafo*
/-meter-/	to measure	diameter/*diámetro*, kilometer/*kilómetro*, odometer/*odómetro*, perimeter/*perímetro*
/-photo-/	light	photoelectric/*fotoeléctrico*, photon/*fotón*, photoreceptor/*fotoreceptor*, photosynthesis/*fotosíntesis*
/-pod-/	foot	tripod/*trípode*, arthropod/*artrópodo*, podium/*podio*, therapod/*terépodo*
/-psych-/	mind	psychedelic/*psicodélico*, psychiatric/*psiquiátrico*, psychic/*psíquico*, psychological/*psicológico*
/-ptera-/	wing	coleoptera/*coleóptero*, hemiptera/*hemiptera*, orthoptera/*ortóptero*, pterodactyl/*pterodáctilo*,
/-sphere-/	ball	atmosphere/*atmósfera*, bathysphere/*batisfera*, hemisphere/*hemisferio*, stratosphere/*estratósfera*
/-tele-/	afar	telegraph/*telégrafo*, telephone/*teléfono*, telescope/*telescopio*, televisión/*televisión*
/-therm-/	heat	exothermic/*exotérmico*, endothermic/*endotérmico*, thermal/*termal*, thermos/*termo*

Liliana:	They both have to do with saying something. So, does /-dict-/ mean «*decir*»?
Mr. Cuello:	Exactly! Do you see how comparing words with the same root, like "contradict" and "predict," you can figure out the meaning of the root word? How might these words be related to the word "diction"?
Armando:	Doesn't that have something to do with the way you say something?
Mr. Cuello:	Good thinking, Armando! It does have to do with the way you say something. It has to do with how clearly you say something. Now, do you guys see how all these words are related?
Class (Assorted students):	Yes, Mr. Cuello. We understand it!

In the dialogue, Mr. Cuello explained that the two words, "contradict" and "predict," have the meaning of the root word, /-dict-/, as part of their definitions. Students used the meanings of those words to guess the meaning of the root word. Mr. Cuello then concluded the lesson by introducing the related word, "diction," illustrating two of the benefits of knowing root words: they help students understand the meanings of new words and they also help them see the semantic relationships among words with the same root.

Mr. Cuello also made the point that many words with the same root word are cognates, which offers a powerful advantage to bilingual learners. Whenever these students see a known root in an unknown word, they can think of a Spanish cognate that is spelled the same or almost the same, and then make sense of the new word in English.

> **LESSON PLAN**
>
> Planting Stories: The Life of Librarian and Storyteller Pura Belpré
> (Denise, 2019)
> Lizzy Demands a Seat!: *Elizabeth Jennings Fights for* Streetcar Rights
> (Anderson, 2020)
> Noah Webster & His Words
> (Ferris, 2015)

To extend the lesson and check for understanding, Mr. Cuello went to the Cognate Companion to find picture books that contain cognates possessing the root word, /-dict-/. For his language arts class, he pointed out the word, «*benediction*», which contains the root word, /-dict-/, while reading the Américas Award picture book, Planting Stories: The Life of Librarian and Storyteller Pura Belpré (Denise, 2019). On another day, Mr. Cuello taught his class the word, "verdict," another word with the root word, /-dict-/. He did this while reading from the Notable Social Studies book, Lizzy Demands a Seat!: Elizabeth Jennings Fights for Streetcar Rights (Anderson, 2020). Later in the semester as he read aloud another Notable Social Studies book, Noah Webster & His Words (Ferris, 2015), Mr. Cuello taught his students that the word, "dictionary" is another cognate having the root word, /-dict-/. Mr. Cuello's cognate morphology instruction is an example of how a teacher can provide the reinforcement and generalization for the learning of root words through the read-alouds of culturally and socially relevant books.

REINFORCING THE LEARNING OF PREFIXES AND ROOT WORDS

We have found several activities that are useful for reinforcing the learning of cognate prefixes and root words. These activities are particularly effective following a picture book read-aloud and its related vocabulary learning. Among these are flashcards, word banks, word sorts, sentence completion exercises, word searches, cognate spelling bees, cognate bingo, and anchor charts for illustrating morphological and spelling rules. Let's take a look at a few types of review exercises to specifically help solidify cognate prefix and root word lessons.

Flashcards and Word Banks

Flashcards provide a quick and easy way to learn cognate vocabulary. Teachers can create flashcards for cognate prefixes and root words by printing the English on one side and its Spanish cognate on the other. As teachers walk around the classroom, they can survey student understanding and identify words that are easy for students, as well as those that are not. By observing students as they learn their vocabulary words from flashcards, teachers can correct any problems the students may have in a timely manner.

Flashcards are also useful because students can save them in word banks and study them in their free time. Students often enjoy drawing pictures on the flashcards to help them recall word meanings and should be encouraged to do so. Flashcards also can be adapted for use in word sorts as discussed as follows.

Word Sorts

Primary school teachers can use word sorts to teach students about cognates (Hernández & Montelongo, 2018). For reinforcing the learning of cognate prefixes, teachers can distribute two different sets of cards to each student. One set of flashcards might contain eight to ten English words while the other set of flashcards has the matching Spanish cognates, as in Figure 4.1. The students first match the English words with their Spanish cognates, and then they match the Spanish words with their English cognates. Once they have done this, they can sort the cognate pairs by prefix or word root.

A parallel activity is to sort cognates by root words as shown in Figure 4.2.

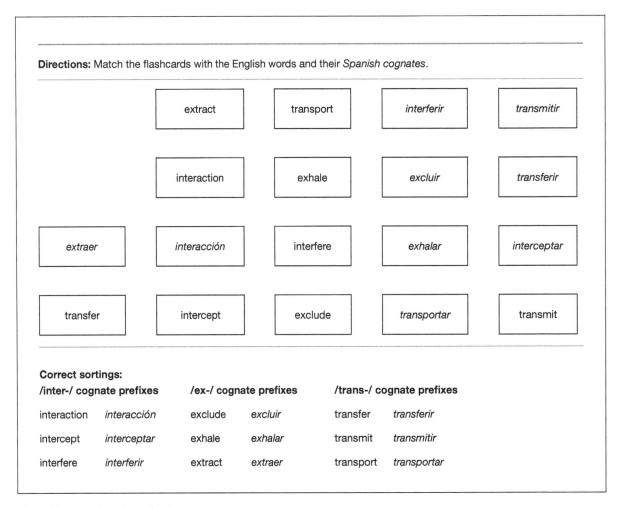

Figure 4.1.   Cognate prefix word sorts.

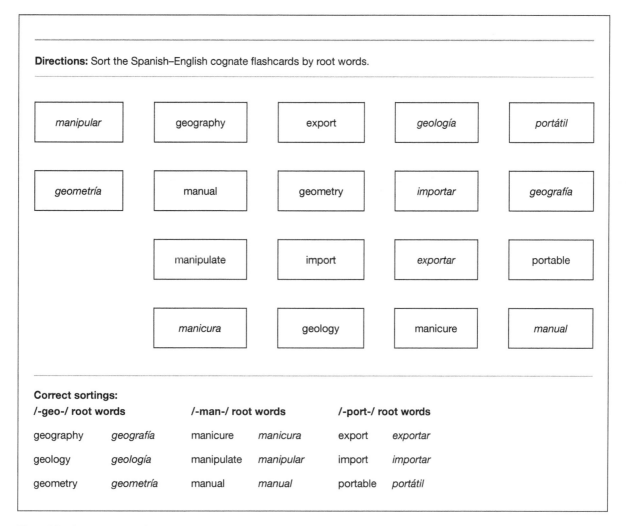

Directions: Sort the Spanish–English cognate flashcards by root words.

manipular	geography	export	*geología*	*portátil*
geometría	manual	geometry	*importar*	*geografía*
	manipulate	import	*exportar*	portable
	manicura	geology	manicure	*manual*

Correct sortings:

/-geo-/ root words		/-man-/ root words		/-port-/ root words	
geography	*geografía*	manicure	*manicura*	export	*exportar*
geology	*geología*	manipulate	*manipular*	import	*importar*
geometry	*geometría*	manual	*manual*	portable	*portátil*

Figure 4.2. Cognate root word sorts.

Formation Exercises

After a lesson on English and Spanish cognate prefixes and root words, teachers can assess student understanding of these rules by having students combine the prefixes with other words. For this activity, students are first presented with the meaning of a prefix. Then they complete the prefix–word combinations and give the meaning of the resulting word, as shown in Figure 4.3. For example, students are taught that the English prefix, /dis-/, means "to do the opposite of." When /dis-/ is combined with the word "appear," it yields the word "disappear," which means to "do the opposite of appear." Similarly, when the Spanish prefix, /des-/, is combined with the word, «aparecer», the resulting word, «desaparecer», means «hacer lo contrario de aparecer».

Similarly, students can be presented with root words in combinations with different prefixes and suffixes, like those shown in Figure 4.4. The task for the students is to combine the prefixes and the root words to generate new words. After having done so, the students are asked to provide a meaning for each of the root words. To illustrate, all of the English words possessing the root word, /-phon-/, have the word "sound" in their meanings. Therefore, students can intuit that the meaning of /-phon-/ is "sound." In like manner, students can guess that Spanish words having the root word, /-fono-/, have something to do with "sound."

Cognate Prefix Exercises

Directions: Fill in the blanks with your best guess of the missing words.

/dis-/ (do the opposite of)	=	***/des-/ (hacer lo contrario de)***
/dis-/ + /-appear-/	=	*/des-/ + /-aparecer/*
/dis-/ + /-cover/	=	*/des-/ + /-cubrir/*
/dis-/ + /-obey/	=	*/des-/ + /-obedecer/*
/dis-/ + /-approve/	=	_____
_____	=	*/des-/ + /-conectar/*
_____	=	*/des-/ + /-embarcar/*
/dis-/ + /-infect/	=	_____
/re-/ (do over again)	=	***re- (hacer de nuevo)***
/re-/ + /-use/	=	*/re-/ + /-usar/*
/re-/ + /-iterate/	=	*/re-/ + /-iterar/*
/re-/ + /-invent/	=	*/re-/ + /-inventar/*
_____	=	*/re-/ + /-grupar/*
/re-/ + /-form/	=	_____
_____	=	*/re-/ + /-sellar/*
/re-/ + /-unite/	=	_____

Figure 4.3. Prefix meanings and combinations.

Cognate Root Words

Directions: Combine the cognate prefixes and cognate root words to generate new words. Then guess the meaning of the root word. See the first example, /-phon/, which means "sound."

/homo-/ + /-phone/ = with the same sound	*/homó-/ + /-fono/ = con el mismo sonido*
/sym-/ + /-phony/ = sound together	*/sin-/ + /-fonía/ = conjunto de sonidos*
/tele-/ + /-phone/ = distant sound	*/telé-/ + /-fono/ = sonido de distancia*
/-phon/ = sound	***/-fono/* = _____**
/geo-/ + /-logy/ = study of the earth	*/geo-/ + /-logía/ = estudio de la tierra*
/geo/ + /graph/ = graph of the Earth	*/geo/ + /grafía/ = gráfico de la tierra*
/geo/ + /metry/ = measurement of Earth	*/geo/ + /metría/ = medición de la tierra*
/geo-/ = _____	***/geo-/* = _____**
/bi-/ + /-nom/ /-ial/ = having two names	*/bi-/ + /-nom/ /-ial/ = tener dos nombres*
/poly-/ + /-nom/+ /-ial/ = having many names	*/poly-/ + /-nom/+ /-ial/ = tener muchos nombres*
/tri-/ + /-nom/ + /-ial/ = having three names	*/tri-/ + /-nom/ + /-ial/ = tener tres nombres*
/-nom/ = _____	***/-nom/* = _____**

Figure 4.4. Root word combinations and meanings.

SUMMARY

Spanish–English cognates are often words that are morphologically complex. That is, they are often made up of a prefix, a root word, and a suffix. Knowing the meanings of these word parts can help students deconstruct unfamiliar words to make meaning of them. New words can be generated by interchanging the word parts and creating new meanings.

Learning the meanings of prefixes and root words is made easier for bilingual learners when teachers use familiar Spanish–English cognates. Using known cognates facilitates learning because students can focus on combining prefixes and root words without having to also learn the meaning of the resulting word. Many lesson plans in the Cognate Companion provide suggestions for which prefixes and/or suffixes to teach with a specific picture book.

Our focus in this chapter has been on Latin and Greek cognate prefixes and root words that make up a large part of the cognate vocabulary in English, especially words used primarily for academic purposes. We also recommend the teaching of Germanic prefixes because words with Germanic prefixes usually signal words that are not Spanish–English cognates.

> ### Did you know?
>
> Teachers can use the Cognate Companion to find award-winning picture books that contain precisely the prefix or root word they want to highlight during picture book read-alouds, not only during language arts but also in other K–5 content-area instruction, such as science, social studies, and mathematics.

This chapter shows teachers how to engage bilingual learners with cognate prefix and root word instruction. Bilingual and monolingual English-speaking teachers can use the examples of classroom dialogue in bilingual, general education, and ESL classrooms to stimulate their thinking about how to teach important morphological concepts to the bilingual learners in their own classes. We also explored activities to encourage student application of the prefixes and root words they learn.

REFLECTION AND ACTION

1. Choose a picture book. Enter its title into the text box of the Cognate Companion. Review the list of cognates that the book includes. Consider how you might teach a given prefix rule or root word using concept induction.

2. Identify several prefixes that you already teach to which cognate rules apply or select a prefix from Tables 4.1 and 4.2. Use the Cognate Companion to find one or two picture books that include these prefixes. Using the example dialogues as a model, create a sample dialogue to teach your identified prefixes as a part of a pre-reading or post-reading activity.

3. Choose one or two cognate root words you already teach or select a root word from Tables 4.3 and 4.4. Using the Cognate Companion, find an appropriate picture book to teach your selected root word(s). Plan your lesson following the example dialogue for teaching a root word such as /-dict-/, /-tract-/, or /-cycle/. Be sure to teach the root word with cognate examples within the read-aloud.

5

Teaching Cognate Suffixes

Cognate Play

For the following Spanish cognates, write the English cognates. Then identify the suffix in the Spanish and English cognates. What commonalities do you see between the cognates? Answers can be found in bold on the bottom of the next page.

Spanish Cognate	English Cognate
transportación	_____
información	_____
celebración	_____
Sufijo _____	Suffix _____

S uffixes are an important element in the study of morphology. The usual role of suffixes is to change a word's part of speech, unlike prefixes and root words that affect a change in meaning. There are suffixes in English that are similar in spelling and meaning to suffixes in Spanish. These cognate suffixes can be used to figure out the meanings of unfamiliar words. They can also be used to convert words from English to Spanish and from Spanish to English. For example, the noun, "glory," becomes the adjective, "glorious," with the addition of the suffix, /-ous/. Similarly, the Spanish noun, «gloria», becomes the adjective, «glorioso», because of the suffix, /-oso/. Indeed, many English words ending in /-ous/ are the cognates of Spanish words ending in /-oso/ and vice versa. There are approximately forty such rules for converting words to their cognate equivalents. Learning these conversion rules will enhance students' abilities not only to recognize cognates, but to also generate new ones from one language to the other. In this chapter, we will learn about these useful cognate suffixes and the part they play in recognizing cognates and transforming words from one language to the other. We will also review ways to teach cognate suffix conversion rules using picture books in language arts and other content areas.

SUFFIXES AND THE GENERATIVE NATURE OF LANGUAGE

English and Spanish use prefixes and suffixes in combination with root words to create new words. These languages are said to be generative because it is possible to generate new words by combining the different word parts in a rule-governed way. When teachers introduce students to the generative nature of language, bilingual learners can dramatically build vocabulary in two languages.

Teaching students about suffixes builds competence as students learn variations of words that can be used syntactically in different ways. When students look up a word in the dictionary, they will find headwords, the main entries in a dictionary, and variant words, those formed with suffixes that change the headwords into different parts of speech. For example, the headword and verb "create" has four variants: an adjective "creativity," an adverb "creatively," and two nouns "creator" and "creation." Once they learn about suffixes, the patterns they follow, and the rules that govern them, students will be able to generate hundreds of other cognates. Examples of headwords and their variants are presented in Table 5.1.

Table 5.1. Academic vocabulary headwords and their adjective, verb, and noun variants

Headword	Variants	Variants	Variants
abstract (adj.):	abstract**ive** (adj.)	abstract**ly** (adv.)	abstrac**tion** (n.)
create (v.):	creat**ive** (adj.)	creat**or** (n.)	crea**tion** (n.)
expand (v.)	expand**able** (adj.)	expans**ive** (n.)	expan**sion** (n.)
final (adj.)	final**ist** (n.)	final**ly** (adv.)	final**ity** (n.)
indicate (v.)	indicat**ive** (adj.)	indicat**or** (n.)	indica**tion** (n.)
mental (adj.)	mental**ist** (n.)	mental**ly** (adv.)	mental**ity** (n.)
predict (v.)	predict**able** (adj.)	predict**or** (n.)	predict**ability** (n.)
transit (n.)	transit**ory** (adj.)	transit**ive** (adj.)	transi**tion** (n.)

Answers:

Spanish Cognate	English Cognate
transportación	transportation
información	information
celebración	celebration
Sufijo **ción**	Suffix **tion**

Cognate Suffix Rules in English and Spanish

One reason that cognate suffixes are so helpful is because they can often be used to change an English word to its Spanish cognate or vice versa. Some cognate suffix conversion rules are obvious because the English suffixes are spelled the same as their Spanish cognate equivalents. In the case of the cognate suffix rule, /al-/ → /-al/, meaning "relating to," the English suffix is the same as the Spanish suffix. This is seen in the cognate pairs: natural/*natural*, special/*especial*, and tropical/*tropical*. More often, however, there are orthographic differences. In the case of the cognate suffix rule, /-ly/ → /-mente/, defined as in what manner, the English and Spanish suffixes are different, as illustrated by the cognate pairs, finally/*finalmente*, precisely/*precisamente*, and totally/*totalmente*.

To provide readers with a sampling of the generative potential of cognate suffix instruction, Table 5.2 includes examples of suffix rules for converting English words into Spanish words and the converse. Most common suffixes listed in the table are used to form nouns or adjectives. Two of them, /-ify/ and /-ize/, are used to make verbs, while /-ly/ is used to create adverbs. With few exceptions, most examples of the words formed by the common suffixes are abstract academic

Table 5.2. Cognate suffix conversion rules

Rules	Examples
/-able/ → /-able/	deplorable/*deplorable*, inevitable/*inevitable*, notable/*notable*
/-act/ → /-acto/	contact/*contacto*, exact/*exacto*, tact/*tacto*
/-al/ → /-al/	animal/*animal*, central/*central*, principal/*principal*
/-ance/ → /-ancia/	distance/*distancia*, elegance/*elegancia*, tolerance/*tolerancia*
/-ant/ → /-ante/	important/*importante*, participant/*participante*, vibrant/*vibrante*
/-ar/ → /-ar/	lunar/*lunar*, popular/*popular*, spectacular/*espectacular*
/-ary/ → /-ario/	contrary/*contrario*, glossary/*glosario*, sedentary/*sedentario*
/-ate/ → /-ar/	accelerate/*acelerar*, operate/*operar*, terminate/*terminar*
/-ence/ → /-encia/	difference/*diferencia*, influence/*influencia*, sequence/*secuencia*
/-ent/ → /-ente/	continent/*continente*, latent/*latente*, reverent/*reverente*
/-gy/ → /-gía/	chronology/*cronología*, mythology/*mitología*, zoology/*zoología*
/-ible/ → /-ible/	audible/*audible*, eligible/*eligible*, permissible/*permisible*
/-ic/ → /-ico/	academic/*académico*, gothic/*gótico*, tragic/*trágico*
/-ical/ → /-ico/	critical/*crítico*, musical/*músico*, technical/*técnico*
/-id/ → /-ido/	hybrid/*híbrido*, rapid/*rápido*, vivid/*vívido*
/-ify/ → /-ificar/	diversify/*diversificar*, modify/*modificar*, simplify/*simplificar*
/-ile/ → /-il/	fragile/*frágil*, infantile/*infantil*, versatile/*versátil*
/-ism/ → /-ismo/	centralism/*centralismo*, hypnotism/*hipnotismo*, optimism/*optimismo*
/-ist/ → /-isto/	artist/*artista*, harpist/*arpista*, terrorist/*terrorista*
/-ity/ → /-idad/	clarity/*claridad*, identity/*identidad*, visibility/*visibilidad*
/-ive/ → /-ivo/	consecutive/*consecutivo*, productive/*productivo*, tentative/*tentativo*
/-ly/ → /-mente/	basically/*básicamente*, frankly/*francamente*, simply/*simplemente*
/-ment/ → /-mento/	cement/*cemento*, element/*elemento*, rudiment/*rudimento*
/-or/ → /-or/	creator/*creador*, horror/*horror*, professor/*profesor*
/-ory/ → /-orio/	directory/*directorio*, satisfactory/*satisfactorio*, territory/*territorio*
/-ous/ → /-oso/	disastrous/*desastroso*, luminous/*luminoso*, prestigious/*prestigioso*
/-sion/ → /-sión/	conclusion/*conclusión*, illusion/*ilusión*, omission/*omisión*
/-sis/ → /-sis/	analysis/*análisis*, emphasis/*énfasis*, synthesis/*síntesis*
/-tion/ → /-ción/	appreciation/*apreciación*, definition/*definición*, pollution/*polución*

Figure 5.1a. Anchor chart of suffix rule /-tion/ → /-ción/.

Figure 5.1b. Examples of students' sticky notes to contribute additional cognates they come across.

words. Therefore, many words that result from the addition of these suffixes are Tier Two or Tier Three words, the majority of which are academic vocabulary words that require explicit instruction.

We teach students suffix conversion rules because they are powerful strategies for increasing vocabulary. When bilingual students learn that cognate suffixes are rule-governed, they are able to guess the meaning of unfamiliar words that follow the cognate suffix rules. For example, suppose a Spanish-speaking bilingual student comes across an unfamiliar word, "intensive," while reading an English text. Knowing that the English suffix /-ive/ has a corresponding Spanish cognate suffix /-ivo/ the student can confidently guess that "intensive" is probably the cognate of the Spanish word, «intensivo», and continue reading.

We also teach our students cognate suffix rules because it gives them the ability to produce or generate new words to communicate their ideas. For example, suppose a Spanish-speaking bilingual learner needs a word to express an idea on an essay. Let us imagine that this student requires an English word that means the same as the Spanish word «creativo». Knowing the cognate suffix rule, /-ivo/ → /-ive/, the student can use «creativo» to form the English word "creative." Although it is possible that a word generated in this manner may not always be correct, knowing the suffix conversion rules provides the student with at least the means to make an intelligent guess. Another cognate suffix rule we teach students is the /-tion/ → /-ción/ as shown in Figure 5.1a. The sticky notes in Figures 5.1a and 5.1b contain cognates students have added to the lists.

Explicitly Teaching Cognate Suffix Rules: An Experimental Study

In our practice, we have found that we need to explicitly teach students the cognate suffix conversion rules. To demonstrate this, we implemented a research study to provide suffix lessons for two classrooms of fourth-graders. The students in the experimental group were explicitly taught the suffix rules for converting words from English to Spanish and from Spanish to English. For example, the experimental group was given the following explicit instruction: "Whenever an English word ends with /-ity/, it usually has a Spanish cognate that ends in /-idad/." We followed this explicit instruction with examples such as community/*comunidad*, personality/*personalidad*, and vanity/*vanidad*. The students in the control were taught the same cognate words but no mention was made of any of the suffix conversion rules. After two weeks of cognate vocabulary instruction, we gave both groups of students a list of previously unseen infrequent English–Spanish cognates possessing the suffix rules that were taught. The students were then asked to transform the words from English to Spanish and vice versa.

Not surprisingly, the experimental group significantly outperformed the control in being able to convert words from English to Spanish and vice versa. The students in the experimental group were able to specify the suffix conversion rules they used to transform the word, and they were also able to communicate this knowledge to their teachers and fellow classmates. In comparison, the few students in the control group who seemed to have learned some of the suffix conversion rules could not explain why they answered as they did. Moreover, they could not explain the processes to their teachers or their fellow classmates. They intuitively knew the rules, but they did not have the vocabulary for expressing their knowledge.

Since that study, we have conducted other similar studies in elementary, middle, and high schools and have found that teaching suffix conversion rules explicitly results in students being able to generate the correct cognates in the other language. In one study, Hillary Vozza found that explicit instruction of cognate suffix rules was effective for English-speaking high school students learning Spanish (Vozza, 2018).

The results of these studies demonstrate the power of explicit cognate instruction and its effects on thinking and talking about language. When students can talk about their languages, in this case about suffix conversion rules, they demonstrate their growing metalinguistic awareness. We have also discovered that the effects of using explicit instruction to teach cognates goes well beyond the classroom. We have observed, for example, that when bilingual learners learn about the cognate conversion suffix rules, they begin to look for other suffix rules. It is as if these students suddenly have morphed into amateur linguists.

TEACHING COGNATE SUFFIX CONVERSION RULES IN ENGLISH AND SPANISH

Now that we have learned about these suffix conversion rules, let's look at techniques for teaching the suffixes. As with prefixes and root words, we use the suffixes found in picture books to create snap-on suffix lessons, which teachers can find on the Cognate Companion. This section shows teachers how to teach cognate suffix rules using picture books. We also draw attention to Germanic suffixes that signal that a word is not a Spanish–English cognate.

> **Did you know?**
>
> Teachers can find lesson plans on the Cognate Companion that show how to teach suffix conversion rules using picture books.

Teaching Cognate Suffix Rules Using Picture Books

Teachers can search the Cognate Companion database to find the picture book they want to read aloud. Once they have chosen the book, they can select the essential cognate vocabulary words to teach. They can also decide upon the suffix rule(s) for the mini lesson they want to accompany the read aloud.

One of the teachers we work with, Mr. Davis, planned to read She Persisted: 13 American Women Who Changed the World (Clinton, 2017) to the bilingual learners in his fifth-grade classroom, which introduces women activists including: Harriet Tubman, Helen Keller, Ruby Bridges, Sally Ride, Oprah Winfrey, and Sonia Sotomayor. In addition to the other literacy activities revolving around the stories of real-life women who did not give up in the face of adversity, Mr. Davis decided to create a mini-lesson for the cognate suffix rule, /-ity/ →/-idad/, using the cognates that appear in the book: ability/*habilidad*, monstrosity/*monstruosidad*, and opportunity/*oportunidad*. Mr. Davis extended the lesson to include

> **LESSON PLAN**
>
> She Persisted: 13 American Women Who Changed the World (Clinton, 2017)

other cognates that followed the same suffix rule: community/*comunidad*, dignity/*dignidad*, necessity/*necesidad*, and tranquility/*tranquilidad*. He found these words in the Find-a-Cognate Database of the Cognate Companion. Mr. Davis's students not only learned the cognate suffix rule, /-ity/ →/-idad/, but also useful Tier Two academic words.

Selecting a Cognate Suffix Rule

A second strategy for building cognate suffix lessons around picture book read-alouds is to decide on a particular suffix rule and then use the Cognate Companion to find a listing of the picture books containing cognate suffixes that reflect the desired rule. To illustrate, Mr. Davis wanted to teach his students the rule, /-ence/ → /-encia/, as an activity to follow the read-aloud. Using the Cognate Companion, Mr. Davis inputted the suffix rule he wanted in the text box. All at once, all cognates that followed the /-ence/ → /-encia/ rule and all the picture books that contained them appeared on the screen. From the list, Mr. Davis selected the picture book, Thurgood (Winter, 2019), a biography of the first Black U.S. Supreme Court Justice, Thurgood Marshall, who argued the 1954 *Brown v. Board of Education* case, which declared the "separate but equal" doctrine unconstitutional. This book was an especially good choice because it was rich enough in /-ence/ → /-encia/ cognates to create a mini-lesson on the rule: difference/*diferencia*, evidence/*evidencia*, experience/*experiencia*, and innocence/*inocencia*.

In a social studies lesson later in the week, Mr. Davis performed a read-aloud of Frederick Douglass: The Lion Who Wrote History (Myers, 2021), a biography of the great social reformer and abolitionist of the 19th century, who escaped slavery and was well-known for his anti-slavery writings. As part of the post-reading activities, Mr. Davis pointed out the cognate, "eloquence," as an example of the /-ence/ → /-encia/ suffix rule. On another occasion, Mr. Davis read from the picture book biography of Ada Lovelace (1815–1852), Ada's Ideas: The Story of the World's First Computer Programmer (Robinson, 2016). Lovelace, the daughter of Lord Byron, helped program the Analytical Engine, a precursor to the modern day computer. As one of his cognate vocabulary words, Mr. Davis selected the word, "influence," which he used to remind his students that it, too, follows the /-ence/ → /-encia/ cognate suffix rule.

The preceding two examples of teaching the cognate suffix rule, /-ence/ → /-encia/, illustrate some of the ways in which teachers can use the Cognate Companion to find the cognates in picture books to design vocabulary lessons on the various suffix conversion rules. Teachers can also find ready-made snap-on lesson plans in the Cognate Companion to accompany a particular picture book.

Did you know?

The Cognate Companion can be used to locate picture books with cognates that match a suffix conversion rule of your choice.

LESSON PLAN

Thurgood (Winter, 2019)
Frederick Douglass: The Lion Who Wrote History (Myers, 2021)
Ada's Ideas: The Story of the World's First Computer Programmer (Robinson, 2016)

Teaching Suffix Rules Through Concept-Induction

One of our favorite stories to read aloud to second-grade students is the Caldecott Award-winning book, Sylvester and the Magic Pebble (Steig, 1969), the story of a donkey who finds a magic pebble that grants the wishes of the person holding it. After discovering the magical powers of the pebble, Sylvester encounters a hungry lion. To avoid being eaten, Sylvester wishes to be transformed into a rock—and he is. To further complicate matters, the magic pebble lands several feet from the rock. Unable to reach out and hold the pebble, Sylvester faces the prospect of spending all eternity as a rock unless someone miraculously places the pebble where Sylvester can touch it, so that he can wish himself to his original form. The odds of that happening were long indeed!

Sylvester's parents and their neighbors searched in vain for the missing Sylvester. Seasons came and went and everyone who knew Sylvester had given up hope of his return. As fate would have it, however, Sylvester's parents chanced upon the magic pebble and placed it on top of the rock that was Sylvester. This permitted Sylvester the opportunity to wish himself back to his former self. Voilà! Sylvester returned as the lovable donkey he once was. Now, there was no need to wish for anything else. Sylvester and his

LESSON PLAN

Sylvester and the Magic Pebble (Steig, 1969)

parents had all they needed or wanted in their love for each other. As for the magic pebble, the happy family stored it in a safe place, never to be used again.

In addition to being an engaging and timeless read-aloud story, <u>Sylvester and the Magic Pebble</u> contains many useful cognate words for creating cognate suffix lessons. Among the vocabulary words from Sylvester, a teacher can teach a Tier Two word, such as "mysterious," as an example of an /-ous/ → /-oso/ suffix conversion rule.

As we saw with prefixes and root words, an especially effective way for teaching suffix regularities is through concept induction, using specific examples that allow students to arrive at the cognate suffix rule and generate other instances of the rule. To illustrate using the concept induction strategy, we will follow the lesson presented by Mrs. Martínez. In the dialogue—part of the post-reading activities for <u>Sylvester and the Magic Pebble</u>—Mrs. Martínez uses the cognate word, "mysterious," as her starting point. Notice the questions that Mrs. Martínez uses to help students induce the suffix conversion rule, /-ous/ → /-oso/:

English	Spanish
mysterious	*misterioso*
fabulous	*fabuloso*
marvelous	*maravilloso*
suspicious	*sospechoso*

Mrs. Martínez:	Class, one of the words we saw in the reading of Sylvester and the Magic Pebble was the word, "mysterious." On the board, I've written words like "mysterious" along with some other English and Spanish words. What can someone tell us about the words in the English and Spanish columns?
Several students:	They're cognates, Mrs. Martínez!
Mrs. Martínez:	That's right! But there's also something special about these cognates.
Paulina:	The English words end in /-ous/ and the Spanish words end in /-oso/.
Mrs. Martínez:	That's correct! There are other English words that end in /-ous/ that are cognates of Spanish words that end in /-oso/. Can anyone think of others beside the ones I have listed on the board?
Marco:	«*Famoso*» and "famous"!
Mrs. Martínez:	Yes, any others?
Leo:	How about «*curioso*» and "curious"?
Mrs. Martínez:	Good, Leo!
Yvonne:	I know one! "delicious" and «*delicioso*».
Mrs. Martínez:	Great, Yvonne! There are lots of English words that end in /-ous/ that have Spanish cognates ending in /-oso/.

In the dialogue, Mrs. Martínez structured the mini-lesson so that students induced the rule, /-ous/ and /-oso/. In doing so, Mrs. Martínez is teaching her students basic lessons in word consciousness and how to learn rules on their own.

Mrs. Martínez followed the lesson on the cognate suffix rule, /ous/→/-oso/, using other picture books found in the Cognate Companion. In her social studies class, Mrs. Martinez read the book, <u>Not Quite Snow White</u> (Franklin, 2019), about a young African American girl whose audition for the part of the lead princess role in a musical play about Snow White is met with glares, whispers, and snickers from the other girls. Mrs. Martínez reminds students that the word, "fabulous," in Not Quite Snow White, is another example of a cognate that follows the rule, /-ous/→/-oso/.

In her science class later in the semester, Mrs. Martínez performed a read-aloud of the picture book, Nothing Stopped Sophie: The Story of the Unshakable Mathematician Sophie Germain (Bardoe, 2018), a biography of the mathematician who did groundbreaking work in physics. This book contains the cognate, "prestigious," which Mrs. Martínez selects as one of her vocabulary words. Since the book also contains the words, "famous" and "mysterious," she provided the class with a second mini-lesson on the cognate suffix rule, /-ous/→/-oso/, as a refresher for her students. By reteaching such cognate suffix rules, Mrs. Martínez is helping her students build a strong foundation for learning cognate morphology.

Teaching Cognate Suffix Rules to Generate Cognates

Teaching bilingual learners about cognate suffix rules is important for developing their ability to recognize cognates. It is also important for developing students' ability to generate new words based upon the cognate suffix rules they know.

The sample mini-lesson presented in the next dialogue illustrates one way to teach students how to generate viable English cognates inductively from the Spanish cognates they already know. The cognate vocabulary discussed in the dialogue was taken from the picture book, The Escape of Oney Judge: Martha Washington's Slave Finds Freedom (McCully, 2007), the inspiring story of a young Black female slave who successfully escaped from the George and Martha Washington household and gained her freedom.

In the vignette, Mr. Davis, the Spanish–English bilingual fifth-grade teacher, models the concept-induction process for using the students' Spanish language to generate English words they have never used before. The first part of the dialogue is devoted to learning the /-ly/ → /-mente/ suffix rule using words from The Escape of Oney Judge.

Mr. Davis:	Class, what is the English word for «honestamente»?
Individual students:	I don't know!
Mr. Davis:	Oh, but you might! Let's see. What is the English word for «terriblemente»?
Dora:	I think it's "terribly."
Mr. Davis:	Yes! Now, let me show you a few more words to see if there's a pattern. [Mr. Davis continues by asking for the English words for «finalmente», «legalmente», and «precisamente». When the class correctly responds with "finally," "legally," and "precisely," Mr. Davis continues the lesson.] Do we see a pattern here?
Diego:	Is it that Spanish words ending in /-mente/ are the cognates of English words ending in /-ly/?
Mr. Davis:	Exactly! Now, what do you do if you need a word in English to express an idea, but you don't know of any that has the meaning you want? One thing you can do is think of a word in Spanish that captures the idea you want to convey. Then, try to make it an English word with your knowledge of prefixes, root words, and suffixes.
Lydia:	I'm not sure I understand!

Mr. Davis:	Let me give you an example. Let's say you want to express an idea—the person was speaking «*francamente*», but you didn't know an English word that means «*francamente*». Let's start by looking at the word «*francamente*» (writes on the board). Is there any prefix, root word, or suffix rule you know that will change this Spanish word to an English word?
Oscar:	I see the suffix, */-mente/.*
Mr. Davis:	Good, Oscar! So, what do you do now?
Oscar:	I would use the English ending, /-ly/, and make the word, "francally."
Mr. Davis:	Not entirely correct, but you are close enough for an English speaker to understand you. Actually, the word you want is "frankly," but you were so close.

Although Oscar's response wasn't entirely correct, it was close enough to an actual English word that it would be understood by an English speaker. And that's okay! Flawlessly generating words from Spanish or English words is an ideal that students can build toward using their knowledge of cognate suffixes. With enough practice, students will become more confident in their ability to create words from the root words and affixes they know.

Teaching Germanic Suffixes

In addition to learning about Latin suffixes, students should also be taught Germanic suffixes. As was the case with Germanic prefixes, most words ending in Germanic suffixes are not Spanish–English cognates. These include words such as "kingship," "neighborhood," and "wretchedness." Instruction on Germanic cognate suffixes enhances students' abilities to distinguish between Spanish cognates and Germanic words. As was the case with Germanic prefixes, we recommend teaching students about Germanic suffixes after they have learned many of the Latin and Greek suffixes so as not to confuse or overburden them. Some of the more frequent Germanic cognate suffixes are shown in Table 5.3.

Table 5.3. Common Germanic suffixes and examples

Anglo-Saxon suffix	Meaning	Examples
/-en/	made of, make	lighten, straighten, wooden
/-ful/	full of	handful, mouthful, spoonful
/-hood/	group, state	brotherhood, knighthood, neighborhood
/-ing/	action, process	laughing, running, singing
/-less/	without	hopeless, penniless, worthless
/-ness/	condition, state	darkness, fairness, homelessness
/-ship/	group, state	craftsmanship, hardship, township

REINFORCING THE LEARNING OF COGNATE SUFFIX RULES

We have found that the activities useful for reinforcing the cognate prefix and root word rules are also valuable for strengthening the learning of Spanish–English cognate suffix conversion rules in Table 5.2. Such activities include flashcards, word sorts, word searches, and anchor charts that display the rules. Here, we expand on two types of exercises to show how they can be specifically used with suffix rules.

Using Formation Exercises as Assessments

After learning a suffix conversion rule, students can be assessed by generating cognates that follow a specified rule. In the example assessment provided in Figure 5.2, students were taught ten suffix conversion rules, such as /-ly/ → /-mente/ and /-ity/ → /-idad/. To test their learning of the rules, the teacher can provide examples of an English word with a blank for students to add the Spanish cognate, or a Spanish word with a blank for students to add the English cognate. To ensure that students are relying on the rules they learned and not on their background knowledge of the individual words, teachers should use less frequent words or realistic pseudo words.

Directions: Fill in the blanks with the cognate for the following English or Spanish words.

English	**Spanish**
1. nebulous	_____
2. _____	*abundantemente*
3. bucolic	_____
4. contrition	_____
5. _____	*vanidad*
6. morbid	_____
7. _____	*penitente*
8. _____	*reducible*
9. transitory	_____
10. _____	*corrosivo*

Answers

1. nebuloso	2. abundantly	3. bucólico	4. contrición	5. vanity
6. mórbido	7. penitent	8. reducible	9. transitorio	10. corrosive

Figure 5.2.   Sample assessment for cognate suffix rules.

Using Anchor Charts to Reinforce the Cognate Suffix Rules

The suffix rules learned through the concept-induction activities can be preserved on anchor charts and displayed throughout the classroom. Teachers can post these charts as students learn them, or they can bring them back at other times throughout the semester to help students review and remember the rules.

We have found that anchor charts work best when there are only one or two rules on each chart. Each rule should consist of at least four or five examples. To keep the learning fresh, various versions of the suffix rules containing different examples of the rules can be created and used at different times of the school year. Of course, the order of the languages should also be alternated. Sometimes the English words can be on the right-hand side, and other times they can be on the left-hand side. This serves to highlight Spanish so it is not seen as a less prestigious language.

Another option is to assign which suffix conversion rule students should work on and have them create their own anchor charts using the

> **Did you know?**
>
> Teachers can use the Cognate Companion to search for lesson plans containing suffix cognates activities to teach different suffix conversion rules.

 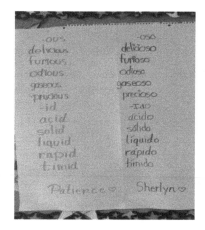

Figure 5.3a. Fourth-grade bilingual learners create anchor charts for two suffix rules: /-id/ → /-ido/ and /-ous/ → /-oso/.

Figure 5.3b. Completed anchor chart for the two suffix rules: /-id/ → /-ido/ and /-ous/ → /-oso/.

Cognate Companion as needed. Students can also work in pairs. After they list all the words on the anchor charts, students should present their cognate word lists and state their particular suffix transformation rule. The butcher paper anchor charts can then be taped to the classroom walls for future reference. Mr. Griego's fourth-grade students created the two suffix anchor charts in Figures 5.3a and 5.3b after he had taught the two suffix rules /-id/ → /-ido/ and /-ous/ → /-oso/.

Family Literacy: Introducing Parents to Cognate Suffixes

Teaching parents and their children about the value of learning cognates can support bilingual learners' vocabulary development in Spanish and English, which can in turn contribute to students' maintenance and development of their home languages. In today's schools, parents of bilingual learners are sometimes told by teachers, administrators, and acquaintances that they and their children should speak only English, not Spanish, at school and at home. In some cases, parents do not allow their children to enter bilingual programs and instead enroll them in general education classrooms. However, a strong home language is a good predictor of a strong new language, especially with respect to literacy. Without support for their home language, children may eventually lose their Spanish. They may not be able to converse with Spanish-speaking peers and elders, enjoy the Spanish lyrics sung in their home language, or read books and newspapers written in Spanish, nor will they be able to engage in academic Spanish. And they will be not be prepared for socioeconomic opportunities that require strong Spanish–English bilingualism and biliteracy.

Recall that Mrs. Martínez is a third-grade teacher in a transitional bilingual program. Mrs. Martínez is always trying to involve her students' parents and guardians as partners in their children's education. Toward this end, Mrs. Martínez holds monthly family literacy nights to discuss language strategies parents can use to assist their children with schoolwork. She recently started to teach the families about cognates, and she encouraged them to support their children as they looked for cognates not only in books at school, but also at home and in the community. In the following vignette, translated from Spanish, Mrs. Martínez interacts with several parents at one of the literacy night meetings.

Mrs. Martínez: Every day, more and more students tell me about the cognates they find around the school and at home. It's really great to see that the Spanish you teach at home is helping them to learn English.

Mrs. Gómez:	Mrs. Martínez, we are happy knowing that we can use our Spanish to help our children with their reading, writing, and spelling. And we are also learning English!
Mrs. Martínez:	Great to hear! Since we have already covered cognate prefixes and root words, tonight I will add cognate suffix rules. [Mrs. Martínez turns on the projector.] Let's look at the word "incredible." It is made up of the prefix, /in-/, which means, "not;" the root word, /-cred-/, which means, "to believe;" and the suffix, /-ible/, meaning "to be able to." When you add up all the different word parts, you get the word, "incredible," which means, "not able to be believed" or "not believable." You can see the same word parts in its Spanish cognate, «increíble».
Mrs. Moreno:	Yes, I see how it works!
Mrs. Martínez:	Suffixes are especially important for generating new words. Take the verb "to invent." Who is the person who "invents"? The "inventor." What does the "inventor" "invent"? The "invention." How can we describe the inventor? "Inventive." See how the suffixes work?
Mrs. Laínez:	Yes! The suffixes all talk about the same invention process. But they have a different focus. One labels the person. Another, the action, and so on.
Mrs. Martínez:	You got it, Mrs. Laínez! Let's compare some English words with some Spanish words. Look at the word "invention." What is "invention" in Spanish? «Invención». What about the word "lotion"? What is it in Spanish? Yes, «loción»! And "nation"? Correct, «nación»! Do you see a pattern?
Ms. Robles:	Is it that English words that end in /-tion/ end in /-ción/ in Spanish?
Mrs. Martínez:	That's it! And the /-tion/ to /-ción/ rule is just one of many rules for changing English words to Spanish ones and vice versa. Tonight, I will show you some of the cognate suffix rules that I will be teaching your children in the next few days. They don't always work, but they work often enough that they're worth learning.

By teaching her students' parents about suffixes and morphology, in general, Mrs. Martínez is showing them that there are rules that can simplify the language-learning process. More importantly, she is making it clear to them that learning Spanish can facilitate learning English.

SUMMARY

To develop the vocabularies of bilingual learners, we suggest that teachers include the instruction of cognate suffix rules as part of their curriculum. Teaching bilingual learners cognate suffix rules as a component of the picture book read-aloud is a powerful way to develop cognate recognition. It is also an effective strategy for teaching students how to produce words in their new language using cognates they already know from their home language.

Teachers can also introduce cognates in their family literacy programs. A family literacy focus on cognates and cognate suffix rules can show parents that there are rules which can make language learning easier.

REFLECTION AND ACTION

| 1 | Choose a picture book. Type the title into the textbox of the Cognate Companion. Review the list of cognates that the book includes. Explain how you might teach a given suffix rule using concept induction strategies. |

| 2 | Identify the suffixes you want your students to learn. Consult the Cognate Companion for books that you want to read aloud and that have the vocabulary words you might want to use to create a snap-on lesson plan. |

| 3 | What activities might you use to help students remember the various cognate suffix rules? |

| 4 | How would you structure a family literacy program on cognate suffix rules to show parents that Spanish can facilitate the learning of English? |

6

Cognate Spelling Rules

OBJECTIVES

☐ Activate metalinguistic awareness through discussion of spelling rules.

☐ Teach the cognate double consonant, consonant digraph, and sibilant consonant blend spelling rules.

☐ Create cognate spelling rule activities to accompany picture book read-alouds and reinforce student learning.

Cognate Play

Read the Spanish–English cognates below and circle the differences in spelling. What commonalities and differences do you see between the cognates?

English–Spanish Cognate Spelling

- possible/*posible*
- photo/*foto*
- special/*especial*

T he preceding chapters on cognate morphology have shown us that learning Spanish–English cognates need not require an endless series of rote exercises. Instead, they illustrate the value of learning powerful rules for recognizing and generating cognates for Spanish and English words. In this chapter, we introduce spelling rules for transforming English words to Spanish words, as well as others that promise the conversion of English or Spanish words to their respective cognates.

SPANISH AND ENGLISH SPELLING RULES

We consider spelling an important part of the development of literacy as well as a revelation of the history and conventions of languages. For example, although the letter "k" in the English word "know" is not pronounced, it provides an important signal of the connection with the meaning of the word "acknowledge," where the letter "k" is pronounced. We see a similar pattern with the letter "g" in the words "sign" and "significant."

You have undoubtedly observed numerous examples of English words that are identical to their Spanish cognates in the way they are spelled, as in the cases of doctor/*doctor* and invisible/*invisible*. Other pairs of cognates are slightly different in spelling but still related in meaning, such as liberty/*libertad.*

This chapter focuses on the teaching and learning of English and Spanish spelling rules, not on the random memorization of word lists as is found in most traditional spelling instruction (Leipzig, 2000). Teaching students about the differences in spelling between English words and their Spanish cognates allows them to discover several important spelling rules for transforming English words into Spanish words and vice versa. In turn, students' understanding of cognate spelling rules can lead not only to improved spelling but also to stronger recognition and generation of cognate words.

Effects of Cognate Spelling Instruction

Over the past several years, we have been investigating the effect of cognate instruction on learning. The teachers we have worked with note that cognate instruction is effective in building the vocabularies of their bilingual learners. Several teachers have suggested that cognate instruction leads to improved English spelling for their students (Hernández et al., 2010). For example, in one 4th-grade transitional bilingual classroom where **English–Spanish cognates** were taught daily for approximately one month, the teacher noticed a major improvement in the spelling of English words by her bilingual learners from Spanish-speaking homes. This piece of anecdotal evidence supports what the empirical research has long suggested: that a student's home language supports the learning of the new language (Cummins, 1981), and the new language in turn supports the student's home language (Hernández, 2001).

With respect to spelling, students learning to read and write in their new language will initially spell by sound, which means that they use their home language to write the new language; consequently, some of their invented spelling is qualitatively different from that of their monolingual English-speaking peers (Helman, 2004). Cognate vocabulary instruction affords teachers strategies they can use to help bilingual learners improve their spelling of English words. This chapter highlights three different types of spelling rules that students can be taught to convert English words to Spanish words, and in one case, to transform Spanish words to English words.

Cognate Spelling Rules

Mr. Gómez, a new bilingual teacher, has been studying the anchor charts Mrs. Martínez has on display throughout her room, several of which are about cognate morphology rules and cognate spelling rules.

Answers:
- po(ss)ible/*po(s)ible*
- (ph)oto/*(f)oto*
- (sp)ecial/*(esp)ecial*

Mr. Gómez:	Ms. Martínez, I like your cognate anchor charts. I've heard that there are some morphology rules about cognates that I could teach to bilingual learners. But you also have spelling rules.
Ms. Martínez:	Yeah! There are a few spelling rules that I like to teach my students. For example, the word "possible" and its cognate *«posible»*. Do you see the difference?
Mr. Gómez:	The English word has the double "s," but the Spanish word does not.
Ms. Martínez:	Yes! Now, think of different/*diferente,* traffic/*tráfico, and* oppose/*oponer.*
Mr. Gómez:	Now I get it. The double English consonants become single consonants in Spanish. Am I right?
Ms. Martínez:	Yes, you are! But it only holds in going from English to Spanish. So, you have to be careful.
Mr. Gómez:	That's still pretty useful; thank you!

Like Mr. Gómez, you may not be familiar with the cognate spelling rules, but they can be useful for bilingual learners. As we see later, some of these rules do not always work for converting Spanish words to their English cognates. This is because English sounds often have more than one letter that can represent them.

TEACHING COGNATE SPELLING RULES

In this section, we present three cognate spelling rules: a) English double consonants, b) consonant digraphs, and c) sibilant consonant blends. For each of the rules, we provide an explanation of the rule, a teaching scenario, an example of an informal assessment, and a discussion of the rule's limitations.

The English Double Consonant Rule

We have found that the English consonant rule is one of the simplest rules to teach. Examine the lists of English and Spanish words below:

English	Spanish
aggressive	*agresivo*
possible	*posible*
common	*común*
button	*botón*
traffic	*tráfico*

What is the difference between the English words and the Spanish words on the list? If you said that the English words have double consonants while the Spanish words have only single consonants, you are correct. The "gg" and the "ss" in "aggressive" become the single graphemes *«g»* and *«s»* in *«agresivo»*. The other cognate pairs differ in the same way, with the English word possessing a double consonant and its Spanish cognate possessing only one.

There is, however, no rule that allows for converting a Spanish word with a double consonant to an English word with a double consonant since English often uses different graphemes, or written letters, to represent the same phoneme, or spoken sound. For example, the English graphemes, "t" and "tt," represent the [t] phoneme. In converting a word such as "attention" from English to its Spanish cognate *«atención»*, the "tt" in the English word can only be changed to the *«t»* grapheme in Spanish. In converting a word from Spanish to English, however, the learner has no way of knowing whether the grapheme *«t»* in the Spanish word *«atención»* is represented by the English

LESSON PLAN

Danza!: Amalia Hernández and El Ballet Folklórico de México
(Tonatiuh, 2017)

grapheme "t" as in "atention" or as the "tt" in "attention." Thus, it is not possible to prescribe a double consonant rule for converting a Spanish word to its English cognate.

One of the reasons that the Cognate Companion is so useful is that many of the picture books included in the database contain hundreds of instances of English–Spanish cognates that follow the double consonant rule. For example, to teach the English double consonant rule, Ms. Galván, a third grade bilingual teacher, uses the cognate vocabulary in *Danza!: Amalia Hernández and El Ballet Folklórico de México* (Tonatiuh, 2017). The book, which is a description of the dancer who founded *El Ballet Folklórico de México*, contains the English words: "expressive," "impressed," "possible," and "professor." These words can be converted to their Spanish cognates by changing the double consonant, "ss" to the single consonant «s» to form the words «expresivo», «impresionado», «posible», and «profesor».

Did you know?

The *Cognate Companion* can be used to find English–Spanish cognates that follow the double consonant rule and the picture books that contain them.

LESSON PLAN

Mae Among the Stars (Ahmed, 2018)
How to Be an Elephant
(Roy, 2017)

Mr. Cuello read the book, Mae Among the Stars (Ahmed, 2018), a biography about the first African American woman in space to his fourth-grade class. Since this book contains a variety of cognates that follow the double consonant rule: accept/*aceptar*, excellence/*excelencia*, officer/*oficial*, and profession/*profesión*, Mr. Cuello created a mini-lesson on transforming English words to Spanish words.

For her third grade science class, Mrs. Martínez read the picture book, How to Be an Elephant (Roy, 2017), about an infant elephant growing up in the wild. Since this book contains several cognates having double consonants: community/*comunidad*, hippopotamus/*hipopótamo*, process/*proceso*, and successive/*sucesivo*, Mrs. Martínez created a mini-lesson on the double consonant rule. More examples of English and Spanish cognates that follow the double consonant spelling rule are presented in Table 6.1. Readers may consult the Cognate Companion for more cognate mini-lessons on the double consonant rule.

The double consonants found in English–Spanish cognates vary in their frequency. Cognates that follow the "pp" → «p», "ss" → «s», and "tt" → «t» rules are among the most frequent

Table 6.1. Double consonant spelling rules from English to Spanish

Books	Spelling rules	Cognate examples
Odd Boy Out: Young Albert Einstein	cc → c	occupy/*ocupar*
Nim and the War Effort		accordion/*acordeón*
La cucaracha Martina		yucca/*yuca*
The Buzz on Bees: Why Are They Disappearing?	ff → f	effect/*efecto*
Angela Weaves a Dream		offer/*ofrecer*
How Santa Got His Job		traffic/*tráfico*
Sneeze	gg → g	aggravate/*agravar*
Parrots Over Puerto Rico		aggressive/*agresivo*
Coyotes All Around		exaggerate/*exagerar*
Nothing	ll → l	dollar/*dólar*
The Twins' Blanket		excellent/*excelente*
Elephants Can Paint, Too		gallon/*galón*
Terrific	nn → n	cannibal/*cánibal*
Welcome to the Ice House		tunnel/*túnel*
Bug Shots: The Good, the Bad, and the Bugly		innocent/*inocente*
What Charlie Heard	pp → p	applaud/*aplauso*
A Monkey Among Us		hippopotamus/*hipopótamo*
Rabbit & Robot: The Sleepover		suppose/*suponer*
Chrysanthemum	ss → s	assign/*asignar*
Each Kindness		pass/*pasar*
Eight Days Gone		mission/*misión*
That Kookoory!	tt → t	attract/*atraer*
John Henry		attack/*atacar*
My Garden		button/*botón*

(e.g., applaud/*aplauso*, assign/*asignar*, and attract/*atraer*). Other double consonant transformations, such as "bb" → «*b*» and "dd" → «*d*», are less common (e.g., rabbi/*rabino* and pudding/*pudín*).

Teaching the English Double Consonant Cognate Spelling Rule

LESSON PLAN

Lily's Purple
Plastic Purse/
*Lily y su bolso de
plástico morado*
(Henkes, 2006)

In this section, we provide a classroom dialogue that can serve as a model for teaching a lesson about the cognate double consonant spelling rules as part of the read-aloud activities for the picture book, Lily's Purple Plastic Purse (Henkes, 2006). The story, written for students in the early primary grades, tells the story of Lily the Mouse, whose musical purse keeps interrupting her favorite teacher as he tries to teach. After several disruptions, Mr. Slinger takes away Lily's purse until the end of the day. In retaliation, Lily slips a nasty drawing of Mr. Slinger into his bag. When Mr. Slinger returns the purse to Lily, she finds that he had written her a kind note. The rest of the story deals with Lily's remorse and her attempts to apologize and make things right again with her favorite teacher.

In the dialogue below, Ms. Smith, an English monolingual second grade teacher of bilingual learners, will use four English cognate examples that follow the common double-consonant cognate rules, "ff" → «*f*», "ll" → «*l*», "ss" → «*s*», and "tt" → «*t*», to help students induce the rule that English words possessing double consonants often have Spanish cognate equivalents with only one of the consonants.

Ms. Smith: Class, I have written today's English and Spanish cognate vocabulary words on the board. What are the differences between the English words and the Spanish words?

English	Spanish
button	*botón*
difficult	*difícil*
excellent	*excelente*
express	*expresar*

Jorge: "Button" has two "t"s but «*botón*» has only one, and "excellent" has two "l"s but «*excelente*» only has one.

Felipe: "Difficult" has two "f"s and «*difícil*» only has one, and "express" has two "s"s but «*expresar*» only has one.

Ms. Smith: Both of you are right! Is there a pattern there?

Hilda: Is it that English words that have a double consonant are cognates of Spanish words that have a single consonant?

Ms. Smith: Hilda, I think you've figured it out. Can we say the rule is that whenever an English cognate has a double consonant, the Spanish cognate probably has only one of the consonants? Does everybody see that? Okay! Let's repeat this rule, everybody!

Ms. Smith writes down the rule: "Whenever an English word has a double consonant, its Spanish cognate often has only one consonant."

In the dialogue, Ms. Smith uses concept induction to lead students to learn the double consonant spelling rule by reviewing English–Spanish cognates that follow the rule. Notice also how she asks the students to review the English and Spanish words for spelling differences. The teacher prompts the students by getting them to define the rule. When they can state it, Ms. Smith writes the rule on the board for them to learn.

Informal Assessment of the Double Consonant Cognate Spelling Rule

As with most lessons that involve the learning of a rule, it is good practice to informally assess student learning by asking the students to apply their understanding of the rule to other words. Ms. Smith has a good grasp of how to assess student learning informally. Notice how

Ms. Smith provides three example words to informally assess student understanding of the English double consonant spelling rule.

Ms. Smith: Let's see if the double consonant works with other words. What would the Spanish cognate spelling be for the English word "mission"?

Hortencia: It would be «*misión*», since it would be spelled with one «*s*» and not two.

Ms. Smith: Very good, Hortencia! How about the Spanish word for "tunnel"?

Roberto: It would probably be spelled with one «*n*» as in «*túnel*».

Ms. Smith: Great job, Roberto! Ok, one more. How would you spell the word "class" in Spanish?

Sylvia: That's easy, Miss! «*c-l-a-s-e*». With only one «*s*».

Ms. Smith: Good, Sylvia! Let's remember the rule: Whenever an English word has a double consonant, its Spanish cognate usually has only one consonant.

Ms. Smith can also develop a worksheet to measure student understanding of the double consonant rule, like the one presented in Figure 6.1. As shown, the worksheet contains examples of four double consonant rules: "ff" → «*f*», "pp" → «*p*», "gg" → «*g*», and "tt" → «*t*».

Double Consonant Spelling Rules

Directions: Read the words on the list. Notice the spelling patterns. Using the patterns, fill in the blanks with a Spanish cognate. Write the double consonant spelling rule.

offer = *oferta*	appear = *aparecer*
tariff = *tarifa*	appendix = *apéndice*
effect = *efecto*	opposite = *opuesto*
difficult = *difícil*	apparatus = *aparato*
buffalo = _____	opportunity = _____
different = _____	hippopotamus = _____
official = _____	appetite = _____
traffic = _____	approve = _____
Rule: _ff_ = _f_	**Rule:** _____ = _____

impossible = *imposible*	attack = *atacar*
classic = *clásico*	silhouette = *silueta*
possessive = *posesivo*	attic = *ático*
express = *expresar*	battle = *batalla*
fossil = _____	letter = _____
glossary = _____	button = _____
classify = _____	lottery = _____
confess = _____	attention = _____
Rule: _____ = _____	**Rule:** _____ = _____

Answers:
búfalo, diferente, oficial, tráfico; Rule: ff=f _____ *oportunidad, hipopótamo, apetito, aprobar*; Rule: pp=p
fósil, glosario, clasificar, confesar; Rule: ss=s _____ *letra, botón, lotería, atención*; Rule: tt=t

Figure 6.1. Activity for the double consonant spelling rules.

Exceptions to the Double Consonant Rule

Earlier, we noted that while most English consonants may appear as double consonants, the only double consonants in Spanish are «cc», «ll», and «rr», and these actually represent different phonemes. The «cc» in words like «acción» represents the phonemes [k] and [s], as in [ak] [sión]. The «ll» grapheme represents the [y] phoneme in Spanish, and the grapheme «rr» represents the [rr] phoneme in Spanish. The lack of correspondence between English words possessing double consonants and their Spanish equivalents renders the double-consonant cognate rule less valuable for converting words from Spanish to English. This limitation is captured in the following dialogue Ms. Smith has with her second grade bilingual learners.

Ms. Smith: Now let's try going from Spanish to English. This is the way you spell the word «possible» in Spanish. (Ms. Smith writes «possible» on the board). What is the English word for «possible»? How is it spelled?

José: I'm not sure if it is "p-o-s-i-b-l-e" or "p-o-s-s-i-b-l-e."

Ms. Smith: José, you've put your finger on the problem. It can be either one of those, unless you know that only "p-o-s-s-i-b-l-e" is the correct word in English and "p-o-s-i-b-l-e" is not. In English, a single consonant or a double consonant are most often represented by a single consonant in Spanish. That means that a single consonant in Spanish may be either a single consonant in English or a double consonant. However, there is no sure way of predicting which spelling is correct.

Raymundo: So, what do we do?

Ms. Smith: The best strategy whenever you want to create a new English word from a Spanish word containing a consonant is to first make an English word having both single and double consonants, then decide.

Felipa: Can you give us an example?

Ms. Smith: Sure, let's try the Spanish word «meteoro». What word is it in English?

Abigaíl: It could be "meteor" or "metteor."

Martín: It is probably "meteor," because "metteor" isn't a word I recognize.

Ms. Smith: Exactly! Do you see how you tried both spellings first and then you decided on the one you think might probably be correct? Thinking that one of the words might be the correct spelling is probably the only way of deciding upon the spelling of the word. That is why it is important for you all to read as much as you can. Usually, the more you read, the better you become at spelling.

This example illustrates one way of explaining the difference between English and Spanish words with respect to the double consonant cognate spelling rule. Most important, the dialogue demonstrates that even though there are limitations on transforming a Spanish word to its English cognate, knowledge of the double consonant cognate rule and its exceptions can often lead to a plausible solution. It's not a perfect strategy, but it may eventually reduce spelling errors.

The Consonant Digraph Rule

A consonant digraph can be defined as two consecutive consonants representing a single speech sound. Consonant digraphs are important because their presence signals to language learners that an unfamiliar English word is possibly the cognate of a Spanish word. A student can use this knowledge to guess that the meaning of an English word is the same or nearly the same as the Spanish cognate.

In English, the common consonant digraphs are "ch," "gh," "kh," "ph," "sh," "th," and "wh." In Spanish, the five consonant digraphs are «ch», «gu», «qu», «ll», and «rr». Only the «ch» digraph is found in English and Spanish. In this section, we begin our discussion of consonant digraphs with English words having the "ph" and "th" digraphs because these are the two most common. Consider the lists of English–Spanish cognate pairs below:

English	Spanish
photogra**ph**	*fotografía*
s**ph**ere	e*sf*era
theater	*t*eatro
pa**th**etic	*patético*

A comparison of the lists illustrates how the digraphs in English words become single consonants in Spanish words. The "ph" digraphs become «f» graphemes regardless of their position in the words, as seen in the examples "photograph" and "sphere." Similarly, the English "th" digraph in words such as "theater" and "pathetic" is converted to a «t» grapheme in Spanish. The converse is not possible because neither the "ph" nor "th" digraphs exist in Spanish. To transform a Spanish word possessing the «f» or «t» grapheme to an English cognate again forces the learner to decide which grapheme, "f" or "ph" or "t" or "th" is correct. This cannot be reliably done because, like the double consonant rule, the consonant digraph rule is restricted to the conversion of English words to their Spanish cognates.

Teaching the Consonant Digraph Rule

Numerous Spanish-English cognates possess the "ph" and "th" digraphs in the picture books included in the Cognate Companion. Animal Poems of the Iguazú/*Animalario de Iguazú* (Alarcón & González, 2008) is a bilingual picture book about the different animals and birds that live in the Argentine national park. English words possessing the "ph" digraph—"alphabet," "hemisphere," and "photo"—become the Spanish cognates: «alfabeto», «hemisferio», and «foto» possessing the «f» grapheme in place of the digraph, "ph."

> **LESSON PLAN**
>
> Animal Poems of the Iguazú/*Animalario del Iguazú*
> (Alarcón & González, 2008) is a bilingual book.
> The Boy Who Invented TV: The Story of Philo Farnsworth
> (Krull, 2014)

Similarly, there are English words with "th"—"enthusiasm," "rhythm," and "theory"—found in the National Science Teaching Association picture book The Boy Who Invented TV: The Story of Philo Farnsworth (Krull, 2014) that can be transformed into Spanish cognates with «t»—«entusiasmo», «ritmo», and «teoría». Other examples of cognate digraph words that may be changed from English to Spanish and the picture books that contain them are presented in Tables 6.2 and 6.3. The first table includes entries for words with initial diagraphs, and the second table shows digraphs occurring later in a word, either in the medial or final positions.

In addition to "ph" → «f» and "th" → «t», there is another word–initial digraph rule: "ch" → «c.» The "ch" → «c» conversion has two associated spelling rules because English words beginning with the digraph "ch" can have either the more familiar [ch] sound as heard in "champion," "channel," and "charity" or the hard [k] sound found in a few words derived from the Greek, such as "characteristic," "chlorophyll," and "choir." For both types of words, the Spanish cognate takes the hard [k] sound: champion/*campeón*, channel/*canal*, and charity/*caridad*, characteristic/*característica*, chlorophyll/*clorofila*, and choir/*coro*. The Latin and Greek cases of the "ch" → «c» are not the only ones containing the word–initial "ch." There is also the case of the English "ch" digraph and the Spanish "ch" digraph containing the sound heard in the cognate pairs chimney/*chimenea*, chimpanzee/*chimpancé*, and chocolate/*chocolate*. An analysis of the frequencies in which these three types of English word–initial "ch" digraphs occur failed to yield a clear-cut choice as to which of these is the most common. As a result, teachers may decide to wait to teach any of these initial "ch" digraph rules until a teachable moment arises.

The situation is similar for the English digraphs "ch" in the medial or final positions, including words that have the same sounds in English and Spanish such as march/*marchar*, porch/*porche*, and trench/*trinchera*. Other cognate pairs have the same [ch] sound for the English word,

Table 6.2. Cognate consonant digraph rule in word-initial positions, from English to Spanish

Book	Spelling rules	Cognate examples
America's Champion Swimmer: Gertrude Ederle A Bad Case of Stripes Rachel Carson and Her Book That Changed . . .	ch → c	champion/*campeón* channel/*canal* charge/*cargar*
If You Hopped Like a Frog The Dinosaurs of Waterhouse Hawkins Brothers	ch ([k]) → c	chameleon/*camaléon* chaos/*caos* character/*carácter*
Nim and the War Effort Houndsley and Catina Little Santa	ch → ch	check/*chequear* chili/*chile* chimney/*chimenea*
Grandma and Me at the Flea The Trouble With Chickens The Hinky-Pink	chr → cr	chrome/*cromo* chronic/*crónico* chrysanthemum/*crisantemo*
Radio Rescue I, Galileo Dark Emperor and Other Poems of the Night	ph → f	phase/*fase* philosopher/*filósofo* photosynthesis/*fotosíntesis*
First Garden: The White House Garden and . . . Even Monsters Need Haircuts Shoes for the Santo Niño	sh → ch	shallot/*chalote* shampoo/*champú* shawl/*chal*
Calling the Doves Odd Boy Out: Young Albert Einstein The Astonishing Secret of Awesome Man	th → t	theater/*teatro* theory/*teoría* thermos/*termo*

but the hard [k] sound for the Spanish word: arch/*arco* and touch/*tocar*. Finally, there are cases in which the medial or final digraphs possess the hard [k] sound in both the English and Spanish cognates: echo/*eco*, mechanical/*mecánico,* and monarch/*monarca*. As was the case with the word–initial "ch" digraphs, an analysis of the frequencies of the medial and final position "ch" digraphs also failed to yield a clear-cut choice for which was the most common. Absent such a

Table 6.3. Cognate consonant digraph rules in medial or final positions, from English to Spanish

Book	Spelling rules	Cognate examples
Monet Paints a Day Snowflake Bentley	ch → c	arch/*arco* rich/*rico*
Honey . . . Honey . . . Lion!: A Story from Africa Papa's Mechanical Fish Nic Bishop Butterflies and Moths	ch ([k]) → c	echo/*eco* mechanical/*mecánico* monarch/*monarca*
All the Water in the World Tales for Very Picky Eaters Stone Soup	ch → ch	avalanche/*avalancha* ranch/*rancho* torch/*antorcha*
How Did That Get in my Lunchbox? The Story. . . One Giant Leap Kate and the Beanstalk	ck → c	pack/*empacar* rock/*roca* sack/*saco*
King Jack and the Dragon What Happens on Wednesdays Man on the Moon: (A Day in the Life of Bob)	ck → que	attack/*ataque* block/*bloque* check/*chequear*
Radio Rescue The Paper Dragon The Biggest Soap	ph → f	telegraph/*telégrafo* triumph/*triunfo* typhoon/*tifón*
Silent Music: A Story from Baghdad Bats at the Ballgame Verdi	th → t	rhythm/*ritmo* sixth/*sexto* python/*pitón*

choice, we once again recommend that teachers postpone introducing any of the medial and final "ch" digraph rules until a teachable moment.

Similarly, words with the "ch" digraph derived from Greek are English words beginning with "chr" can be reliably transformed into Spanish words having the «cr» spelling: chrome/*cromo*, chronic/*crónico*, and chrysalis/*crisálida*. The "chr" is neither a digraph nor a trigraph, but rather the first three letters associated with English words derived from three different Greek roots signifying different meanings: /-chrom-/ (color), /-chron-/ (time), and /-chrys-/ (yellow). Since there are few words in the Cognate Companion that begin with any of these root words, it would perhaps be best if the spelling rule, "chr" → «cr», is taught as part of a lesson on Greek roots and their meanings. Thus, the "chr" → «cr» spelling rule might be taught during a lesson about words derived from the Greek root for time: chronic/*crónico*, chronological/*cronológico*, and chronometer/*cronómetro*.

Another digraph is the English "sh" digraph. The Spanish equivalent of English "sh" is «ch». There are only three examples of the word–initial spelling rule, "sh" → «ch», in the Cognate Companion: shallot/*chalote*, shampoo/*champú*, and shawl/*chal*. In the medial and final positions, only two cases were found: brush/*brocha* and fetish/*fetiche*, the latter signifying a talisman in the alphabet book, A Is for the Américas (Chin-Lee & de la Peña, 1999). With so few cognate equivalents following the spelling rule, "sh" → «ch», we recommend that this rule be taught explicitly only when it is necessary for comprehending the text in a picture book.

LESSON PLAN

A Is for the
Américas
(Chin-Lee & de la
Peña, 1999)

The English consonant digraph sound [ck] occupies only the medial, or final, positions in words. Although primarily found in Germanic cognates—"flock," "sick," and "wreck"—the [ck] consonant digraph sound appears in some common cognates—cockroach/*cucaracha*, rock/*roca*, trick/*truco*, attack/*ataque*, block/*bloque*, and check/*chequear*. The examples of the English cognates possessing the "ck" digraph are illustrative. For some of the English cognates, the "ck" digraph is replaced by the Spanish grapheme «c» whereas in the others it is replaced in Spanish by «que». There are two spelling rules for the English consonant digraph "ck:"

"ck" → «c» and "ck" → «que».

Since neither digraph spelling rule appears to be more frequent than the other, we suggest teaching these two spelling rules separately in the context of a picture book read-aloud vocabulary lesson.

Absent from Tables 6.2 and 6.3 are the English consonant digraph "wh," as well as the ghost digraphs "gn," "kn," and "wr"—so-named because the first letter was pronounced at one time in history and is not pronounced now. Except for a few rare cognates such as gnome/*gnomo*, and English words with *"wh,"* the ghost digraphs can be taught more reliably as signals for Germanic cognate words such as "what," "know," and "wreck."

To summarize this section on consonant digraphs, we suggest that only rules for "ph" → «f» and "th" → «t», in all positions within a word, be explicitly taught. Since there seems to be no apparent most frequent type of digraph involving the different "ch" digraphs for any position, we recommend that these rules be taught as appropriate for student learning. We make the same suggestion for the two spelling rules involving "ck." Finally, there are few instances of the "sh" → «ch» rule to warrant explicit instruction. The Cognate Companion can be used to identify the English and Spanish words for teaching the rules with consonant digraphs.

Classroom Vignette: Teaching the Consonant Digraphs "ph" and "th"

Mr. Hampton, a third grade Spanish one-way immersion teacher whose class is composed of all home language English speakers, engages his students by demonstrating a lesson on the consonant digraph rule. Here is the English translation of his lesson.

Mr. Hampton: Class, I have written today's English and Spanish cognate words on the board. Can someone tell me the difference between the English words and the Spanish words in the two lists below?

	List 1	**List 2**
	thermometer/*termómetro*	phenomenal/*fenomenal*
	method/*método*	telephone/*teléfono*
	north/*norte*	triumph/*triunfo*

Renata: The English words in List 1 all have the letters "t" and "h" together and the Spanish words have only a single «*t*». In List 2, the English words have the "p" and "h" together and the Spanish words have an «*f*» instead of the "ph."

Mr. Hampton: Renata, you're onto something! Before going on, let me just say that letters that are paired together to form one sound are called "digraphs." In List 1, the English words have the digraph "th," but not the Spanish words. In List 2, the English words have the digraph "ph," but not the Spanish words. Is there a letter or letters that the Spanish words have in common to take the place of the consonant digraphs in the English words?

Elizabeth: The «*t*» takes the place of the "th" for the Spanish words in List 1, and an «*f*» takes the place of the "ph" digraph in List 2.

Mr. Hampton: That's it, Elizabeth! Now can you give us a rule for whenever you have a consonant digraph like "ph" or "th" in an English word? I'll write it down while you dictate it.

Elizabeth: I'll try, Mr. Hampton. "Whenever you have an English word that has the consonant digraph 'ph' or 'th,' you can change the 'ph' to an «*f*», or the 'th' to a «*t*», to make its Spanish cognate."

Mr. Hampton: That was very good, Elizabeth. One more thing. Did anyone else notice something about where the "ph" and "th" digraphs occur?

Sean: The diagraphs occur at the beginning of the word.

Penny: Oh, oh, the digraphs also occur in the middle of the words.

Renata: You forgot that they also occur at the end of words.

Mr. Hampton: That's it, all of you are correct. The two digraphs "ph" and "th" can occur in all three positions: beginning, middle, and end, that is, initial, medial, and final positions.

Notice how Mr. Hampton used concept induction to lead students to learn the consonant digraph spelling rule by writing two lists of words on the board that correspond to the three positions of the two different English digraphs. He then asked the students to examine the letter patterns in English compared to Spanish words for spelling differences. Finally, Mr. Hampton wrote down the English cognate consonant diagraph spelling rule for both and the "th" →« *t*» and "ph" → «*f*» as Elizabeth dictated it.

Informal Assessment of the Consonant Diagraph Rule

Once Mr. Hampton's third grade students have had time to learn the rules, he can informally assess student understanding by asking the class to generate the Spanish cognates when they are provided examples of the English words.

Mr. Hampton: Let's try some examples. I will write an English word on the board, and you tell me its Spanish cognate. [Mr. Hampton writes the word "digraph" on the board.]

Anita: Is it «*d-i-g-r-a-f-* (long pause) *o*»?

Mr. Hampton: Great job, Anita! It is «*d-í-g-r-a-f-o*» with the accent on the «*i*». [Mr. Hampton writes «*dígrafo*» on the board.] Do you all see that English cognates having the digraph "ph" are cognates to Spanish words that have an «*f*» instead of the "ph"? Here are some other examples: "telephone" and «*teléfono*», and "photograph" and «*fotografía*». Do you see that every time there's a "ph," it changes to an «*f*» in Spanish?

Teachers can design parallel lessons for the "th" → «*t*» conversion rules using dialogue similar to that for the "ph" → «*f*» rule. These rules should be taught because they are reliable cognate spelling rules. The key to the lesson in the dialogues is to get the students to focus on the consonant digraphs "ph" and "th" in the English words and how they are replaced in the Spanish cognates by the graphemes «*f*» and «*t*».

Teachers can create a formative assessment of the "ph"→ «*f*» and "th" → «*t*» rules such as that presented in Figure 6.2. Because the two digraph rules proceed from the English to the Spanish, all of the exercises move in that direction.

Consonant Digraph Spelling Rules

Directions: Read the words on the list. Notice the spelling patterns. Using the patterns, fill in the blanks with a Spanish cognate. Write the consonant digraph spelling rule.

alphabet = *alfabeto*	panther = *pantera*
apostrophe = *apóstrofe*	theme = *tema*
phrase = *frase*	theory = *teoría*
graph = *gráfica*	enthusiasm = *entusiasmo*
telephone = _____	theater = _____
trophy = _____	hypothesis = _____
pharmacy = _____	thermometer = _____
photograph = _____	mathematics = _____
Rule: ___ph___ = ___f___	**Rule:** _____ = _____

Answers:
teléfono, trofeo, farmacia, fotografía; Rule: ph=f
teatro, hipótesis, termómetro, matemáticas; Rule: th=t

Figure 6.2.   Activity for consonant digraph spelling rules.

Exceptions to the Consonant Diagraph Rule

Earlier, we observed that the cognate double consonant spelling rule reliably predicted the conversion of the English word to its Spanish cognate, but not for transforming Spanish words to their English cognates. The explanation for this difference was that, as a rule, the Spanish language does not have double consonants. Similarly, the consonant digraph rule cannot be generalized to English–Spanish cognates because Spanish words having an «*f*» or «*t*» grapheme are not normally transformed into English words possessing the "ph" or "th" digraphs. The English words, "family" and "temperature," for example, become the Spanish cognates, «*familia*» and «*temperatura*», rather than «*phamilia*» and «*themperatura*». For the sake of completeness, then, some teachers might find it necessary to devote a lesson or mini-lesson to these digraph exceptions.

The purpose of the following dialogue, translated from Spanish, is to teach bilingual learners that the «*f*» → "ph" and the «*t*» → "th" rules cannot be used to convert Spanish words to their English cognates. To demonstrate this, Mr. Hampton uses examples of Spanish words possessing the «*f*» grapheme and English words containing "f" or "ph" spellings.

Mr. Hampton: Now that you know you can change English words having the digraphs "ph" and "th" into Spanish words, it is also possible to ask whether Spanish words having the letter «*f*» or the letter «*t*» can be converted into English cognates having the digraphs "ph" and "th." Let's try a few words. For example, what is the English cognate for the Spanish word «*gráfico*»? How is it spelled?

Adam: I think the word is "graphic!" It is spelled, "g-r-a-p-h-i-c."

Mr. Hampton: Very good, Adam! The English word "graphic" has the "ph" digraph. Now, let's try another! What is the English word for «*transformar*»?

Robert: Would it be "transphorm," "t-r-a-n-s-p-h-o-r-m"?

Mr. Hampton: Good try, Robert! But the English word for «*transformar*» is "transform," "t-r-a-n-s-f-o-r-m." There is no "ph" digraph in Spanish. So, it cannot be «*transphorm*».

Alicia: Why is it that in converting an English word to Spanish that the "ph" digraph is changed to «*f*,» but not so with changing a Spanish word with «*f*» to an English cognate with a "ph" digraph?

Mr. Hampton: It doesn't work because the [f] sound in Spanish can either be spelled as "f" in English, as in "transform," or as "ph," as in "biography." There is no sure way for deciding whether you should use an "f" or a "ph" to form the English word. What you can do with an unfamiliar Spanish word having the [f] sound is to spell it both ways to see if you recognize one of the spellings as correct. And just like the "ph" digraph, the «*t*» in Spanish sometimes becomes "th" in an English word and sometimes it doesn't.

Mr. Hampton then continues the lesson with examples of Spanish words possessing «*t*» graphemes that do become "th," as in *termómetro*/thermometer, and those which do not, as in *therritorio*/territory. Again, even though the cognate consonant digraph spelling rule doesn't necessarily yield reliable results for transforming a Spanish word to an English one, it does provide the students with a strategy for potentially resolving the spelling issue.

Teaching the Sibilant Consonant Blend Rules

Sibilant refers to the hissing sound that appears in words such as "sibilant" and "zip" in English and «*sibilante*» in Spanish. In phonetics, sibilants are a type of "fricative," which is a type of a consonant made by the friction of breath through a narrow opening, producing a turbulent air flow. With this in mind, review the following list of English and Spanish words. How are they the same and different?

English	Spanish
scarlet	*escarlata*
slalom	*eslálom*
smog	*esmog*
special	*especial*
stomach	*estómago*
stress	*estrés*

If you guessed that the English words begin with a consonant cluster and the Spanish words begin with the [e] sound before the [s + consonant], you would be correct. This is due to the fact that words in Spanish cannot begin with the initial sibilant consonant blend sounds: [sl], [sm], [sn], [sp], [spr], [st], or [str].

Teachers who have Spanish-speaking emerging bilingual learners in their classrooms often remark that these students tend to pronounce English words such as "stop" as [estop], and "student" as [estudent]. Since Spanish does not permit the occurrence of word–initial sibilant consonant blends such as [sc], [sl], [sm], [sn], [sp], [spr], [st], or [str], Spanish speakers may insert an [e] sound before the [s + consonant]. Therefore, English words that begin with sibilant consonant blends are often converted to their Spanish cognates by adding «e» before the consonant as in the examples scarlet/*escarlata*, slalom/*eslálom/*, smog/*esmog*, special/*especial*, stomach/*estómago*, and stress/*estrés*.

There are some very common cognate sibilant consonant blends that are used to form numerous Spanish–English cognates (e.g., [sp] and [st]). Other sibilant consonant blends (e.g., [sc] and [sm]) that are not as frequent of the various cognate consonant blend spelling rules and the books that contain them are presented in Table 6.4. Other examples may be found in the Cognate Companion.

Ms. Williams, a monolingual English-as-a-second-language teacher, instructs her fifth-grade bilingual learners in initial cognate sibilant consonant blend rules using the picture book, The First Step: How One Girl Put Segregation on Trial (Goodman, 2016), The book tells the story of a young African American girl who challenged the legality of segregated Boston schools in 1847. A cognate objective for the lesson in the dialogue is to teach students that English words beginning with the initial consonant blends [sp] and [st] often become Spanish cognates possessing an initial [es] sound, resulting in the spellings «esp» and «est».

LESSON PLAN

The First Step:
How One Girl Put
Segregation on Trial
(Goodman, 2016)

Table 6.4.   Examples of sibilant consonant blend spelling rules from English to Spanish

Book	Spelling rules	Cognate examples
Dragon Dancing	sc → esc	scale/*escala*
Freedom School, Yes!		scarlet/*escárlata*
Gugu's House		sculpt/*esculpir*
Rachel Carson and Her Book That Changed the World	scr → escr	script/*escritura*
Classic French Fairy Tales		scruple/*escrúpulo*
Starry Messenger: A Book Depicting the Life . . .		scrutinize/*escrutar*
Hamburger Heaven	sk→ esc	skeptical/*escéptico*
What Do You Do When Something Wants to Eat You?		skink/*escinco*
The Princess and the Admiral		skirmish/*escaramuza*
A Place for Turtles	sk → esq	skeleton/*esqueleto*
Roger and the Fox		ski/*esquí*
Auntie Yang's Great Soybean Picnic	sp → esp	special/*especial*
Growing Patterns: Fibonacci Numbers in Nature		spiral/*espiral*
Fly High, Fly Low		spy/*espiar*
Life in the Boreal Forest	sph → esf	sphagnum/*esfagno*
Look to the Stars		spherical/*esférico*
Gone Wild: An Endangered Animal Alphabet		sphinx/*esfinge*
Milo's Hat Trick	st → est	station/*estación*
Mutt Dog!		stomach/*estómago*
Street Music: City Poems		studio/*estudio*
First Garden: The White House Garden and How it Grew	str → estr	stress/*estrés*
Gone Wild: An Endangered Animal Alphabet		strict/*estricto*
Dinosaur Mountain: Digging into the Jurassic Age		structure/*estructura*

Ms. Williams:	Class, I have written today's English and Spanish cognate words on the board. Can someone tell me the difference between the English words and the Spanish words?	

English	Spanish
special	*especial*
spectator	*espectador*
spirit	*espíritu*
state	*estado*
student	*estudiante*

René: The English words are spelled with "sp" and "st" and the Spanish words are spelled with «*esp*» and «*est*».

Ms. Williams: Yes, René! Very good. The English words begin with the sibilant consonant blends [sp] and [st] and their Spanish cognates begin with «*esp*» and «*est*». We call the sounds in English that are made by combining the two consonants together consonant blends because you can hear each of the consonants in the sound they produce. They are called sibilant consonant blends because the "s" makes a "hissing" sound. Let's see how easy it is to convert an English word with an initial sibilant consonant blend to its Spanish cognate. For example, what would the Spanish word for "space" be?

Rita: «*Espacio*»!

Ms. Williams: Yes, Rita! Can you spell it for us?

Rita: «*E-s-p-a-c-i-o*».

Ms. Williams: Good. "Space" in English is «*espacio*» in Spanish. Do you all see a pattern? Let me write the rule: "If an English word begins with an initial consonant sibilant the consonant blend [sp], then it is possible that it has a Spanish cognate that begins with the [es + p] sound."

Ms. Williams started by introducing two example cognate vocabulary words, each one beginning with a word–initial sibilant consonant blend, before the story read-aloud. Ms. Williams and her students then engaged in a study of the English words with initial sibilant consonant blends, and their Spanish cognate pairs. The dialogue ended with a statement of the spelling rule for initial consonant blend cognate words.

After Ms. Williams is confident that her fifth-grade students have learned the spelling rule, the lesson can be continued with other initial sibilant consonant blend cognates from the story: special/*especial*, spectator/*espectador*, spirit/*espíritu*, state/*estado*, and student/*estudiante*. Another teacher might also choose words that are not from the story but also follow the initial sibilant consonant blend rule. Teachers can use the initial sibilant consonant rules and examples to teach the lesson and use the previous dialogue as a model for their instruction.

> **Did you know?**
>
> The Cognate Companion can be used to find English–Spanish cognates that begin with consonant blends and the picture books that contain them.

Informal Assessment of the Sibilant Consonant Blend Rules

Teachers can use any of the exercises or suggested activities as informal assessments. The assessments asks students to apply their understanding of the rule to other words. We provide three example informal assessments for the two cognate spelling rules in Figure 6.3.

Directions: Read the words on the list. Notice the spelling patterns. Using the patterns, fill in the blanks with an English or Spanish cognate. Write the sibilant consonant blend spelling rule.

esponja = sponge   student = *estudiante*

spinach = *espinacas*   stamp = *estampilla*

space = *espacio*   sterilize = *esterilizar*

spiral = *espiral*   stable = *estable*

_____ = *especificar*   _____ = *estómago*

_____ = *espina*   _____ = *estéreo*

spirit = _____   statue = _____

special = _____   state = _____

Answer:
Rule: ___sp___ = ___esp___   Rule: _____ = _____

Figure 6.3. Activity for sibilant e spelling rule.

Dual Nature of the Sibilant Consonant Blend Rules

Unlike the cognate double consonant and consonant digraph spelling rules, the sibilant cognate consonant blend rules are reliable for transforming Spanish words to their English cognates. As with all of the lessons in this book, teachers can use the Cognate Companion to find a picture book that contains vocabulary words for teaching this spelling strategy. The bilingual picture book Magic Windows/*Ventanas mágicas/* (Lomas-Garza, 1999), for example, contains several Spanish–English cognates for teaching the «*esp*» → "sp" rule: *especie*/species, *especial*/special, *especia*/spice, *espiral*/spiral, *espina*/spine, and *espíritu*/spirit. Ms. Martínez, a third grade teacher in a transitional bilingual program, has decided to use this picture book to teach the initial cognate sibilant consonant rule for transforming Spanish words into English.

> **LESSON PLAN**
>
> Magic Windows/ *Ventanas mágicas* (Lomas-Garza, 1999) is a bilingual book.

Ms. Martínez: Class, we have learned how to transform English words containing the initial consonant blend into their Spanish cognates. Today, we are going to learn how to convert Spanish words into English cognates containing initial consonant blends. Let's try the word «*especie*». How can we transform this word to its English cognate?

Andrea: To convert an English word into a Spanish word, you have to change the sibilant consonant blend and add the [e] sound to form [es]. So, for changing a Spanish word to an English cognate, you probably have to do the opposite.

Ms. Martínez: Okay, Andrea. I think you might be onto something. Let's see if it works the way you say for the Spanish word «*especies*».

Andrea: If we start by leaving off the «e» in «*especies*», you will have a word that begins with the consonant blend [sp]—"species." Is that right?

Ms. Martínez: You're right. The rule is: "To transform a Spanish word to an English word beginning with the sibilant consonant blend, you usually just have to drop the 'e' in the Spanish word."

Teachers can then try using some of the less frequent cognate sibilant consonant blend words in the story to assess student learning: *especial*/special, *especia*/spice, *espiral*/spiral, *espina*/spine, and *espíritu*/spirit. The lesson can be extended to other sibilant consonant blend rules that signal cognates, especially "st" → «*est*» and "str" → «*estr*».

REINFORCING THE LEARNING OF COGNATE SPELLING RULES

We have found many activities for reinforcing the learning of cognate spelling rules, and they are particularly effective after a picture book read-aloud and its related cognate vocabulary learning. Among these are flashcards, word banks, word sorts, and word searches, which were introduced in an earlier chapter. In the next few paragraphs we take a look at a type of activity that is not used nearly enough—analogy exercises, which teachers can use to help students deepen their learning of the three distinct cognate spelling rules discussed in this chapter: the double consonant rules; the consonant digraph rules, "ph" → «*f*» and "th" → «*t*»; and the initial sibilant consonant blend rules.

Analogy Exercises

One activity for reviewing the cognate spelling rules is an analogy activity such as the one shown in Figure 6.4. There are several steps for finding the analogy. First, the student considers each analogy, figures out which cognate spelling rule is being depicted, and then selects the example analogy that follows the same rule. The analogies in the figure should be read with the single colon meaning "is to" and the double colon meaning "as." Therefore, item 1 (suggest/*sugerir*) should be read, "suggest" is to «*sugerir*», as "attack" is to «*atacar*», since both are examples of the double consonant rule. The cognate pairs that follow the double consonant rule in items 1, 5, and 9 are attack/*atacar*, express/*expresar*, and missile/*misil*, respectively. Each of the English words in the pair contain a double consonant while the Spanish word in each pair is a single consonant. Items 2, 4, and 8 are intended to model the consonant digraph rule. Finally, the sibilant consonant rule is found in items 3, 6, and 7.

Analogy exercises can be used as a pretest prior to instruction on the different cognate spelling rules if students are familiar with them. As a formative assessment tool, analogy exercises can also be used to decide which rule(s) need to be retaught and reinforced. After administration of this activity, teachers should review the correct answers with their students.

Cognate Word Walls

Teachers can create a cognate spelling rule word wall to remind students of the three cognate spelling rules we have presented in this chapter. To do this, teachers first need to divide the word wall into three sections. One section should be devoted to cognate pairs that follow a double consonant rule, such as "ss" → «*s*». A second section should include those that follow the digraph rules "ph" → «*f*» and "th" → «*t*». The final section should be devoted to the sibilant consonant blend rules, especially "sl" → «*esl*,» "sp" → «*esp*», "spr" → «*espr*», "st" → «*est*», and "str" → «*estr*».

Teachers can improve the value of the word walls by constantly adding new cognate pairs to each section of the rules. Teachers also can make the word wall more dynamic by having students contribute cognate pairs they discover in their classroom assignments and outside readings.

Spelling Bees

Another good way to reinforce the application of the spelling rules is for the teacher to have their students participate in cognate spelling bees. Following our belief that spelling is learned through repeated practice, we suggest the use of cognate spelling bees after teaching each of the rules. Spelling bees provide a way of reviewing cognate vocabulary and are especially useful because they require that students concentrate on the similarities and differences between the English and Spanish spellings, many of which are rule governed.

Directions: Choose the cognate pair that shares the same relationship as the italicized pair.

1. **suggest : *sugerir* ::**
   a. sugar : sugary   b. **attack : *atacar***   c. special : *especial*

2. **phantom : *fantasma* ::**
   a. dollar : *dólar*   b. distance : *distancia*   c. **method : *método***

3. **station : *estación* ::**
   a. **space : *espacio***   b. telephone : *teléfono*   c. possible : *posible*

4. **thermometer : *termómetro* ::**
   a. immigration : *inmigración*   b. **phrase : *frase***   c. spirit : *espíritu*

5. **massive : *masivo* ::**
   a. theater : *teatro*   b. scene : *escena*   c. **express : *expresar***

6. **slogan : *eslogan* ::**
   a. **student : *estudiante***   b. pharmacy : *farmacia*   c. attention : *atención*

7. **strict : *estricto* ::**
   a. **scorpion : *escorpión***   b. essential : *esencial*   c. thermal : *termal*

8. **photo : *foto* ::**
   a. smog : *esmog*   b. **thermos : *termo***   c. appear: *aparecer*

9. **traffic : *tráfico* ::**
   a. aphid : *áfido*   b. **missile : *misil***   c. python : *pitón*

Note: The answers are in bold print.

Figure 6.4. Analogy assessment for the cognate spelling rules.

SUMMARY

Three different spelling rules for transforming English words into Spanish were discussed in this chapter. The first rule provided a strategy for converting English words containing double consonants to Spanish words having a single consonant. It was found that this type of transformation was reliable for changing an English word to its Spanish cognate, but not for changing Spanish words to their English cognates. This lack of bidirectionality is due to Spanish not allowing double consonants. Further, it was suggested that teachers focus more on the frequent English double consonants such as "pp," "ss," and "tt" and less on those such as "bb," "dd," and "gg," which are not common.

The second spelling rule for transforming an English word into its Spanish cognate involved consonant digraphs. Here, we demonstrated that consonant digraphs found in English words can be reliably transformed into their Spanish cognates using the spelling rules "ph" → «f» and "th" → «t». Once again, however, converting Spanish words to English is not possible because the "ph" and "th" digraphs do not exist in Spanish.

The third spelling rule examined the reliability of the English cognate sibilant consonant blends as predictors of Spanish cognates. Furthermore, the majority of these consonant blends can be converted to their English cognate equivalents. Furthermore, they are reliable for transforming words from English to Spanish and from Spanish to English.

Teachers can use the English–Spanish cognate vocabulary in the award-winning picture books listed in the Cognate Companion to create spelling lessons. This practice will allow language learners to recognize English–Spanish cognates when they encounter them. This will also facilitate the language learner's efficiency in transforming words from one language to another.

REFLECTION AND ACTION

1.   How can using the three cognate spelling rules presented in this chapter help your bilingual learners?

2.   Select one of the three spelling rules presented in this chapter. Then using the Cognate Companion or the examples in this chapter, identify three example English words and their Spanish cognate equivalents. How might you teach the selected spelling rule?

3.   How might you organize a cognate spelling bee that incorporates the three spelling rules?

7

Planning Cognate Lessons Using Picture Books

OBJECTIVES

☐ Select picture books and plan cognate vocabulary lessons that accompany read-alouds.

☐ Examine and explain a sample cognate lesson plan for a picture book.

☐ Design the outline for a cognate vocabulary lesson that you can integrate into your classroom instruction.

Cognate Play

You are a literacy coach and you have been asked to create activities to accompany the read-aloud of the picture book, <u>When Aidan Became a Brother</u> (Lukoff, 2019), which tells the story of a transgender boy as he adjusts to his new life as a male and as a soon-to-be brother of a new baby. The cognates you have chosen from this picture book are:

LESSON PLAN

<u>When Aidan Became a Brother</u> (Lukoff, 2019)

adjust/*ajustar*	exclaim/*exclamar*
announce/*anunciar*	experiment/*experimento*
decide/*decidir*	transgender/*transgénero*
exactly/*exactamente*	trapped/*atrapado*

What activities would you suggest or create for a third grade class to accompany this picture book? For example, would you create a mini-lesson on the cognate prefixes: /ad-/, /ex-/, or /trans-/? Perhaps a mini-lesson on the roots: /-claim-/, /-gen-/, /-jus-/, or /-nounce/, or on the cognate suffixes /-ly/ or /-ment/? Perhaps a spelling lesson on double consonants such as "nn" or «*pp*»? Write down your ideas here.

_____

_____

_____

_____

Picture books are an integral part of literacy instruction in elementary school. This chapter illustrates how teachers can create cognate lesson plans using picture books for all content areas. A sustained focus on cognates helps bilingual learners expand their academic vocabularies and develop metalinguistic awareness—the ability to objectify language by discussing features in one or two of their languages (Baker, 2011; Bialystok, 2007).

Did you know?

Teachers can find more than 300 cognate lesson plans on the Cognate Companion that illustrate instructional and assessment strategies for converting Spanish cognates and their constituent parts (i.e., prefixes, roots, suffixes) to English and from English to Spanish.

T his chapter models our lesson planning process using award-winning picture books for language learning and literacy instruction with cognates and cognate recognition strategies. Sample lesson plans for more than 300 picture books are provided in the Cognate Companion. We also include a blank lesson planning template so teachers can create their own cognate lessons tailored to their students' language and literacy needs.

CHOOSING PICTURE BOOKS AND COGNATES FOR A READ-ALOUD

In the elementary schools where we have worked with teachers, we have found that many decisions about what to teach are made by the people who create and write the national, state, and district curriculum standards. Textbook publishers take these standards and commission their curriculum writers to design, scope, and sequence materials to create grade-level language and content-area textbooks. At the school district level, administrators, content-area experts, and teachers select a textbook series for each of the content areas. At the school level, instructional coaches and teachers follow the lesson plans and suggestions contained in their textbooks' teacher manuals to prepare the lessons they teach.

We have been fortunate to work in schools that grant their elementary grade-level teachers some leeway when designing instruction and assessment, particularly for bilingual learners. We have found that such teachers typically follow the curriculum guides in their textbooks and adapt the curriculum to meet the needs of their students while working to ensure that the national, state, and district standards are embedded and addressed in each unit of instruction. This applies to teachers who use English as a medium of instruction as well as those who teach bilingually.

Elementary grade teachers who know their students and their content areas well sometimes feel that the textbooks adopted by their districts do not adequately address the needs of their students. These teachers often supplement their instruction with picture books to create materials, lessons, and assessments they feel will enhance student learning. This chapter provides guidance for teachers who choose to develop cognate lesson plans that target the language, literacy, and cultural needs of their bilingual learners in the content areas.

Cognate Lesson Planning Using the Cognate Companion

We have found a wide range of expertise about cognates and cognate instruction among the teachers that we have collaborated with. Teachers who are just beginning to learn about using cognates in their classrooms can likely find advice from their colleagues to draw on. An easy way to tap into this knowledge is to find ways to encourage teachers to talk about cognate teaching and learning when opportunities arise as in the following vignette.

Mrs. Martínez, a Spanish–English bilingual teacher in a third grade transitional bilingual program, is busy cleaning her classroom at the end of a long school day when her colleague at the school, Ms. Jones, comes in to ask advice on writing cognate lesson plans. Let's listen in on their conversation.

Ms. Jones: Hi, Mrs. Martínez! I was wondering if you could give me some advice.

Mrs. Martínez: Sure, I'd be glad to.

Ms. Jones: I attended some sessions on Spanish–English cognates at the bilingual conference last week and I wanted to implement some of the cognate activities that were presented. I especially wanted to ask you about writing lesson plans for cognates.

Mrs. Martínez: Sure! I include cognate lessons in almost all of my classes. I use them for my language arts, science, and social studies classes. I even use cognates in math classes. Every time I do a picture book read-aloud, I create a cognate lesson plan. I feel it's important for my bilingual learners to build their English and Spanish vocabularies. I use a snap-on cognate lesson planning template to integrate my cognate instruction into my regular lesson plans.

Ms. Jones: I'd love to see the template.

Mrs. Martínez: Sure. The template has space for pre-reading, during reading, and post-reading cognate activities, the actual cognates to use, and how to assess the students. You can try it out, and let me know what you think.

Finding the Right Picture Book for Your Purposes

Teachers' manuals generally divide the units of instruction into their component lessons, complete with the learning objectives designed to meet the curriculum standards. To evaluate each of the component lessons suggested in the teachers' manual, teachers must evaluate the adequacy of each lesson plan for their students in terms of the materials, procedures, and assessments, as well as for its linguistic and cultural responsiveness.

> **Did you know?**
>
> Teachers can use the picture books in the Cognate Companion to design lessons, materials, and assessments featuring the English–Spanish cognates in those texts to improve instruction.

Textbook writers and publishers know their lessons may not be entirely adequate for all students, particularly bilingual learners. It is for this reason that textbooks often contain suggestions for auxiliary online or text resources that teachers can use to make their instruction more effective for learners. Among the materials most often suggested are picture books. Using the Cognate Companion, teachers can supplement their textbook's picture book recommendations.

The Cognate Companion database is comprised of over 3,000 award-winning books. The books are catalogued using the subject headings for each book as they appear in WorldCat, a comprehensive database of library books (https://www.worldcat.org/). Teachers can search the Cognate Companion for books by subject just by inputting the subject headings. Suppose a teacher wanted a book on dogs, they need only type in the subject and titles of books having the subject heading, "dog," would appear along with all of the Spanish–English cognates contained in these particular books. Once a book has been identified through this process, the teacher can check in the school or public library catalog for its availability.

> **Did you know?**
>
> Teachers can search the Cognate Companion by subject headings to find relevant picture books and cognates.

Another popular strategy for finding a book to read aloud is to visit the school or public library for a book and then check to see if it is in the Cognate Companion database. The advantage of this method is that a teacher can read the entire text and peruse the illustrations to judge the suitability of the picture book without having to worry about its availability.

Identifying the Cognate Vocabulary for the Lesson

After teachers have selected a picture book, they are ready to create a cognate vocabulary lesson. What questions does a teacher ask in choosing the appropriate words for a cognate vocabulary lesson for their students? In our practice, we ask basic questions concerning the frequency and utility of the cognate vocabulary words such as, "Which cognates in the picture book are Tier One words that require no explicit instruction?" "Which words are general academic Tier Two words that require explicit instruction and will be found in other subjects?" "Which academic Tier Three words require discipline-specific instruction?" "Which cognates support foundational skills such as word analysis?"

> **Did you know?**
>
> Teachers can review the cognate vocabulary in picture books in the Cognate Companion to design lessons to teach cognates.

We also ask questions about morphology, spelling, and context clues. Specifically, we ask, "Which cognates possess a prefix, a root word, or a suffix?" "Which of the cognates in the picture book follows a spelling rule that can be taught in a mini-lesson?" "Which cognates might best be taught using context clues?"

LESSON PLAN

Up in the Garden
and Down in the Dirt
(Messner, 2017)

LESSON PLAN

Seeds Move
(Page, 2019)

LESSON PLAN

The Sun Is Kind of
a Big Deal
(Seluk, 2018)

LESSON PLAN

The Mangrove Tree:
Planting Trees to
Feed Families
(Roth & Trumbore,
2021)

LESSON PLAN

Are Trees Alive?
(Miller, 2003)

Consider the case of Mr. Cuello, a fourth-grade teacher in a bilingual program, who is teaching a science unit on plants and wants to find an appropriate picture book on the topic of photosynthesis. Using the Cognate Companion, Mr. Cuello enters the search terms, "plants," "trees," and "photosynthesis," in the subject field and finds several books: Up in the Garden and Down in the Dirt (Messner, 2017), Seeds Move (Page, 2019), The Sun Is Kind of a Big Deal (Seluk, 2018), The Mangrove Tree: Planting Trees to Feed Families (Roth & Trumbore, 2021), and Are Trees Alive? (Miller, 2003). After reviewing the books, he selects the book, Are Trees Alive?, an ILA Teachers' Choice Award Book.

To find the appropriate vocabulary words, Mr. Cuello consults the Cognate Companion for the list of cognates in Are Trees Alive? (Miller, 2003). There he discovers the Tier Two words he knows will be useful for his students to learn: characteristic/*característica*, diversity/*diversidad*, massive/*masivo*, and signify/*significar*. He believes these words are useful not only for understanding the science content of the picture book, but they can be applied across other subject disciplines such as social studies and language arts. Mr. Cuello also decides to teach the Tier Three cognate pair, stoma/*estoma*, since it is essential for understanding the text.

Cognate Objectives and Assessments to Measure Them

Teachers include cognate objectives, activities, and assessments in their lesson plans. In the Cognate Companion the lesson plans include cognate objectives and activities. These cognate activities can also be used as formative and summative assessments of bilingual learners' progress in meeting the cognate objectives.

One important cognate objective is for students to learn the association between the English and Spanish forms of the cognate pairs. We want bilingual learners to remember the Spanish–English cognate associations forward and backward. When presented with the English word, "rapid," they should respond with the cognate, «*rápido.*» When presented with «*rápido,*» they should answer "rapid." To achieve this objective, we employ methodology from the early days of psychology—paired-associates learning and its time-tested vehicle for learning associations, the flashcard. We include the use of flashcards to associate the English and Spanish cognate words in almost every activity. Almost every snap-on lesson plan in the Cognate Companion includes a flashcard activity as a formative assessment.

> **Did you know?**
>
> Each snap-on lesson plan on the Cognate Companion includes an award-winning picture book, cognate objectives, cognate activities, and cognate assessments.

Another important objective is for bilingual learners to be able to use their newly acquired cognate vocabulary words accurately and in the appropriate context. To this end, we employ another common activity of the language arts classroom as a formative or summative assessment—the sentence completion worksheet.

Among the laws of psychology is the one stating that comprehension precedes production. With respect to vocabulary, this implies that before learners can create meaningful utterances or sentences, they must understand the meaning of words. Therefore, after students demonstrate their comprehension of the cognate vocabulary in the context of the picture book read-aloud, we ask them to generate original sentences—in English and Spanish. We find these sentences to be useful as assessments of their academic language development in either or both languages.

Objectives to Deepen Student Understanding of Cognates

The snap-on cognate lesson plans should include morphology and spelling objectives to give students opportunities to improve their literacy skills. We also focus on teaching context clues for students to guess the meanings of unfamiliar words. The teaching of morphology and context clues provides students with strategies to improve their ability to make meaning of the text.

After selecting a picture book for a read-aloud, teachers should define the objectives for the lesson plans to accompany the read-aloud. One of the first objectives of cognate instruction is for bilingual learners to be able to deconstruct unfamiliar cognates into their component parts to make meaning of them. To do this, there are specific lesson plans to address this objective. The Cognate Companion includes lesson plans for teaching students to break up words into root words and affixes in meaning-making ways.

> ### Did you know?
>
> Lesson plans with morphology and spelling conversion rules can help students deepen their understanding of cognates.

Another morphological objective is for bilingual learners to be able to convert English words to their Spanish cognates and vice versa using the cognate suffix rules. This will help students recognize cognates and, equally importantly, generate cognates they can use to express themselves intelligently. Many of the lesson plans in the Cognate Companion are included for the purpose of teaching the specific cognate suffix rules.

> **LESSON PLAN**
>
> Ruth Objects: The Life of Ruth Bader Ginsburg (Rappaport, 2020)

For example, Ms. Galván, a third grade teacher who teaches the English component in a bilingual program, wants to conduct a read-aloud of Ruth Objects: The Life of Ruth Bader Ginsburg (Rappaport, 2020). In reviewing the list of cognates for the book using the Cognate Companion, Ms. Galván notices that three of the cognates, nervous/*nervioso*, prestigious/*prestigioso*, and rigorous/*rigoroso*, follow the /-ous/ →/-oso/ suffix rule. Since teaching cognate suffix rules, such as /-ous/→/-oso/, is one of the essential cognate objectives, Ms. Galván develops a mini-lesson on this rule as an activity to accompany her read-aloud. Ms. Galván can also consult the Cognate Companion for other picture books containing cognates that follow this suffix rule and use those in a mini-lesson to reinforce the learning of the /-ous/→/-oso/ rule.

Teachers want their students to become better spellers. To get this done, they should create lesson plans that teach spelling rules such as the double consonant and consonant digraph rules for transforming English words to Spanish words. Teaching students about the cognate sibilant consonant blends will also help them become better spellers.

> **LESSON PLAN**
>
> The Librarian Who Measured the Earth (Lasky, 1994)

Teachers often discover that cognates in a particular picture book can be used to design a mini-lesson on a cognate spelling pattern. Ms. Williams, who teaches fifth-grade English as a second language to bilingual learners, finds that The Librarian Who Measured the Earth (Lasky, 1994), a picture book she will be reading aloud, contains the cognates: stadium/*estadio*, stomach/*estómago*, student/*estudiante*, and studio/*estudio*, each one of which begins with a sibilant consonant blend. Reflecting on this discovery, Ms. Williams decides she will create a mini-lesson using these vocabulary words to teach the cognate spelling rule, "st" → «est,» to accompany her read-aloud.

It is important for students to be able to use context clues to guess the meanings of unfamiliar words, and our experience suggests this needs to be practiced regularly. Too often we find that the teachers and students do not know the different types of context clues. This is unfortunate given that one of the characteristics of good readers is their ability to guess the meanings of unfamiliar words using context clues. Therefore, teachers should strive to include lessons that teach students how to use cognate context clues as another meaning-making strategy. Suggestions for such lesson plans are included in the Cognate Companion.

The classroom vignettes of Mr. Cuello, Ms. Galván, and Ms. Williams illustrate some of the ways teachers can use the cognates in the award-winning picture books in the Cognate Companion for developing cognate mini-lesson plans to accompany their read-alouds.

Table 7.1.   A sampling of the 300 lesson plan inventory in the Cognate Companion

Book title	Grade level	Discipline/Subject matter	Cognate objective(s)	Cognate assessments
La tortilla corredora	K–2	Literature: Retelling of *The Gingerbread Boy*	Tier two cognates; Compare/Contrast	Compare/Contrast; Vocabulary
Side by Side/*Lado a lado*: The Story of Dolores Huerta and Cesar Chavez/*La historia de Dolores Huerta y Cesar Chavez*	2–4	Social Studies	Tier two cognates; /-tion/ → /ción/	Compare/Contrast; Sequence; Vocabulary; Cognate production
Dealing with Bullying/*Que hacer con los bravucones*	K–5	Social Studies Informational Text	Tier two cognates; Text structures; Main ideas and supporting details; Summary	Summarize text; Text Comprehension; Vocabulary test
When the Wolves Returned: Restoring Nature's Balance in Yellowstone	2–5	Science	Tier two cognates; Vocabulary in context; /-eco-/ → /-eco-/	Cause and effect relations; Vocabulary test; Root Word /-eco-/ → /-eco-/ study
One Grain of Rice: A Mathematical Folktale	1–4	Mathematics; Folktale	Tier two cognates; Vocabulary in context;	Exponent problems; Sequence of events; Vocabulary test
Nasreen's Secret School: A True Story from Afghanistan	2–5	Social Justice	Tier two cognate vocabulary; /-ic/ → /-ico/	Text to self-connection; *Suffix* /-ic/ → /-ico/ study Cognate production

Such individual efforts can be enhanced when teachers have a space in which to share their discoveries and cognate activity ideas. Such collaboration allows teachers to coordinate lessons and stories across grades and subjects, thus building a coherent program of cognate study. Table 7.1 provides a sampling of the lesson plan inventory included on the Cognate Companion that teachers can work with individually and in teams or professional learning communities.

DESIGNING A LESSON WITH THE COGNATE LESSON PLAN TEMPLATE

Now that we have explored the parts of cognate lesson plans (cognate objectives, cognate vocabulary, pre-and post-reading activities, and cognate assessments), let's look at the lesson plan overall. This section provides a step-by-step guide for creating one's own snap-on cognate lesson plans using the cognate lesson plan template we have used in our work, including the lesson plans on the Cognate Companion. The lesson plan template serves two purposes. First, it serves as a flexible framework that teachers can use to create their own cognate lesson plans, which they can regularly integrate into content-area instruction. The completed template can also facilitate communication among administrators, coaches, and other teachers about cognate vocabulary instruction in their classroom practice.

In the next section, we follow Mrs. Martínez to see how she uses the cognate lesson plan template to create a cognate lesson for her third-grade bilingual class to accompany the read-aloud of the award-winning picture book, <u>Pancho Rabbit and the Coyote: A Migrant's Tale</u> (Tonatiuh, 2013). The lesson plan template that Mrs. Martínez created for the book, <u>Pancho Rabbit and the Coyote: A Migrant's Tale</u> (Tonatiuh, 2013) is presented in Figure 7.1.

LESSON PLAN

<u>Pancho Rabbit and the Coyote: A Migrant's Tale</u> (Tonatiuh, 2013)

TITLE *Pancho Rabbit and the Coyote: A Migrant's Tale*

AUTHOR	ILLUSTRATOR	GRADE LEVEL
Duncan Tonatiuh	Duncan Tonatiuh	3rd (3.8)

THEME OR BIG IDEA

In this allegory of the plight of undocumented workers, Pancho Rabbit faces many dangerous situations in searching for his father, a migrant worker in the United States.

COGNATE VOCABULARY TERMS	**COGNATE OBJECTIVES**
appear/*aparecer* distance/*distancia* emerge/*emerger* exhausted/*exhausto* finally/*finalmente* instrument/*instrumento* migrant/*emigrante* normally/*normalmente*	Students will be able to: • Compose an original sentence for each cognate vocabulary pair in English and Spanish. • Use the cognate vocabulary words in sentence completion exercises. • Transform English words ending in /-ly/ to the Spanish cognates ending in /-mente/ and the converse by invoking the /-ly/ = /-mente/ rule, as in the cognates finally/*finalmente*. • Deconstruct Spanish–English cognates consisting of the prefix /e-/ and cognate root words to derive the meanings of words such as emerge/*emerger*. • Apply the cognate double consonant spelling rule for transforming English words to Spanish words, such as appear/*aparecer*.

PRE-READING COGNATE ACTIVITIES

• **Activate background knowledge:** Introduce the title of the story. Discuss the plight of farmworkers in the United States. Discuss how the *coyotes* mistreat the migrant farmer workers on the journey to the United States border and how farmers abuse them with low wages.

• **Frontload the cognate vocabulary:** Teachers present the English word of the cognate vocabulary pairs and ask the students to guess their Spanish cognates. Next, teachers provide the Spanish cognates and ask students for their English equivalents.

The Read-Aloud

POST-READING COGNATE ACTIVITIES AND ASSESSMENTS

• **Review cognate vocabulary and instruction:** Have students: a.) cut out, review, and test themselves using their flashcards; b.) compose original sentences with the cognate vocabulary words; or c.) complete a fill-in-the-blanks sentence completion activity.

• **Cognate vocabulary assessment:** The students will complete a summative fill-in-the-blanks exercise using the cognate vocabulary words.

• **Cognate mini-lesson:** Teachers use concept induction exercises to introduce students to the cognate suffix rule /-ly/ = /-mente/ using cognates such as the vocabulary pair, finally/*finalmente*.

• **Cognate vocabulary assessment:** The students will transform unfamiliar English words that follow the /-ly/ = /-mente/ into their Spanish cognates and the converse.

• **Cognate mini-lesson:** Teachers can use concept induction exercises to teach students that the cognate prefix, /e-/, means "out" as in the cognate pair, emerge/*emerger*.

• **Cognate vocabulary assessment:** The students will guess the meaning of unfamiliar English and Spanish cognate words that contain the prefix, /e-/.

Figure 7.1.   Lesson Plan for Pancho Rabbit and the Coyote: A Migrant's Tale.

Identifying Important Information about the Picture Book

Teachers like Mrs. Martínez can begin using the cognate lesson plan template by completing the important information about the picture book, including the title, author, and illustrator. For example, the book Pancho Rabbit and the Coyote: A Migrant's Tale was written and illustrated by Duncan Tonatiuh.

Mrs. Martínez will also want to include what grade level the picture book targets. Most picture books do not come with a grade level assigned to them, so teachers usually have to consult outside sources. A useful tool for finding this information is the Renaissance: Accelerated Reader Bookfinder (http://www.arbookfind.com), which is published online by the same people who produce the Accelerated Reader (AR) program. The Advantage-TASA Open Standard (ATOS) book level rating was developed by Renaissance Learning and Touchstone Applied Science Associates for identifying the grade level of picture books. The ratings describe the level of reading a student would need to independently read a certain book; the numbers reflect the grade and month of the school term. For example, Pancho Rabbit has an ATOS rating of 3.8, signifying that this book is suitable for readers having the skills of an average reader in the eighth month of third grade. For teachers wanting to know the range of student levels for a given picture book, they can use the reading level conversion chart published by Action Potential Learning (https://www.aplearning.com/images/DownloadPDFs/Lexile-Conversion-Chart.pdf). This conversion chart uses the ATOS reading level of a book to provide its grade-level ranges. According to this chart, Pancho Rabbit is suitable for students whose reading grade levels range from 1.7 to 5.0, which correlates highly with the reading levels in Mrs. Martínez's classroom.

Amazon is another source for identifying the general reading level of a book. Each webpage for a picture book usually contains a book review from an established periodical such as *Booklist* and *School Library Journal* that is typically accompanied by a suggested grade level. On the same page, Amazon also provides an age range that can be used to judge the suitability of a particular book for students at a certain grade level. According to the Pancho Rabbit webpage at Amazon, the picture book is appropriate for students whose ages are six to nine and in grade levels one through four. Both the reading level conversion chart and the Amazon websites suggest that *Pancho Rabbit* is appropriate for Mrs. Martínez's third-grade students.

Articulating the Lesson Objectives

Having selected the book to read aloud and determined its readability, Mrs. Martínez turns her attention to the content, language, and cognate vocabulary objectives she will focus on after she has closely read the picture book. The guiding question for this section is, "What should the students learn from the story or information in this book?"

Main Ideas and Themes

In informational texts, the main idea is defined as the message the author wants to convey about the topic. Main ideas are present in every paragraph and are proved or explained by supporting details: facts, reasons, examples, and opinions. Finding the main ideas in informational passages is essential to the comprehension and summarization of text and is an explicit focus of the English language arts and literacy standards.

In a narrative story, like Pancho Rabbit, the theme is the message or lesson an author wants to convey. Of course, picture books often have more than one theme to communicate. Sometimes, the students take away a theme that may or may not have been intended by the author, but that connects with students' prior knowledge or experiences. Whether the theme is intended by the author, targeted by the curriculum, or connected to students' worlds, students need to learn how to identify themes, support them with evidence from the text, discuss intertextual connections, and negotiate meaning with the other students and the teacher in the class.

Mrs. Martínez identified the theme or big idea of Pancho Rabbit. On the lesson plan template, she writes: "Undocumented migrant workers face many dangers as they look for work in the United States." Because some of the students and their family members may have experienced migration or are undocumented themselves, students are likely to have rich linguistic and cultural funds of knowledge around this theme. Mrs. Martínez knows that she needs to address this topic with respect and care.

Cognate Word Selection

After writing out the main idea or theme of the text, Mrs. Martínez moves to selecting the cognate vocabulary words. The selection of the vocabulary is important because the chosen cognate words should be those that will first help the students understand the text. Additionally, the selected vocabulary words will inform the choice of activities or lesson plans that will accompany the picture book read-aloud.

We suggest that teachers select four to nine cognates for each picture book read-aloud. Picture books appropriate for the youngest students often have as few as four cognates that may be deemed important for understanding the text. On the other hand, there are science and social science picture books for upper elementary students that contain more. The majority of the lesson plans in the Cognate Companion list between four and nine cognate vocabulary words.

To decide on cognate vocabulary objectives for her read-aloud of <u>Pancho Rabbit and the Coyote: A Migrant's Tale</u>, Mrs. Martínez closely examined the list of cognates provided in the Cognate Companion to select the vocabulary words using the question, "What are the Tier Two or Tier Three cognates that are essential for my students to comprehend the story?"

After reviewing the cognates listed in the Cognate Companion, Mrs. Martínez chose the following eight cognates: appear/*aparecer*, distance/*distancia*, emerge/*emerger*, exhausted/*exhausto*, finally/*finalmente*, instrument/*instrumento*, migrant/*emigrante*, and normally/*normalmente*. Now Mrs. Martínez is ready to create the cognate objectives for the lesson that could be used to strengthen the learning of the individual vocabulary words and meaning-making strategies.

Cognate Objectives

Mrs. Martínez is now at the point our literacy coach was in the opening activity to this chapter. Now, she must decide what cognate objectives she will include as part of her read-aloud activities. We can see the five cognate objectives that Mrs. Martínez chose (Figure 7.1). The first two objectives ask students to 1) use cognate vocabulary words in a sentence completion exercise, and 2) compose an original sentence with each one of the cognates in English and Spanish. Both of these objectives allow teachers to assess students' understanding of word meanings.

Cognate objectives three and four are morphological. To reach objective 3, Mrs. Martínez chose to teach her students the suffix rule, /-ly/→/-mente/ using the adverbs, "finally" and "normally," along with other adverbs Mrs. Martínez might want to include. A review of the vocabulary list in Figure 7.1 shows that Mrs. Martínez could also have chosen to teach the suffix rules, /-ance/→/-ancia/ using the cognate nouns, distance/*distancia*; the rule, /-ment/→/-mento/, with the noun cognates, instrument/*instrumento*; or another noun rule, /-ant/→/-ante/, exemplified by the cognates, migrant/*emigrante*. When asked why she chose the /-ly/→/-mente/ suffix rule over the others, Mrs. Martínez replied that her students needed more practice with it than with the other rules.

Because Mrs. Martínez also believed that her students would profit from learning about the prefix, /e-/, a variant of the prefix, /ex-/, which means, "out, away, or forth," she included objective 4. The cognate vocabulary word, emerge/*emerger*, means "to arise out of." She could have also created a mini-lesson by using the prefix, /ex-/, which is found in the cognates, exhausted/*exhausto*, which literally means "to draw out." Mrs. Martínez could have opted for the prefix, /ap-/, which is a variant of /ad-/, meaning "before," as in the cognate vocabulary words, appear/*aparecer*. There were also several root words Mrs. Martínez could have used to build a mini-lesson. The root, /-stan-/, in distance/*distancia*, means "to stand or to remain." The /-fin-/ in finally/*finalmente* means, "end," the /-stru-/ in instrument/*instrumento* means "to build," the /-migr-/ in migrant/*emigrante* means "to move to a new place," and the /-norm-/ in normally/*normalmente*, means "a rule or pattern." There were several morphological rules Mrs. Martínez could have incorporated in her read-aloud activities. These were the ones Mrs. Martínez felt her students needed the most work on.

In her lesson plan template, Mrs. Martínez also included the double consonant spelling rule as cognate objective 5, specifically, the "pp" → «*p*» spelling rule seen in the Spanish–English cognates, appear/*aparecer*. She believed that learning this rule would help her bilingual learners translate from English to Spanish.

Creating Pre-reading Activities

The next sections in the lesson plan template focus on the procedures and activities for teaching and assessing the lessons before, during, and after the picture book read-aloud. In the first part of the lesson plan template, teachers plan the pre-reading activities that will occur before the actual read-aloud of the award-winning picture book and specify how the activities relate to the objectives of the lesson. To do this, teachers can provide a chronology of the procedural steps that are as detailed as possible, not only for themselves, but for their supervisors.

As is common practice with the read-alouds of picture books, teachers begin with the introduction of the book title and the author. The purpose of discussing the title with students is to activate prior knowledge of the subject matter to be discussed in the story. Teachers can provide some of the ideas they want to discuss with their students for the introduction of the title and the author on the lesson plan template. Next, teachers introduce the purpose(s) for reading the book. Teachers will discuss their reasons for selecting the book with the students as a means of motivating them to listen and learn from the book. The inclusion of information about the purpose for the read-aloud is also useful to coaches, mentors, or supervisors working with the teacher, because they can focus their observations and feedback on this purpose in the teachers' actual classroom practice.

To heighten their interest and motivation for reading the book and learning more about migration, Mrs. Martínez told her students that she was going to read them a fascinating picture book that "she just couldn't put down." She then introduced the title of the book, <u>Pancho Rabbit and the Coyote: A Migrant's Tale</u>, provided the background information they needed to understand the story, and explained how their work would address the content and language objectives of their lesson as well as the specific cognate objectives of the snap-on lesson plan.

After activating students' background knowledge, the teacher introduces the cognate vocabulary words one by one on cards written in the language of the text. As each card is presented, the teacher asks the students if they know what the word is in the other language. In the case of Mrs. Martínez' read-aloud of <u>Pancho Rabbit and the Coyote: A Migrant's Tale</u>, the text is written in English. Therefore, she asks if the students know what each word is in Spanish. When the majority of students respond with their answers, Mrs. Martínez reinforces their correct responses by telling them that they are correct and, more importantly, points out that the English and Spanish words are cognates.

When students do not respond with the correct answer or do not respond at all, Mrs. Martínez presents them with the word in the other language and asks them if they know what that word means. If students don't know the meaning of either word, then Mrs. Martínez offers them an explanation of the word's meaning and provides examples.

One of our objectives is that students should know the words in both languages. Therefore, once all of the vocabulary words have been presented in one language, the teacher mixes up the order of the words and presents them in the other language. Since Mrs. Martínez presented the English words first, she presents them in Spanish the second time around and reviews the responses with the students. Once the process is finished, Mrs. Martínez places the cards in the pocket chart displaying the card English side out since the text is in English. After the teacher is confident that the students have a working knowledge of the vocabulary words, the teacher can begin to read the book aloud.

Post-reading Activities

Teachers design their post-reading activities to help students deepen their comprehension of the picture book read-aloud and extend student learning beyond the text. Of course, the purposes of the activities will likely vary by content area in important ways. For example, immediately after the read-aloud of a picture book in a language arts class, the teacher and the students might discuss the characters, plot, and setting of the story. They might do a close read of a particular part of a narrative or informational text to gather evidence from that text for specific purposes. In a social studies class, the post-reading activities might ask students to explain orally and in writing why an important event occurred and what happened as a result. In all cases, it is important for a teacher to clearly relate the purposes of the post-reading activities in the lesson plan template to the content, language, and cognate objectives. These kinds of post-reading activities can also function as assessments because they provide evidence of student performance relative to the cognate objectives for the lesson.

After the discussion of the story and the post-reading assessment activities related to the content objectives, teachers like Mrs. Martínez can return to the cognate objectives and the cognate vocabulary words. Sometimes, Mrs. Martínez uses the strategy of presenting the cognates in context to help students remember them. To do this, she returns to the picture book and presents students with the cognate vocabulary as they occurred in the picture book and has the students recall the meanings of the words using the context of the sentences and, if applicable, the picture. At other times, Mrs. Martínez points to the cards on the pocket chart and has the students respond with the cognates of the vocabulary words.

To reinforce the associations between the English words and their Spanish cognates, Mrs. Martínez prepared individual sheets of cardstock with the cognates printed on them. The English words were printed on one side of the sheet with the Spanish words printed on the back. After every student received a sheet, they cut out the flashcards. When all the flashcards were cut out, the students reviewed them and tested themselves and each other for a few minutes. Mrs. Martínez walked around observing the students, stopping to test some of the students to ensure that they are learning the cognate pairs. After the students finished reviewing their flashcards and have tested themselves, they gathered the flashcards and placed them in their large-size personal sandwich bag, which served as a cognate word bank and stored them at their desks for future activities.

For the next post-reading activity, Mrs. Martínez had her students complete an activity whereby the students finish sentences with the appropriate cognate vocabulary words—the so-called sentence completion activity. After the students completed the activity, Mrs. Martínez reviewed the answers with them and had them correct their wrong answers. Then, Mrs. Martínez asked the students to compose a sentence with each vocabulary word in English and Spanish. As they wrote their sentences, Mrs. Martínez made her way around the room, providing students with any help they might need.

The post-reading activities Mrs. Martínez had her students complete are standard fare in most elementary school classrooms. They can be used as formative assessments of student progress. She could have had her students work on creating more polished sentences as a formative assessment for a grade. Mrs. Martínez could have created other cognate vocabulary worksheets and activities using the same vocabulary words to arrive at a summative assessment of their learning.

After the suffix lesson, Mrs. Martínez taught her students the cognate spelling rule for converting the double consonants in English words to the Spanish cognates. Once again, she employed the list of Spanish–English cognates for which the students had to induce the rule.

Mrs. Martínez introduced a morphology mini-lesson on the cognate suffix rule, /-ly/ = /-mente/. Prior to the lesson, Mrs. Martínez wrote a list of four Spanish–English cognate pairs on the board, two of which were the vocabulary words, finally/*finalmente* and normally/*normalmente*. The other two pairs that followed the /-ly/ = /-mente/ rule came from other cognates in the book.

As is the case with most of the teaching vignettes throughout the book, we suggest that teachers use the strategy of concept induction to teach the various morphological and spelling rules. Following this strategy, Mrs. Martínez first had her students examine the lists of cognates to see if they could recognize the word patterns. She then responded affirmatively to answers that closely approximated the /-ly/ = /-mente/ rule. For answers that were incorrect, Mrs. Martínez provided corrective feedback. Mrs. Martínez informed the students why the answer was not correct and built upon the answer to achieve a more desirable end.

> **Did you know?**
>
> Teachers can use the Cognate Companion to search for cognate suffixes like /-ly/ or /-mente/

Once the students discovered the rule, Mrs. Martínez asked her students to provide further examples of the /-ly/ = /-mente/ suffix rule. Since the students were unable to provide examples, Mrs. Martínez offered some of her own, "regularly" and «regularmente.» To assess the learning of the rule, Mrs. Martínez provided students with other English words ending in /-ly/, for which the students wrote the corresponding Spanish cognates. She also presented them with a list of Spanish words ending in /-mente/ and had her students write the English cognates in their cognate notebook. After the lesson, Mrs. Martínez assessed their cognate vocabulary learning by having her students generate responses to infrequent words that followed the /-ly/ = /-mente/ rule. Since the students had never heard or seen these words before, Mrs. Martínez was confident that her students demonstrated their learning of the rule and that they were not simply responding from memory.

Mrs. Martínez's cognate lesson plan around the picture book <u>Pancho Rabbit</u> contains the parts we would expect from a cognate lesson plan. Students learned new cognate vocabulary, a morphological rule, and a spelling rule. Students practiced using the cognate vocabulary in context while also composing sentences in English and Spanish. This is just a single example of how a teacher can use a picture book to create a powerful cognate lesson plan for their bilingual learners.

Adapting Lesson Plans for Different Classes

The example lesson plan we have presented was particularly suited for Mrs. Martínez's third-grade transitional bilingual class. Other teachers finding themselves in either Mrs. Martínez's teaching situation or in different language programs at various grade levels should feel free to adapt the lesson plans to meet the needs of their students.

For example, Ms. Galván, a third grade bilingual teacher, may have chosen different cognate vocabulary words to frontload. She might also have decided to teach a different morphological or spelling rule than those of Mrs. Martínez or chosen a picture book in Spanish, as she often does. We believe that the choices should be left up to the teachers who know their students best.

Teachers in the upper primary grades can also adapt the lesson plan Mrs. Martínez created. The context of the students' educational needs should be the guiding force when choosing to use or adapt an existing lesson plan. For example, Mr. Hampton, who teaches Spanish to his third-grade English speakers, might create a cognate lesson plan that focuses on context clues. Mr. Cuello, a fourth grade teacher, may believe his students already know some of the cognates selected by Mrs. Martínez; therefore, he may choose to include more challenging targeted cognate vocabulary words.

> **Did you know?**
>
> Teachers can search the Cognate Companion for books in Spanish and bilingual books.

In summary, teachers know their students' abilities best. They can use or adapt the cognate lesson plans in the Cognate Companion to create the lessons students need, or they can use the blank lesson plan template to create their own plans for other stories in the Cognate Companion. Many of the cognate prefix, root word, suffix, and spelling rules presented throughout this book are included in the lesson plans found in the Cognate Companion.

SUMMARY

Throughout the chapter, we described the ways that teachers can use the Cognate Companion to locate read-aloud books and create cognate lesson plans that are appropriate for their students. We began by recommending strategies for locating read-aloud books, as well as ways for selecting cognate vocabulary words for instruction. We described the morphological and spelling objectives that can be included in a lesson plan, as well as the context clues to help students guess the meaning of unfamiliar words. Then we introduced a template for designing snap-on cognate lesson plans featuring the Spanish–English cognates found in award-winning picture books. We concluded the chapter by presenting activities that could be used to strengthen the learning of the Spanish–English cognates, including flashcards, sentence completion exercises, context clue activities, and sentence writing.

REFLECTION AND ACTION

1. Review and discuss the sample lesson plan for Pancho Rabbit. How can this sample lesson plan help you create lessons for your students? How might you include cognate vocabulary instruction in your current lessons?

2. Search the Cognate Companion for picture books that you already use. Choose one or two of the books and identify the cognates you could teach and the assessments you could use.

2. Search the Cognate Companion for lesson plans you might use for picture book read-alouds. Select one lesson plan and determine how you might modify it for your students.

8

Designing Content-Area Thematic Units

OBJECTIVES

☐ Explain how teachers can create a content-area thematic unit of instruction using picture books found on the Cognate Companion.

☐ Integrate cognate instruction in a content-area thematic unit that you can use in your classroom.

Cognate Play

Crosswords puzzles are a staple of the elementary school classroom. Cognate puzzles like the bilingual example that follows are especially entertaining for students (and teachers!) because they can be used to reinforce vocabulary in both languages.

Directions: Complete the bilingual crossword puzzle, Animals/*Animales*. For the clues provided in English, write down their Spanish cognates. Likewise, for the clues provided in Spanish, write down the English cognate.

See the footnote on the next page for the answers.

Animals/*Animales*

Down:
1. elephant in Spanish
2. gorilla in Spanish
3. *león en inglés*
5. *rinoceronte en inglés*
7. hyena in Spanish

Across:
4. *tigre en inglés*
6. *jirafa en inglés*
8. *hipopótamo en inglés*
9. leopard in Spanish
10. zebra in Spanish

M any of the topics we have been discussing throughout this book, such as cognate awareness, cognate recognition, cognate generation, and cognate morphology, may be found among state content standards (e.g., the Common Core Standards) for teaching vocabulary. To help teachers meet these standards, we devote this chapter to designing content-area thematic units featuring cognate instruction using the picture books in the Cognate Companion. A thematic unit is a curriculum or set of lesson plans built around a specific topic or theme. In designing thematic units, teachers create a series of integrated lessons on the topic or theme. There are many examples of content-area thematic units across the various grade levels and disciplines. For instance, there are thematic units on butterflies, Dr. Seuss, bodies in outer space, and Groundhog Day. More sophisticated thematic units, such as those on the American Civil War, the solar system, and women's history, can be found in the upper elementary grades.

> **Did you know?**
>
> Teachers can use the Cognate Companion to create thematic units that feature cognate instruction using award-winning picture books.

This chapter showcases content-area thematic units for first through fifth grade that include cognate lesson plans using award-winning picture books and the cognates they contain. Teachers can adapt and use these grade-level units, or create their own.

DESIGNING A CONTENT-AREA THEMATIC UNIT

The first step in designing a content-area thematic unit is to decide upon the theme for instruction. The theme selected should be one that fits with the curricular standards prescribed at the federal, state, and district levels, which include the standards for reading and language arts, mathematics (e.g., Common Core State Standards), social studies (part of English Language Arts and Literacy Standards), and science standards (e.g., the Next Generation Science Standards). Dual language teachers may also want to refer to Strand 3 Instruction within the Guiding Principles for Dual Language Education, third edition (https://www.cal.org/resource-center/publications-products/guiding-principles-3).

Selecting a Topic or Theme

Engaging in the creation of a cognate content-area thematic unit can be an important turning point for teachers who want to help their students improve their vocabulary. Ms. Smith and Ms. Rivers, two monolingual English-speaking second grade teachers who work at different schools, have just attended a workshop on literacy sponsored by their district. Both of them teach the English component in dual language programs. Let's listen in on their conversation:

Ms. Rivers: I wish that just for once, the district would provide us with activities we can use with our bilingual students, like some tips on teaching them vocabulary.

Ms. Smith: Do you ever use cognates in your lessons?

Ms. Rivers: You mean those English words that are the same in Spanish?

Ms. Smith: Yeah, those! Well, I have been teaching with cognates through picture books. I especially like it because it makes it pretty easy to create thematic units. Once I settle upon a topic I want to teach, I go to the Cognate Companion and I search for picture books on the topic. The database provides the grade levels for each book and gives you the list of cognates included in that particular book. Then I choose the cognates I want to teach.

Answers:

Down	Across
1. *elefante*	4. tiger
2. *gorilla*	6. giraffe
3. lion	8. hippopotamus
5. rhinoceros	9. *leopardo*
7. *hiena*	10. *cebra*

Ms. Rivers: So, did you find the picture books and the cognate vocabulary you want to teach for your thematic unit.

Ms. Smith: Not only that! The database also comes with over 300 lesson plans teachers can use to create mini-lessons for your thematic unit. This week, I did a thematic unit on the different variations of the Gingerbread Man folktale. I not only taught the students a lot of Spanish–English cognates, but I also taught them cognate morphology rules and spelling rules for changing words from English to Spanish.

Ms. Rivers: That sounds great! I'd like to observe your class and see how you do it.

> **Did you know?**
>
> Teachers can search the Cognate Companion by topic or theme to find picture books for their classes.

The majority of this chapter shares thematic units that feature cognate lessons designed by teachers we have collaborated with in real-life classrooms. These examples reflect a framework and routine for creating thematic units based on the read-aloud activities for picture books that focus on a central theme. In addition, we describe the design and implementation of grade-level cognate activities to accompany the thematic units.

The thematic units we describe use a set of picture book read-alouds focused on topics found in the elementary school curriculum grades one through five. Specifically, we present thematic units on gardens, the gingerbread man tale, the butterfly life cycle, the lives of scientists, and those of migrant farmworkers. These thematic units weave together the lists of cognates found in the books in the Cognate Companion with the many lesson plans included there to make the teaching of Spanish–English cognate vocabulary, morphology, and spelling rules easier for teachers.

The books, vocabulary words, and activities listed in the tables for this and the other thematic units in the book are only suggestions. The same is true of the scoping and sequencing of the books and the associated activities. We believe that teachers are the best judges of their students' literacy strengths and needs. Therefore, it should ultimately be left up to teachers to decide which books to use in their thematic units and how they will sequence them.

A First-Grade Thematic Unit on Gardens

Among the thematic units that are regularly taught in the first grade are those having a garden theme. Garden units range from the actual growing of a garden to the interactions of the insects and plants typically found there. Since garden themes are common in the early primary grades, there are numerous award-winning picture books dedicated to this subject. It is because of the popularity of garden themes that we followed first grade teacher, Mrs. García, as she developed a unit on the flowers, insects, and animals that can be found in gardens. As noted earlier, Mrs. García is a Spanish–English bilingual teacher who teaches the Spanish language component in a dual language classroom with students from English-speaking, Spanish-speaking, and bilingual homes.

> **Did you know?**
>
> Teachers can search the Cognate Companion for picture books related to gardens.

To create the unit, Mrs. García first consulted the Cognate Companion for books about flowers, insects, and animals usually found in a garden to use as read-alouds. Once she identified the picture books she wanted to use to create the unit, Mrs. García checked to see if the books were available in the school or public libraries. Next, she **scoped and sequenced** the picture books she was able to locate to fit the objectives of the unit. Mrs. García consulted the Cognate Companion to review the cognates contained in each of the selected books. After examining the lists, she chose the cognates she needed for generating the lessons. The picture books and the cognates culled from each of the books and the order in which they were presented are given in Table 8.1.

Scoping and Sequencing the Books

Mrs. García chose to scope and sequence the books from the easiest and most general to the more difficult and most specific. In the table, the cognate vocabulary words are located beneath the titles

Table 8.1. Vocabulary words for Mrs. García's first-grade thematic unit on the garden

Over Under in the Garden	A Seed Is Sleepy	How Groundhog's Garden Grew
Cognate vocabulary	**Cognate vocabulary**	**Cognate vocabulary**
garden/*jardín*	air/*air*	breeze/*brisa*
iris/*iris*	energy/*energía*	delicious/*delicioso*
jacket/*chaqueta*	generous/*generoso*	exclaim/*exclamar*
mosquito/*mosquito*	mountain/*montaña*	fertilizer/*fertilizante*
obedient/*obediente*	photosynthesis/*fotosíntesis*	idea/*idea*
plant/*planta*	temperature/*temperatura*	nectar/*néctar*
rose/*rosa*	**Activities**	**Activities**
yucca/*yuca*	Color the pictures	Flashcards
Activities	Flashcards	Cognate matching
Color the pictures	Word sort	Sentence completion
Flashcards	Cognate matching	Compose sentences in English and
Word search	Sentence completion	Spanish
Cognate matching		

Up in the Garden and Down in the Dirt	Secrets of the Garden: Food Chains and the Food Web in our Backyard	Planting the Wild Garden
Cognate vocabulary		**Cognate vocabulary**
color/*color*	**Cognate vocabulary**	boot/*bota*
insect/*insecto*	connected/*conectado*	family/*familia*
plan/*planear*	different/*diferente*	float/*flotar*
pollen/*polen*	discover/*descubrir*	oval/*óvalo*
secret/*secreto*	nutrient/*nutriente*	pass/*pasar*
tunnel/*túnel*	plant/*planta*	sweater/*suéter*
Activities	tomato/*tomate*	**Activities**
Flashcards	**Activities**	Flashcards
Sentence completion	Flashcards	Sentence completion
Compose sentences in English and Spanish	Sentence completion	Compose sentences in English and Spanish
	Compose sentences in English and Spanish	Cognate spelling bee for unit words
Review cognates for unit test	Unit test: sentence completion for cognate vocabulary	Spelling test
		Compose sentences

of the books. The cognate activities meant to accompany the picture book read-alouds are also presented, as are a few content-area activities. Each of the picture books listed in Table 8.1 has its own lesson plan in the Cognate Companion. Thus, the vocabulary words, related cognate activities, and mini-lessons correspond to those given in the lesson plans.

Mrs. García began her thematic unit with the introductory alphabet book, Over Under in the Garden (Schories, 1996). This book is excellent as an introduction because it presents informative facts and pictures of plants and animals found in gardens. Mrs. García chose cognates that not only pertained to the subject of gardening—garden/*jardín*, iris/*iris*, mosquito/*mosquito*, rose/*rosa,* and yucca/*yuca* but also others she felt her students should know: jacket/*chaqueta* and obedient/*obediente*.

The next book in Mrs. García's series of read-alouds was A Seed Is Sleepy (Aston, 2014). This picture book offered rich illustrations and interesting facts, including the processes by which seeds become plants. Among the cognates selected for study are the Tier Two words energy/*energía* and generous/*generoso*, as well as the Tier Three cognate, photosynthesis/*fotosíntesis*.

After A Seed Is Sleepy, the next three picture books described the processes involved in growing a garden. The most basic of the three was How Groundhog's Garden Grew (Cherry, 2003). It was followed by Up in the Garden and Down in the Dirt (Messner, 2017) and then by Secrets of the Garden: Food Chains and the Food Web in Our Backyard (Zoehfield, 2012).

LESSON PLAN

How Groundhog's
Garden Grew
(Cherry, 2003)

LESSON PLAN

Up in the Garden
and Down in the Dirt
(Messner, 2017)

LESSON PLAN

Secrets of the
Garden: Food Chains
and the Food Web
in Our Backyard
(Zoehfield, 2012)

LESSON PLAN

Planting the Wild
Garden
(Galbraith, 2015)

How Groundhog's Garden Grew provided an especially interesting treatment of how to plant and maintain a garden from the viewpoints of the garden's animals. The picture book contained two cognate pairs specific to the subject of gardens: fertilizer/*fertilizante* and nectar/*néctar*. There were also more general words important for bilingual learners to know—breeze/*brisa*, delicious/*delicioso*, exclaim/*exclamar*, and idea/*idea*.

Up in the Garden and Down in the Dirt (Messner, 2017) relates the story of a grandmother and her granddaughter as they maintain their garden from the time of planting until it is ready to be harvested. The book focuses on what happens to seeds "down in the dirt," where earthworms and insects do their work. It is not surprising, therefore, to find cognates such as insect/*insecto*, pollen/*polen*, and tunnel/*túnel* among the cognate vocabulary words for this book.

Secrets of the Garden: Food Chains and the Food Web in Our Backyard (Zoehfield, 2012) follows a family's activities through the planting process. This picture book included descriptions of the interactions that take place in the garden such as those between animals, insects, and the vegetation; hence, the cognate pairs connected/*conectado* and nutrient/*nutriente*. The "wild" in Planting the Wild Garden (Galbraith, 2015) is what makes this picture book different from the other picture books Mrs. García chose for her read-alouds. In Planting the Wild Garden, Galbraith provides information about what happens to seeds when they are washed away by the rain or when animals transport them from one place to another.

Post-reading Activities

After each read-aloud, Mrs. García and her students discussed the picture books for the main ideas and facts on gardening. Once the contents of each picture book had been discussed, Mrs. García reviewed the cognate vocabulary words in Spanish and English. She especially focused on the words students found most difficult by reviewing them in context. For some books, Mrs. García simply showed the pictures of the vocabulary words in context and provided elaborations of the meanings of the words.

Once the students demonstrated an understanding of the cognates, Mrs. García distributed a worksheet containing the pictures of the animals and plants in the vocabulary list for the students to color and label. This was followed by the flashcard activity in which students cut out their own flashcards, tested themselves and each other, and then stored the cards away in sandwich bags for later review.

Mrs. García also prepared a word search puzzle for her students. The students' task was to find the hidden English cognates for the Spanish words. Finally, to ensure that they had learned the cognate pairs, the students matched the list of English words with their Spanish cognates. If the text had been in Spanish, the students would have been asked to match Spanish words with their English cognates.

Most of the above activities—pictures to color and label, flashcards, and cognate matching—were also included in the activities following the read-aloud for A Seed Is Sleepy. For this picture book, however, Mrs. García had her students sort the vocabulary words in alphabetical order. Additionally, she created a sentence completion worksheet for the cognate vocabulary words to get students to demonstrate their understandings of the words while providing them with practice for using the cognate words in a meaningful way.

The post-reading activities for the next four books (see Table 8.1) included flashcard and sentence completion activities. For these picture books, Mrs. García also had her students write original sentences in English and Spanish with the cognate words.

Then Mrs. Garcia provided her students with a review of the content information and the cognate vocabulary. The students used their flashcards to review the cognates. After the review, she tested her students on the content-area information. She also gave the students a test over the unit's cognate vocabulary in the form of a sentence completion activity, as well as a spelling test. To assess their writing skills, Mrs. García also had the students write sentences in both languages using the cognate words. At the end of the thematic unit, Mrs. García administered a unit test over the Spanish–English cognates, apart from a test of the content. This cognate test included sentence completion exercises, a spelling test, and a sentence composition test.

Second-Grade Thematic Unit on the Folktale *The Gingerbread Man*

Ms. Smith, a monolingual teacher who teaches second grade bilingual learners from Spanish-speaking homes, decided to create a thematic unit on the tale of the Gingerbread Man using picture books. As is often the case with folktales, the Gingerbread Man story is an especially popular one that has been told in several ways with different characters, plots, and outcomes. The school library where Ms. Smith teaches has various versions of the folktale in its collection.

> **Did you know?**
>
> Teachers can search the Cognate Companion for multicultural folktales.

Ms. Smith wanted to teach students the lesson that tales are often repeated in different forms and often with different outcomes. Through the Gingerbread stories, she also wanted to teach students to compare and contrast the different versions of the tale featuring different settings, characters, plots, and, in the case of the Gingerbread stories, refrains. Teachers may recognize this as an example of Common Core standard, CCSS.ELA-Literacy.RL3.9: Compare and contrast the themes, settings, and plots of stories written by the same author about the same or similar characters.

During the planning phase of the Gingerbread Man thematic unit, Ms. Smith checked the Cognate Companion to see how many versions of the folktale were included in the database. Then she visited the school library's online catalog for books on the Gingerbread Man. As luck would have it, six of the seven books in the Cognate Companion were available from the school library.

Scoping and Sequencing the Books

Ms. Smith used the languages in which the picture books were written and the content of the stories to sequence the read-alouds, as shown in Table 8.2. Readers will recall that Ms. Smith is a monolingual English teacher and that most of the bilingual learners in her class are Spanish speakers at different stages of English language development. Since the Gingerbread Boy story is a cumulative tale with much repetition, Ms. Smith confidently decided that she could begin the thematic unit with a read-aloud of the Spanish version of the story, *La tortilla corredora* (Herrera, 2010). Since *La tortilla corredora* would provide her students with the basic schema for the Gingerbread stories, Ms. Smith opted to follow the Spanish book with the bilingual book about a runaway Mexican pig-shaped sweet bread, The Runaway Piggie/*El cochinito fugitivo* (Luna, 2010), which she would read in English. For students who struggled to comprehend what she was reading, Ms. Smith would read those parts in Spanish. Next came the English picture books: The Runaway Tortilla (Kimmel, 2016), The Gingerbread Cowboy (Squires, 2006), The Gingerbread Man on the Loose in the School (Murray, 2011) and The Gingerbread Girl (Ernst, 2006). The sequencing of the books, the cognate vocabulary words, the activities for the unit, and the unit test are presented in Table 8.2.

Each of the picture books used by Ms. Smith has a lesson plan in the Cognate Companion. The vocabulary words and most of the activities she used came directly from there. Like Mrs. García above, Ms. Smith presented the vocabulary words prior to the read-aloud of each story. She also conducted a picture walk before reading each story to support and scaffold the students' background knowledge, which students use to better comprehend the story.

LESSON PLAN

La tortilla corredora
(Herrera, 2010)

LESSON PLAN

The Runaway Piggie/*El cochinito fugitivo*
(Luna, 2010)

LESSON PLAN

The Runaway Tortilla
(Kimmel, 2016)

LESSON PLAN

The Gingerbread Cowboy
(Squires, 2006)

LESSON PLAN

The Gingerbread Girl
(Ernst, 2006)

Table 8.2. Cognate vocabulary words for second-grade thematic unit on the Gingerbread Boy fable

La tortilla corredora	The Runaway Piggie/*El cochinito fugitivo*	The Runaway Tortilla
Cognate vocabulary	**Cognate vocabulary**	**Cognate vocabulary**
escape/*escapar*	coffee/*café*	arroyo/*arroyo*
exclaim/*exclamar*	cross/*cruzar*	cactus/*cactus*
prepare/*preparar*	fresh/*fresco*	canyon/*cañón*
propose/*proponer*	guitar/*guitarra*	confess/*confesar*
save/*salvar*	music/*música*	rock/*roca*
Activities	perfect/*perfecto*	promise/*prometer*
Flashcards	**Activities**	**Activities**
Sentence completion	Flashcards	Flashcards
Compose sentences in English and Spanish	Sentence completion	Sentence completion
	Compose sentences in English and Spanish	Compose sentences in English and Spanish
The Gingerbread Cowboy	**The Gingerbread Man Loose in the School**	**The Gingerbread Girl**
Cognate vocabulary	**Cognate vocabulary**	**Cognate vocabulary**
corral/*corral*	announce/*anunciar*	aroma/*aroma*
coyote/*coyote*	gymnasium/*gimnasio*	attention/*atención*
decide/*decidir*	ingredient/*ingrediente*	fabulous/*fabuloso*
javelina/*jabalí*	mention/*mencionar*	implore/*implorar*
ranch/*rancho*	spectacular/*espectacular*	insist/*insistir*
rodeo/*rodeo*	spy/*espiar*	suggest/*sugerir*
Activities	**Activities**	**Activities**
Flashcards	Flashcards	Flashcards
Sentence completion	Sentence completion	Sentence completion
Compose sentences in English and Spanish	Compose sentences in English and Spanish	Compose sentences in English and Spanish
Review cognates for unit test	Double consonant spelling rule	Double consonant spelling rule
	Unit test: sentence completion for cognate vocabulary	Spelling test
		Compose sentences

Post-reading Activities

Inspection of Table 8.2 reveals the commonalities among the picture books in terms of post-reading activities. For all picture books, there is a flashcard activity, a sentence completion activity, and a writing activity for students to compose sentence in English and Spanish. For the last two picture books in the sequence, The Gingerbread Man on the Loose and The Gingerbread Girl, Ms. Smith added a mini-lesson on the double consonant spelling rule.

As was the case with Mrs. García's unit test, Ms. Smith's test provided for a review of the cognate vocabulary and the mini-lessons learned throughout the unit. Included in the unit test was a sentence completion activity and a writing component that called for students to compose original sentences in English and Spanish. A spelling test was also given for assessing student performance on transforming English words with double consonants to their Spanish cognates.

The various versions of the Gingerbread folktale lent themselves to activities exclusive to picture books that are variations of the same theme. As outlined by Ms. Smith, there were several opportunities with which to compare and contrast the versions of the gingerbread theme. Among the activities for this unit were those that required students to compare the different "Gingerbread" stories in terms of the characters, settings, problems, and solutions. Ms. Smith also had the students create plot timelines, and contrast the refrains from each of the stories.

Third-Grade Thematic Unit on Butterflies

> **LESSON PLAN**
>
> The Butterfly House
> (Flint, 2019)

> **LESSON PLAN**
>
> A Butterfly Is Patient
> (Aston, 2015)

> **LESSON PLAN**
>
> Butterflies in the Garden
> (Lerner, 2002)

> **LESSON PLAN**
>
> It's a Butterfly's Life
> (Kelly, 2007)

> **LESSON PLAN**
>
> What's the Difference between a Butterfly and a Moth?
> (Koontz, 2007)

> **LESSON PLAN**
>
> Nic Bishop: Butterflies and Moths
> (Bishop, 2009)

Mrs. Martínez, a Spanish–English bilingual teacher, chose to create a thematic unit on butterflies in English for her third-grade transitional bilingual classroom. Specifically, she wanted to teach her students about their life cycles, their migrations, and how they differ from moths.

To create the unit, Mrs. Martínez went to the library to search for picture books about butterflies and found many possibilities. She also consulted the Cognate Companion to see if any of the selected library books were included in the database. It turned out that six of the books were in the Cognate Companion database: The Butterfly House (Flint, 2019), A Butterfly Is Patient (Aston, 2015), Butterflies in the Garden (Lerner, 2002), It's a Butterfly's Life (Kelly, 2007), What's the Difference between a Butterfly and a Moth? (Koontz, 2007), and Nic Bishop: Butterflies and Moths (Bishop, 2009). In addition to having all the cognates in each book listed, every one of these books also has a lesson plan in the database.

Scoping and Sequencing the Books

In deciding upon the arrangement of the read-alouds, Mrs. Martínez opted to order the books from the introductory to the more advanced. She began the series with the more general The Butterfly House and ended it with the two more detailed books that compare butterflies and moths, What's the Difference between a Butterfly and a Moth? and Nic Bishop: Butterflies and Moths. The sequencing of the read-alouds, the cognate vocabulary drawn from each picture book, and suggested post-reading activities are presented in Table 8.3.

The Butterfly House is a wonderfully illustrated book that follows the development of the butterfly from the egg to adult. It also provides information on the migration patterns of the monarch butterfly and discusses the differences between butterflies and moths. A Butterfly Is Patient presents information about the butterfly's body and its means of protection and its role in pollination. Butterflies in the Garden delves into the interactions between butterflies and the flowers that coexist in a garden. It's a Butterfly's Life, rated an Outstanding Science Book for Children by the National Science Teachers Association (NSTA), begins with the subject of the metamorphosis of butterflies and ends with a description of butterflies that migrate. What's the Difference between a Butterfly and a Moth? compares and contrasts the life cycles of butterflies and moths through illustrations, while the more advanced Nic Bishop: Butterflies and Moths features lush photographs of these two related insects.

Cognate Activities

Mrs. Martínez brought in pictures of different kinds of butterflies to the classroom to help her students build background knowledge about butterflies. She displayed a map of the world to show the migration patterns of the monarch butterfly and other butterfly species. Mrs. Martínez also conducted picture walks of the books to prime students for listening to the read-aloud. Mrs. Martínez frontloaded the vocabulary by introducing the cognate vocabulary words, one by one, in English (since all of the texts were written in English) and then repeated the vocabulary review with the Spanish words presented first.

Mrs. Martínez selected mainly Tier Two and Tier Three cognate words to teach in her thematic unit. Tier Two words such as absorb/*absorber,* accumulate/*acumular,* distinct/*distinto,* and member/*miembro* can be found throughout the unit. And as one would expect from a unit on the life cycles of animals, the Tier Three science words required explicit instruction: chrysalis/*crisálida,* gland/*glándula,* metamorphosis/*metamorfosis,* and perennial/*perenne.*

Mrs. Martínez used several of the cognate vocabulary words as springboards for cognate morphology lessons. To introduce the idea that there are English cognate prefixes that have

Table 8.3. Cognate vocabulary words for third-grade thematic unit on the butterfly life cycle

The Butterfly House	A Butterfly Is Patient	Butterflies in the Garden
Cognate vocabulary	**Cognate vocabulary**	**Cognate vocabulary**
adaptation/*adaptación*	absorb/*absorber*	certain/*cierto*
appearance/*apariencia*	chrysalis/*crisálida*	common/*común*
comparison/*comparación*	emerge/*emerger*	cosmos/*cosmos*
cycle/*ciclo*	evolution/*evolución*	include/*incluir*
distinctive/*distinto*	patient/*paciente*	member/*miembro*
habitat/*hábitat*	predator/*predador*	perennial/*perenne*
nectar/*néctar*	species/*especies*	petal/*pétalo*
pupa/*pupa*	spectacular/*espectacular*	transplant/*trasplantar*
transformation/*transformación*	**Mini-lesson** Teach root word /-spec-/	**Mini-lesson** Teach prefix /per-/ meaning, "through"
Mini-lesson Teach /-tion/→ /-ción/ suffix ending rule		
It's a Butterfly's Life	**What's the Difference between a Butterfly and a Moth?**	**Nic Bishop: Butterflies and Moths**
Cognate vocabulary	**Cognate vocabulary**	**Cognate vocabulary**
accumulate/*acumular*	adult/*adulto*	camouflage/*camuflaje*
antenna/*antena*	camouflage/*camuflaje*	chemical/*químico*
attack/*atacar*	creature/*criatura*	distinct/*distinto*
attract/*atraer*	metamorphosis/*metamorfosis*	fertilize/*fertilizar*
opposite/*opuesto*	monarch/*monarca*	gland/*glándula*
pattern/*patrón*	nocturnal/*nocturno*	migrate/*emigrar*
pollen/*polen*	thorax/*tórax*	nutrient/*nutriente*
pollution/*polución*	process/*proceso*	sensor/*sensor*
Mini-lesson: Double consonant spelling rule	**Mini-lesson:** Consonant digraph spelling rules	vivid/*vívido*
		Mini-lesson: Context clues to guess the meanings of unfamiliar words
Review cognates for unit test	Unit test: sentence completion for cognate vocabulary; spelling test	Sentence composition in English and Spanish
		Test morphology and spelling rules

Note: All of the picture books included the following activities: flashcards, sentence completion exercises, and the composition of sentences in English and Spanish.

equivalent Spanish cognate prefixes, she incorporated the example of the prefix, /per-/, meaning "through," as in the cognate pair perennial/*perenne* found in Butterflies in the Garden, along with other cognate pairs from the Cognate Companion possessing this prefix—permit/*permitir*, perpetual/*perpetuo*, persist/*persistir*, and perspective/*perspectiva*.

Mrs. Martínez taught the root word, /-spect-/, meaning, "to look," found in spectacular/*espectacular* from A Butterfly Is Patient, to teach the rule, /-spec-/ → /-espec-/ with the cognates specify/*especificar*, spectator/*espectador*, spectrograph/*espectrógrafo*, and spectrum/*espectro*. The root word, /-trac-/ → /-traer-/, observed in attract/*atraer* from the picture book, It's a Butterfly's Life, was also taught through the cognate pairs, contract/*contraer*, distract/*distraer*, extract/*extraer*, and subtract/*sustraer* to support the learning of this rule.

Finally, Mrs. Martínez crafted a /-tion/ → /ción/ suffix mini-lesson using the cognate pair adaptation/*adaptación* and transformation/*transformación* from The Butterfly House. The suffixes were later reinforced by the cognates, evolution/*evolución*, from A Butterfly Is Patient and pollution/*polución* from It's a Butterfly's Life. As further examples of the /-tion/ → /-ción/ rule, Mrs. Martínez included the cognate word pairs, accumulation/*acumulación*, attraction/*atracción*, creation/*creación*, and fertilization/*fertilización* from other books in the Cognate Companion.

In addition to the morphology rules, Mrs. Martínez taught several spelling rules using the cognate vocabulary words drawn from the butterfly books. For example, the entire list of vocabulary words from It's a Butterfly's Life was used to teach the double consonant rule. The consonant digraph spelling rules, "ph" → «f» and "th" → «t», were taught through the cognates metamorphosis/*metamorfosis* and thorax/*tórax* from What's the Difference between a Butterfly and a Moth?

Mrs. Martínez found other examples of these spelling rules to bolster the learning. For the "ph" → «f» rule, she taught the pairs emphasis/*énfasis*, pharmacy/*farmacia*, photography/*fotografía*, and phrase/*frase*. For the "th" → «t» rule, she used hypothesis/*hipótesis*, theory/*teoría*, thermometer/*termómetro*, and thesaurus/*tesauro*. Finally, the cognate pairs, species/*especies* and spectacular/*espectacular*, found in the picture book <u>A Butterfly Is Patient</u>, served to illustrate the "*sp*" → «*esp*» cognate initial sibilant consonant blend rule. Examples such as special/*especial*, spirit/*espíritu*, and sponge/*esponja* were drawn from other picture books in the Cognate Companion to extend the lesson.

For the vocabulary words in <u>Nic Bishop: Butterflies and Moths</u>, Mrs. Martínez presented a mini-lesson on the context clues: antonyms, appositive phrases, definitions, examples, and synonyms. She then had the students consult a dictionary to find a more precise definition.

To assess student performance on the cognate portion of the unit, Mrs. Martínez created a summative sentence completion worksheet and a spelling test including the important cognate vocabulary from the entire unit. She also had her students compose original sentences using the cognates in English and Spanish. To test students on the morphology rules, Mrs. Martínez provided her students with lists of English and Spanish words and asked them to convert these to their Spanish and English cognates respectively. For the cognate spelling rules, double consonant rules, and consonant digraph rules, Mrs. Martínez had her students transform English words to Spanish words, since only English words can be predictably converted to their Spanish cognates. Finally, Mrs. Martinez created context clues exercises for guessing the meanings of unfamiliar words.

Mrs. Martínez utilized some of the general vocabulary activities we described in earlier thematic units for reinforcing the learning of the cognate vocabulary words. These included learning the cognate vocabulary terms, their spellings, and word usage through Spanish–English flashcards, sentence completion exercises, and sentence composition activities in English and Spanish.

Fourth-Grade Thematic Unit on the Biographies of Scientists

Mr. Cuello, a fourth grade bilingual teacher working with Spanish and English speakers in a bilingual classroom, is one of the most inspirational teachers we have worked with. As a teacher who works with students from working class family backgrounds, he continuously encourages them to prepare for college so that they may become professionals, thereby increasing their opportunities for careers of their choosing. Professionals from the community often come to his classroom to deliver motivational speeches on the importance of earning good grades in school and graduating from college. Further evidence of Mr. Cuello's strong beliefs in a college education is provided by the many pennants from the most prestigious universities and colleges that adorn the walls of his cramped portable classroom.

To inspire his students to think about careers in science, Mr. Cuello decided to create a thematic unit on the lives of scientists using picture book read-alouds. Since he firmly believes in teaching Spanish–English cognates to his bilingual students, he included activities that featured cognate vocabulary words as part of the unit. Like the other teachers, Mr. Cuello began his preparation for the thematic unit by consulting the Cognate Companion for picture books on scientists. Having decided upon the books that he felt would be inspirational for his students, Mr. Cuello searched the library's catalogue to see if they had copies of the books.

Scoping and Sequencing the Books

Upon his careful study of the picture books, Mr. Cuello sequenced the biographies in the chronological order of the scientists' lives beginning with Gregor Mendel and ending with the environmental scientists, Jacques Cousteau, Rachel Carson, and Sylvia Earle. In creating his lesson plans for his thematic unit, Mr. Cuello used the Cognate Companion. Since each of the biographies in his thematic unit is included in the Cognate Companion, he selected the cognates he wanted to teach, as well as the mini-lessons to accompany the read-aloud from the individual lessons plans for each book. The sequencing of the books, words, mini-lessons, and activities are presented in Table 8.4.

Mr. Cuello began his unit with the rich, informative biographies of two of the foremost scientists in history: Gregor Mendel: The Friar Who Grew Peas (Bardoe, 2015), and Odd Boy Out: Young Albert Einstein (Brown, 2008). Gregor Mendel: The Friar Who Grew Peas, is the biography of the monk who meticulously experimented with the characteristics of peas and revolutionized the study of genetics. The second book, Odd Boy Out: Young Albert Einstein contains anecdotes from Albert Einstein's quirky childhood.

The third book Mr. Cuello selected, Queen of Physics: How Wu Chien Shiung Helped Unlock the Secrets of the Atom (Robeson, 2019), is the picture book biography of the Chinese-American physicist, Chien-Shiung Wu (1912–1997), who overcame sexism and racial prejudice in the United States to become one of the premier particle physicists in the world.

Table 8.4. Cognate activities for fourth-grade thematic unit on scientists

Gregor Mendel: The Friar Who Grew Peas	Odd Boy Out: Young Albert Einstein	Queen of Physics: How Wu Chien Sung Helped Unlock the Secrets of the Atom
Cognate vocabulary	**Cognate vocabulary**	**Cognate vocabulary**
dominant/*dominante*	brief/*breve*	electricity/*electricidad*
evidence/*evidencia*	cruel/*cruel*	exceptional/*excepcional*
gene/*gen*	frustrate/*frustrar*	explore/*explorar*
generation/*generación*	insist/*insistir*	expression/*expresión*
geneticist/*genetista*	occupy/*ocupar*	hypothesis/*hipótesis*
perpetual/*perpetuo*	phenomenal/*fenomenal*	parity/*paridad*
philosopher/*filósofo*	solitude/*solitud*	physics/*física*
recessive/*recesivo*	theory/*teoría*	prejudice/*prejuicio*
Mini-lesson	**Mini-lesson**	university/*universidad*
Teach root word /-gen-/	Teach spelling rules "ph" → «f» and "th" → «t»	**Mini-lessons**
		Teach suffix rule: /-ity/ → /-idad/
		Teach prefix rule: /ex-/ → /ex-/
The Fantastic Undersea Life of Jacques Cousteau	**Rachel Carson and Her Book That Changed the World**	**Life in the Ocean: The Story of Oceanographer Sylvia Earle**
Cognate vocabulary	**Cognate vocabulary**	**Cognate vocabulary**
accept/*aceptar,*	academic/*académico,*	communication/*comunicación,*
apparatus/*aparato,*	consider/*considerar,*	direction/*dirección,*
create/*crear,*	diagnose/*diagnosticar,*	expedition/*expedición,*
educate/*educar,*	fragrant/*fragante,*	investigation/*investigación,*
fascinate/*fascinar,*	naturalist/*naturalista,*	space/*espacio,*
frigid/*frígido,*	putrid/*podrido,*	spiral/*espiral,*
illuminate/*iluminar,*	refuge/*refugio,*	study/*estudio,*
impose/*imponer,*	territory/*territorio,*	spherical/*esférico*
Mini-lessons	**Mini-lesson**	**Mini-lesson**
Teach suffix rule, /-ate/ → /-ar/	Context clues	Teach initial sibiliant consonant spelling rule: "sp" → «esp» and "st" → «est»
Teach double consonant rule		
Review cognates for unit test	Unit test: sentence completion for cognate vocabulary	Sentence composition
	Spelling test	Test morphology and spelling rules

Note: All of the picture books included the following activities: flashcards, sentence completion exercises, and composition of sentences in English and Spanish.

The lives of three environmental scientists followed next: The Fantastic Undersea Life of Jacques Cousteau (Yaccarino, 2012), Rachel Carson and Her Book That Changed the World (Lawlor, 2014), and Life in the Ocean: The Story of Oceanographer Sylvia Earle (Nivola, 2012). The first of these biographies relates the story of Jacques Cousteau, who as a sickly little boy was encouraged to swim in the ocean. As a result, he developed a desire to study the oceans and fought against the dumping of atomic waste into the seas.

Rachel Carson and Her Book That Changed the World depicts Rachel Carson as a young girl who was so fascinated with the natural world that she became a marine biologist at a time when few girls were working in science. She then proceeded to lead the fight against the use of pesticides in the environment. Although Rachel Carson's life and death preceded those of Cousteau, her placement in Mr. Cuello's schedule of read-alouds permitted a better comparison with the third marine scientist, Sylvia Earle.

In Life in the Ocean: The Story of Oceanographer Sylvia Earle, readers learn about the life story of a young girl who followed her passion for exploring the ocean's depths to become a marine scientist. Earle, like Cousteau and Carson, is notable for her fight against the polluting of oceans and the rapid extinction of sea life.

Cognate Activities

To prime the students for each biography, Mr. Cuello taught his students that scientific theories are often the result of many years of painstaking work. For example, Gregor Mendel conducted his meticulous experiments on peas for seven years to establish his findings on heredity.

When the students were ready for the vocabulary lesson and the read-aloud, Mr. Cuello began as usual by introducing the cognate vocabulary words. He presented the cognate words one by one, asking the students for the word in Spanish that meant the same as the presented English word. After all the cognate pairs had been introduced, he performed the read-aloud.

In addition to being rich in content, Mr. Cuello's biographies also include many Spanish–English cognates, which allowed for the creation of lessons on morphology and spelling. Mr. Cuello used the cognates in Gregor Mendel: The Friar Who Grew Peas to teach the cognates possessing the root word, /-gen-/, found in the words: gene/gen, generation/generación, and geneticist/genetista. He presented a spelling mini-lesson on the consonant digraph rules, "ph" → «f» and "th" → «t» with the cognates, phenomenal/fenomenal and theory/teoría, from the book Odd Boy Out: Young Albert Einstein. He also created a mini-lesson on the suffix rule, /ity/ → /-idad/, and a mini-lesson on the prefix, /ex-/ → /ex-/, using the cognates culled from the Queen of Physics biography of Chien-Shiung Wu.

Mr. Cuello used the cognate vocabulary items drawn from The Fantastic Undersea Life of Jacques Cousteau to teach the double consonant spelling rule. He used the cognate pairs, create/crear, educate/educar, and illuminate/iluminar to teach the word-ending rule, /-ate/ → /-ar/. In addition, Mr. Cuello developed context clues exercises to introduce the cognates in the picture book, Rachel Carson and Her Book That Changed the World. The cognates: space/espacio, spiral/espiral, study/estudio, and spherical/esférico from Life in the Ocean: The Story of Oceanographer Sylvia Earle were used to teach the spelling rule, "sp" → «esp».

Like Mrs. Martínez, Mr. Cuello included a summative sentence completion test, a spelling test, and an activity for creating English and Spanish sentences. As noted below Table 8.4, the flashcard, sentence completion, and sentence writing activities seen in our previous thematic units were included in this unit also. Mr. Cuello's summative unit test for the cognate objectives included a test of the vocabulary words, as well as tests of the morphology and spelling rules taught during the unit.

To assess students on the morphology rules, Mr. Cuello presented his students with lists of English and Spanish words and asked them to convert these to their Spanish and English cognates. Because only English words can be converted to their Spanish cognates using the double consonant and consonant digraph rules, Mr. Cuello presented his students with lists of English words that they were to transform into Spanish words. For testing the initial sibilant consonant rule, he gave them lists of English and Spanish words and had them convert these to their cognates. Finally, Mr. Cuello created activities using context clues to evaluate his students' ability to guess the meanings of unknown words.

Fifth-Grade Unit on Migrant Farmworkers

Ms. Williams, a fifth-grade teacher of English as a second language, wanted to teach her diverse classroom of bilingual learners about the history of migrant farmworkers and their battle for social justice. Like the other teachers we have described, Ms. Williams consulted the Cognate Companion to search for the books she would use for her thematic unit. After finding a few promising ones, she searched the library's catalog to see if they were available. Ms. Williams was able to check out several books on migrant farmworkers, including several that were written about two of the heroes of the labor movement—César Chávez and Dolores Huerta.

Pre-reading Activities

Teachers can prime their students for reading this next group of books by first explaining to them about the difficult lives migrant farmworkers lead as they travel from farm to farm in search of work. Teachers can then introduce the cognate vocabulary words by reminding them that the following pairs of words are cognates, or words that have the same or nearly the same meaning and spelling. Having done so, teachers can proceed to present each English word first, and then ask the students for its cognate pair. They can then prompt the students for the meanings of each cognate pair. When the students do not know the meaning of a cognate pair, teachers can provide them with an informal student friendly definition of the words and examples whenever possible.

Scoping and Sequencing the Books

Ms. Williams chose to start off her unit with the picture book biographies of the leaders of the farmworker movement. She began with a read-aloud of <u>Dolores Huerta: A Hero to Migrant Workers</u> (Warren, 2012), the story of the schoolteacher who became a prominent leader in the farmworkers' movement. She followed this book with the biography of César Chávez: <u>Harvesting Hope: The Story of César Chávez/*Cosechando Esperanza: La historia de César Chávez*</u> (Krull, 2003) and the story depicting the different roles Huerta and Chávez played in the bilingual book, <u>Side by Side: The Story of Dolores Huerta and César Chávez/*Lado a lado: La historia de Dolores Huerta y César Chávez*</u> (Brown, 2010).

Ms. Williams continued with three consecutive bilingual books. The first of these, *La frontera: El viaje con papá/*<u>My Journey with Papa</u> (Mills & Alva, 2018) is the story of a father and son's journey from their farm in Mexico to find work in the United States. On their journey, they are cheated out of their money by the coyote who was hired to take them there. The duo faced other troubles until they were able to send back enough money to Mexico to bring the rest of the family to the United States four years later. Ms. Williams performed the read-aloud of

LESSON PLAN

<u>Dolores Huerta: A Hero to Migrant Workers</u>
(Warren, 2012)

LESSON PLAN

<u>Harvesting Hope: The Story of César Chávez</u>
(Krull, 2003)

LESSON PLAN

<u>Side by Side: The Story of Dolores Huerta and César Chávez/*Lado a lado: La historia de Dolores Huerta y César Chávez*</u>
(Brown, 2010)

LESSON PLAN

La frontera: El viaje con papá/<u>My Journey with Papa</u>
(Mills & Alva, 2018)

LESSON PLAN

The Christmas Gift/
El regalo de Navidad
(Jiménez, 2000)

LESSON PLAN

My Diary from Here
to There/Mi diario de
aquí hasta allá
(Pérez, 2009)

La frontera: El viaje con papá/My Journey with Papa in Spanish. She also had the students learn the vocabulary words in Spanish. The next story in the unit is the sad personal narrative of a young boy who dreams of receiving a red rubber ball for Christmas, The Christmas Gift/*El regalo de Navidad* (Jiménez, 2000). The sequence of books about the migrant farmworkers' experiences ends with My Diary from Here to the There/*Mi diario de aquí hasta allá* (Pérez, 2009), which is told from a young girl's point of view. The sequencing of the picture books, the vocabulary words, activities, mini-lessons, and assessments for this thematic unit are presented in Table 8.5.

Ms. Williams used the six books about the plight of migrant farmworkers to infuse a social justice perspective into the curriculum. Through these picture books, she discussed the issues of oppression, equality, and opportunity related to this historical and still current and relevant topic of immigration.

The choice of books and the scope and sequence of the picture books afforded Ms. Williams the opportunities to teach students history and language arts. The stories of Huerta, Chávez, and the farmworkers are real and need to be learned and understood. The personal narratives of Jiménez and Pérez provide students with contrasting perspectives on their lives as farmworkers' children.

Table 8.5.   Cognate activities for fifth-grade thematic unit on migrant workers

Dolores Huerta: A Hero to Migrant Workers	**Harvesting Hope: The Story of César Chávez**	**Side by Side: The Story of Dolores Huerta and César Chávez**
Cognate vocabulary	**Cognate vocabulary**	**Cognate vocabulary**
decide/*decidir*	association/*asociación*	approval/*aprobación*
fortune/*fortuna*	conflict/*conflicto*	comprehend/*comprender*
invite/*invitar*	dedicate/*dedicar*	cultivate/*cultivar*
organize/*organizar*	entire/*entero*	obtain/*obtener*
predict/*predecir*	justice/*justicia*	politician/*político*
treat/*tratar*	publicity/*publicidad*	salary/*salario*
violence/*violencia*	respond/*responder*	unite/*unirse*
	suspicious/*sospechoso*	
Mini-lessons		**Mini-lessons**
Teach word ending rule /-ence/ → /-encia/	**Mini-lesson**	Teach root word /-tain-/
Teach root word /-orga-/	Context clues	Teach prefix /-com-/
Search dictionaries for etymologies		
***La Frontera: El viaje con papá*/My Journey with Papa**	**The Christmas Gift/*El regalo de Navidad***	**My Diary from Here to There/*Mi diario de aquí hasta allá***
Cognate vocabulary	**Cognate vocabulary**	**Cognate vocabulary**
astute/*astuto*	anxious/*ansioso*	boycott/*boicot*
commence/*comenzar*	fragile/*frágil*	culture/*cultura*
station/*estación*	mend/*remendar*	enormous/*enorme*
state/*estado*	governor/*gobernador*	opportunity/*oportunidad*
function/*funcionar*	nervous/*nervioso*	pack/*empacar*
maintain/*mantener*	north/*norte*	patrol/*patrulla*
solitare/*solitario*	offer/*ofrecer*	recognize/*reconocer*
timid/*tímido*	pure/*puro*	union/*union*
Mini-lessons	**Mini-lesson**	**Mini-lesson**
Teach suffix rule /-ido/ → /-id/	Teach suffix rule /-ous/ → /-oso/	Teach word ending rule /-ity/ → /-idad/
Teach initial sibilant consonant rule		
Review cognates for unit test	Unit test: sentence completion for cognate vocabulary	Sentence composition in English and Spanish
	Spelling test	Test morphology and spelling rules

Note: All of the picture books included the following activities: flashcards, sentence completion exercises, and composition of sentences in English and Spanish.

Pre-reading Activities

Ms. Williams and her students discussed the plight of farmworkers in the United States. They talked about aspects of their difficult lives such as having to leave their home countries to live and work in a country where the dominant culture and language was different from their own. They also talked about the fact that farmworkers worked under oppressive conditions and were paid very little for their hard work.

To pique student interest for the read-aloud, Ms. Williams conducted a picture walk for each book. She then presented the cognate vocabulary words, displaying those that corresponded to the language of the text first, followed by a review of the words in the other language.

Post-reading Activities

Having readied her students for the read-alouds, Ms. Williams read the picture books, discussed their contents, and then moved on to the cognate vocabulary activities and mini-lessons. In the following paragraphs, we discuss the cognate activities and mini-lessons for each of the books in the unit and conclude with a description of the unit tests.

Ms. Williams designed a mini-lesson for the root word, /-orga-/, using cognates such as organize/*organizar*, from <u>Dolores Huerta: A Hero to Migrant Workers</u>. She also created a mini-lesson on the word ending rule, /ence/ → /encia/, around the cognate word pair; violence/*violencia*, from the same picture book. Ms. Williams included an activity requiring students to look up the etymologies of the cognate words.

Ms. Williams used the vocabulary from <u>Harvesting Hope: The Story of César Chávez</u> to teach a mini-lesson on using different types of context clues. For the <u>Side-by-Side</u> picture book, she included a mini-lesson on the root word, /-tain-/, meaning "to hold," as exemplified by the word pair, obtain/*obtener*, and a mini-lesson on the prefix, /com-/, a variant of the prefix, /con-/, meaning "with," as found in the cognates, comprehend/*comprender*.

For the picture book, *La frontera: El viaje con papá*/<u>My Journey with Papa</u>, Ms. Williams provided a mini-lesson on transforming Spanish words to their English cognates using the suffix rule, /*-ido*/=/-id/, as well as a mini-lesson on the initial sibilant consonant spelling rule as exemplified by the cognates, *estación*/station, and *estado*/state. She featured the cognate pairs, anxious/*ancioso* and nervous/*nervioso*, from <u>The Christmas Gift</u>/*El regalo de Navidad* to teach the /-ous/ → /*-oso*/ suffix rule. For the last book in the thematic unit, <u>My Diary from Here to There</u>/*Mi diario de aquí hasta allá,* she created a mini-lesson using the suffix rule, /-ity/ → /*-idad*/.

Readers will recognize the framework for Ms. William's unit test. Like Mrs. Martínez and Mr. Cuello, Ms. Williams included a summative sentence completion test, a spelling test, and an activity for creating English and Spanish sentences in English and Spanish. She also used flashcards, sentence completion exercises, and sentence writing activities. Her summative unit test for the cognate objectives consisted of a test of the vocabulary words, as well as tests of the morphology and spelling rules taught during the unit.

To test students on the various morphology rules, Ms. Williams gave her students lists of English and Spanish words to convert to their respective Spanish and English cognates. Since only English words can be converted to their Spanish cognates using the double consonant and consonant digraph rules, she presented her students with lists of English words that they were to change into Spanish words. For testing the initial sibilant consonant rule, she gave them lists of English and Spanish words and had them convert these to their cognates. Ms. Williams also created context clues exercises for evaluating her students' ability to guess the meanings of unfamiliar words.

SUMMARY

The thematic units we have presented share a common process in their creation. Teachers first decide upon the theme(s) they want to teach. Then, they search for a set of picture books that revolve around these themes. Once the books for the read-alouds have been selected, teachers review the list of cognates in each one of the picture books. Next, teachers scope and sequence the books according to their own criteria and the standards they are following. Then, they plan the content-area activities and select the cognate words that they want to incorporate into their lessons as well as the cognate morphology and spelling rules that will be featured in the thematic unit.

The Cognate Companion is an excellent resource for creating content-area thematic units. To design these thematic units, teachers can use the Cognate Companion to identify the picture books related to the content topic and the cognates they feel are important to teach. Teachers can also consult the Cognate Companion for ready-made lesson plans.

REFLECTION AND ACTION

1   Design a plan for creating a content-area thematic unit on a topic of your choice. Use the Cognate Companion to choose the picture books you will read aloud. Select the cognates for instruction and write down some ideas for the mini-lessons to accompany the read-aloud and the supporting activities you will use to strengthen the learning. Finally, design formative and summative assessments for your thematic unit.

2   Share your thoughts on the merits of integrating cognate instruction into content-area thematic units. What future possibilities can you imagine for your classroom?

9

Designing an Introductory Cognate Unit of Instruction

Cognate Play

Directions: Search the letter soup for the English cognate of each listed Spanish word and write it in the blank. Write down the prefix rule represented by each list.

bienal _____	*producir* _____	*simbiosis* _____
bilateral _____	*progenie* _____	*simetría* _____
binocular _____	*proyectil* _____	*síntoma* _____
prefix = _____	**prefix** = _____	**prefix** = _____

See the footnote on the next page for answers.

```
x y b k h b p p c e
t t i s p i r m s b
c a n y r l o s y i
p z o m o a j y m e
r y c p d t e m b n
g n l o c r t e o i
e k a m e a i t s a
n s r u g l l r i l
y t j c l s e y s q
```

The idea for this chapter came from Mr. Cuello, one of the teachers that we have worked with and who is featured throughout the book. Mr. Cuello identified the need for a cognate-focused unit of instruction that provides opportunities for students to develop some background knowledge on cognates at the beginning and build on that knowledge over the year.

Mr. Cuello:	Hello, Dr. Montelongo.
Dr. Montelongo:	Hi, Mr. Cuello. How are your classes going?
Mr. Cuello:	They're going great. This year has been especially different from years past. For one thing, students never used to seem excited about learning new vocabulary. One of the things I've noticed this year is that they're really into cognates. I mean really excited! They're always pointing out words that are cognates. They shout out things like, "Hey, mister, that's a cognate!" Or, they tell me about some of the cognates that came up in their readings.
Dr. Montelongo:	Wow! That's great to hear. Thanks for letting me know. I'll tell the other authors!
Mr. Cuello:	Just one suggestion.
Dr. Montelongo	What's that?
Mr. Cuello:	You need to have an introductory thematic unit on cognates. Instead of building up the concepts of cognates over several months, you should give students a general overview of cognates at the beginning and then keep reinforcing the concepts throughout the year.
Dr. Montelongo:	Hmm! I think you may have something there, Mr. Cuello. Thanks for the idea!

We (José Montelongo, Anita Hernández, and Roberta Herter) discussed Mr. Cuello's idea among ourselves and agreed that a thematic unit on Spanish–English cognates would be good. As Mr. Cuello suggested, we felt that providing students a general overview of the cognates early instead of giving them bits and pieces here and there might be more productive.

CREATING A THEMATIC UNIT ON SPANISH–ENGLISH COGNATES

In creating the cognate thematic unit, we wanted to impress upon students how important and ubiquitous Spanish–English cognates are. We wanted the students to learn some of the useful terms for discussing cognate vocabulary, word meanings, morphology, and spelling in their two languages. Most important, we wanted them to know that there are rules they can use to convert English words to their Spanish cognates and vice versa, which would increase their vocabulary, foster word consciousness, and strengthen their metalinguistic awareness.

Designing a Fourth-Grade Unit on Cognates

In this section, we describe the processes for creating an introductory thematic unit on cognates. The purpose of the unit is to emphasize for students the ubiquity of cognates and the rule-governed nature of cognate morphology and orthography we have written about in this book. To accomplish this, we first selected the picture books, and then we scoped and sequenced the unit into six sections: Section 1 has introductory lessons on the prevalence of cognates; sections 2 through 4 contain mini-lessons for understanding the rule-governed morphology

---

Answers:

biennial	produce	symbiosis
bilateral	progeny	symmetry
binocular	projectile	symptom
/bi-/	/pro-/	/sym-/

of cognates; and sections 5 and 6 include lessons for understanding the rule-governed orthography of cognates. The books, vocabulary words, mini-lessons, and activities for the thematic unit are presented in Table 9.1.

The Ubiquity of Cognates

For the first lessons on cognates, we wanted students to learn how common and general cognates are. Therefore, we wanted to perform read-alouds of two different picture books that contained cognates from different semantic categories. To find these, we searched the Cognate Companion and reviewed the lists of cognates in individual picture books for the words that would suit this purpose.

Scoping and Sequencing the Books

LESSON PLAN

Crown: An Ode
to the Fresh Cut
(Barnes, 2017)

LESSON PLAN

The Hole Story
of the Doughnut
(Miller, 2016)

Table 9.1 shows the order of the books used in this lesson. The picture book, Crown: An Ode to the Fresh Cut (Barnes, 2017), tells of the uplifting experience young black men have from getting their hair cut. The cognates we selected as vocabulary words were different in frequency of usage and were drawn from diverse semantic categories: attention/*atención,* design/*diseño,* finally/*finalmente,* geography/*geografía,* ode/*oda,* presidential/*presidencial,* protect/*proteger,* and scorpion/*escorpión.* The second book, The Hole Story of the Doughnut (Miller, 2016), relates the story of Hanson Gregory, who claimed to have invented the doughnut in the 1800s. The cognates selected for this story were: appetite/*apetito,* captain/*capitán,* fried/*frito,* indgestion/*indigestión,* invent/*inventor,* legend/*leyenda,* prepare/*preparar,* and satisfied/*satisfecho.* The theme and vocabulary words in The Hole Story of the Doughnut were very different from those in Crown.

The read-alouds for the two picture books were conducted on separate days. For the first book, Crown: An Ode to the Fresh Cut, we asked the students to examine the title and cover illustration to predict what this picture book is about. Most students responded by telling us that the word, "crown," and the expression of pride on the young man's face suggested that the book is about the experience young people have from getting a super-cool haircut. We then presented the students with the eight English cognate vocabulary words and asked the students for their Spanish cognates. This was followed by the read-aloud.

After the read-aloud, we handed out sheets of flashcards for the students to cut out and use for practice. Once we were confident that the students had learned and tested themselves on the cognate pairs, we presented them with a sentence completion activity. To complete the sentences, the students filled in the blanks with the correct vocabulary words. After reviewing their answers, the students were asked to write a sentence in English and Spanish with each of the vocabulary terms.

After students completed the three activities, we discussed the fact that cognates occur at all word frequencies, semantic categories, and parts of speech. Some cognates are common, while others are rare. For example, the word, "attention," is frequent, while the word, "ode," is more specialized. Some cognates can be categorized as animals (scorpion/*escorpión*), while others have to do with safety (protect/*proteger*). Finally, the cognates represented all the different parts of speech: nouns (geography/*geografía*), verbs (commence/*comenzar*), adjectives (presidential/*presidencial*), and adverbs (finally/*finalmente*).

We followed the same procedures for the picture book, The Hole Story of the Doughnut. We began with the question, "Who invented the hole in a donut?" to pique student interest. This was followed by a lively discussion. Finally, we presented the cognate vocabulary words.

The cognate vocabulary words for the Hole Story of the Doughnut also came from different frequency levels, semantic categories, and parts of speech. "Captain," for example, is common, while "mariner" is not. "Fried" is associated with cooking, while "satisfied" is a state of mind. "Indigestion" is a noun, "risk" is a verb, and "frigid" is an adjective. Furthermore, the picture

Table 9.1.   A thematic unit on English–Spanish cognates

Ubiquity of cognates	Cognate prefixes	Cognate root words
1. Crown: An Ode to the Fresh Cut **Cognate vocabulary** attention/*atención* design/*diseño* finally/*finalmente* geography/*geografía* ode/*oda* presidential/*presidencial* protect/*proteger* scorpion/*escorpión* **Activities** Flashcards Sentence completion exercises Compose sentences with each cognate in both English and Spanish **2. The Hole Story of the Doughnut** **Cognate vocabulary** captain/*capitán* fried/*frito* *frigid/frígido* *indigestion/indigestión* *invent/inventar* mariner/*marinero* risk/*arriesgar* satisfied/*satisfecho* **Activities** Flashcards Sentence completion exercises Compose sentences with each cognate in both English and Spanish.	**3. Her Right Foot** /con-/→/con-/ construct/*construir* convince/*convencer* **4. On a Beam of Light: A Story of Albert Einstein** /dis-/→/des-/ disappear/*desaparecer* discover/*descubrir* **5. Lion of the Sky: Haiku for All Seasons** /ex-/→/ex-/ exhale/*exhalar* explode/*explotar* **6. Mario and the Hole in the Sky: How a Chemist Saved Our Planet** /in-/→/in-/ incredible/*increíble* invisible/*invisible* **Activities** Flashcards Sentence completion exercises Compose sentences with each cognate in both English and Spanish.	**7. The Bluest of Blues: Anna Atkins and the First Book of Photography** /-duc-/→/-duc-/ education/*educación* introduce/*introducir* produce/*producir* **8. How to Swallow a Pig** /-jec-/→/-yec-/ inject/*inyectar* project/*proyecto* **9. Hidden Figures: The True Story of Four Black Women and the Space Race** /-naut-/→/-naut-/ aeronautics/*aeronáutica* cosmonaut/*cosmonauta* **10. The Fantastic Ferris Wheel: The Story of Inventor George Ferris** /-spec-/→/-spec-/ spectator/*espectador* spectacular/*spectacular* **Activities** Flashcards Sentence completion exercises Compose sentences with each cognate in both English and Spanish.

Cognate Suffix Rules	Cognate Spelling Rule	Cognate Spelling Rules
11. Marie Curie /-ate/→/-ar/ calculate/*calcular* celebrate/*celebrar* create/*crear* fascinate/*fascinar* graduate/*graduar* excavate/*excavar* exterminate/*exterminar* indicate/*indicar* **Activities** Flashcards Sentence completion exercises Compose sentences with each cognate in both English and Spanish	**12. Away with Words: The Daring Story of Isabella Bird** double consonant rule attention/*atención* buffalo/*búfalo* concession/*concesión* finally/*finalmente* mission/*misión* possibility/*posibilidad* suffer/*sufrir* suggestion/*sugerencia* suppose/*suponer* **Activities** Flashcards Sentence completion exercises Compose sentences with each cognate in both English and Spanish	**13. Someday Is Now: Clara Luper and the 1958 Sit-ins** "sp"→«esp»; "st"→«est»; special/*especial* spice/*especia* spirit/*espíritu* state/*estado* student/*estudiante* **14. Odd Boy Out: Young Albert Einstein** "ph"→«f»; "th"→«t» mathematics/*matemáticas* method/*método* north/*norte* phenomenal/*fenomenal* photon/*fotón* theory/*teoría* **Activities** Flashcards Sentence completion exercises Compose sentences with each cognate in both English and Spanish
Unit Test	Sentence completion Compose sentences in both English and Spanish	Test on cognate morphology Test on cognate orthography

books belong to different genres. Whereas <u>Crown: An Ode to the Fresh Cut</u> is fiction, <u>The Hole Story of the Doughnut</u> is historical fiction. After the read-aloud of <u>The Hole Story</u>, the students cut out the flashcards, studied them, and tested themselves and each other for recall. Then, we presented them with a sheet of sentence completion exercises to test their grasp of the meanings of the cognate vocabulary words. As with <u>Crown</u>, students composed English and Spanish sentences with each cognate vocabulary pair.

After concluding the activities, we discussed the ubiquity and usefulness of cognates. Students were impressed by the range of cognates and with their importance as demonstrated in the following vignette:

Authors: In the last few days, we've read two stories and learned about some of the cognate vocabulary words in those stories. What can you say about the cognate words? Why don't you take out your flashcards and look over the words you have? Do you see any differences between the cognates and other words? Take a few minutes to look over the vocabulary words. Discuss them with the classmates next to you.

(After a few minutes had passed, we queried the students.)

Well, what do you all think?

Daniela: Well, they seem just like all the other words except that you can tell they're similar to Spanish words.

Authors: That's right. Besides being similar to Spanish words, did you all notice anything else about them? For example, are they words that are more frequent or less frequent than the words that don't look like Spanish words? Look over your words again.

Salvador: Not really! Some are pretty common and some I've never heard of. But overall, they seem just like normal words.

Authors: Okay! So, they seem just like other words. Now, are the cognates all from one category? For example, are they all words associated with, say, getting a haircut or baking donuts? Look at your words.

Margaret: No! These words seem like they can be used in any other story. I think that "captain" and "mariner" are related to sailors, but the others don't seem to be from one category.

Authors: Okay, good! Now, are the cognates more of one part of speech than the others? I mean are they more often nouns than adjectives? Or are they more frequently verbs?

Jorge: I don't think so. Looking over the flashcards on my desk, I can see that there are some nouns and some adjectives and some verbs, not just one type.

Authors: Okay! So, they seem to be just like the other words. Not more frequent, not from one category, and not just from one part of speech. And this is true. Cognates are everywhere. You can find some that are very frequent and some that are rare. They come from all categories. You'll find cognates in books on sports, on science, and even in mathematics. Some will be nouns, some will be verbs, adjectives, and adverbs. In the next few days, you will be learning some strategies for recognizing cognates in things you read and, sometimes, in the things you hear.

Cognate Morphology: Prefixes

After the introduction on the ubiquity of cognates, we taught the students some of the morphological rules for prefixes, root words, and suffixes in separate lessons. As was the case with the first two lessons on the prevalence of cognates, we used different books to introduce students to the different morphological rules. Our first topic was cognate prefixes. Our objective was to teach students that certain prefixes are the same or nearly the same in English and Spanish and that it is possible to convert English words to Spanish words and the converse using these prefixes. To do this, we taught students the following rules using English cognate prefixes that were the same or similar to their cognate Spanish prefixes:

/con-/→/con-/

/dis-/→/des-/

/ex-/→/ex-/

/in-/→/in-/.

To find the illustrative words and picture books that contained them, we searched the Cognate Companion. However, it proved difficult to find more than two instances of cognates exemplifying each rule in any one book, so we opted to use two examples from each of four different picture books to teach the rules. We taught the lessons over two days.

Scoping and Sequencing the Books

LESSON PLAN
Her Right Foot (Eggers, 2017)

Table 9.1 above shows the order of the books used in this lesson. It also includes the prefix rule introduced in each book and the cognate pairs that exemplify the rule. For teaching the prefix rule, /con-/→/con-/, which means "with" or "together," we selected Her Right Foot (Eggers, 2017). This picture book focuses on the Statue of Liberty's right foot, which suggests that Lady Liberty is in midstride. The book's author hypothesizes that this was done purposely by the sculptor to show movement as the "shining beacon of hope" for immigrants. The cognate examples for this prefix rule were construct/*construir* and convince/*convencer*. The meanings for these words are:

construct = with + build (to build with)

convince = with + conquest (to overcome with)

LESSON PLAN
On a Beam of Light: A Story of Albert Einstein (Berne, 2013)

"Construct" and "convince" are both Tier Two vocabulary words, and important for the students to know—across content areas.

The second picture book, On a Beam of Light: A Story of Albert Einstein (Berne, 2013) was used to teach the cognate prefix rule, /dis-/→/des/, which means, "do the opposite of." The example cognates we chose to exemplify the rule were disappear/*desaparecer* and discover/*descubrir*, reflecting the etymological meanings:

disappear = do the opposite of appear

discover = do the opposite of cover

LESSON PLAN
Lion of the Sky: Haiku for All Seasons (Salas, 2019)

Both of the cognates, disappear and discover, are Tier Two vocabulary words and are used across content areas.

Lion of the Sky: Haiku for All Seasons (Salas, 2019) presents riddles in haiku poems to celebrate the seasons. The cognate pairs, exhale/*exhalar* and explode/*explotar*, serve as the example words for the prefix rule, /ex-/→/ex-/, which means, "out." The etymological meanings of these words are:

exhale = out + breathe (breathe out)

explode = out + clap (clap out)

LESSON PLAN
Mario and the Hole in the Sky: How a Chemist Saved Our Planet (Rusch, 2019)

One of the meanings of the prefix, /in-/, is "not." To teach the cognate rule, /in-/→/in-/, we performed a read-aloud of the picture book, Mario and the Hole in the Sky: How a Chemist Saved Our Planet (Rusch, 2019). It tells the story of the Mexican chemist, Mario Molina (1943–2020), who won the Nobel prize for his part in discovering the threat to the Earth's ozone layer caused by fluorocarbons. The book contains two words that can be used to teach the /in-/→/in-/ rule: incredible/*increíble* and invisible/*invisible*, that have the etymological meanings:

incredible = (not + credible)

invisible = (not + visible)

Again, both of these are academic vocabulary words.

Post-reading Activities

We followed the same basic procedure in the read-alouds of all the picture books in these lessons as we had in all the read-alouds throughout this book. After the read-aloud of each of the four books, we discussed the readings with the students. After the discussions, we then proceeded to teach the cognate prefix lessons using the two vocabulary words drawn from each book, as well as other examples drawn from other sources.

To strengthen the learning of the prefix regularities, we distributed a cardstock sheet containing the eight cognate vocabulary words after the last of the two-day sessions. The students cut out the flashcards, studied them, and then tested themselves and each other. We also had the students complete a worksheet of sentence completion exercises and had them compose English and Spanish sentences using the vocabulary words. To assess the understanding and application of the prefix rules, we tested the students by presenting them with a list of Spanish cognates and their English definitions. The students were to match the Spanish word with its corresponding definition. We also tested the students by presenting them with a list of English cognates that they had to match with their definitions.

Cognate Morphology: Root Words

<table>
<tr><td>

LESSON PLAN

The Bluest of Blues: Anna Atkins and the First Book of Photography
(Robinson, 2019)

</td></tr>
</table>

For our next morphology lessons, we taught the students about cognate root words. As was the case with the prefix rules, we read four picture books over two days to introduce the root word rules with each book, contributing two cognate examples to the learning of each rule.

Scoping and Sequencing the Books

As shown in Table 9.1, the first read-aloud we performed was The Bluest of Blues: Anna Atkins and the First Book of Photography (Robinson, 2019). Atkins (1799–1871) was the first woman to publish a book on photography. We used her biography as the vehicle for teaching the root word rule, /-duc-/→/-duc-/, where the root word, /-duc-/, means "to lead." The book contains the cognates: education/*educación*, introduce/*introducir*, and produce/*producir*, which we used as examples of the rule.

<table>
<tr><td>

LESSON PLAN

How to Swallow a Pig
(Jenkins and Page, 2015)

</td></tr>
</table>

During the same class period, we also taught the rule, /-jec-/→/-yec-/, where the root word, /-jec-/, means "to throw," using the cognates: inject/*inyectar* and project/*proyecto*. These pairs were culled from the picture book How to Swallow a Pig (Jenkins & Page, 2015), which reveals the skills some animals use to survive in the wild.

<table>
<tr><td>

LESSON PLAN

Hidden Figures: The True Story of Four Black Women and the Space Race
(Shetterly & Freeman, 2018)

</td></tr>
</table>

On the following day, we performed a read-aloud of Hidden Figures: The True Story of Four Black Women and the Space Race (Shetterly & Freeman, 2018), the story of mathematicians at NASA who overcame gender and racial barriers to help make John Glenn's Friendship 7 flight possible. We also selected this book to teach the root word /-naut-/, meaning "related to ships and sailors." The cognate models we used were aeronautics/*aeronáutica* and cosmonaut/*cosmonauta*.

In our final session on cognate root words, we taught the cognate rule for the root word, /-spec-/, which means "to look at" using the cognates spectator/*espectador* and spectacular/*espectacular*. These were taken from The Fantastic Ferris Wheel: The Story of Inventor George Ferris (Kraft, 2015), a picture book on the invention and construction of the Ferris wheel for the 1893 World's Fair and its inventor.

Post-reading Activities

After the two days of read-alouds and mini-lessons on cognate root words, we distributed a set of flashcards printed on cardstock for the students to cut out, review, and test themselves and each other. We also provided students with a sentence completion activity and we had them compose sentences in English and Spanish using the cognate words.

To assess student understanding and their abilities to apply the root word rules, we created a root word transformation assessment parallel to the one used for the learning of the prefix rules. Students were provided with a list made up of English and Spanish words and were asked to match these with their definitions.

Cognate Morphology: Suffixes

Next, we taught students the cognate suffix rule, /-ate/→/-ar/ as an accompaniment to the read-aloud for the picture book, Marie Curie (Demi, 2018), a biography of the great scientist. As we have for most of our mini-lessons, we used the concept induction teaching strategy to teach the cognate suffix rule. We then extended the lesson by including words drawn from other picture book lists contained in the Cognate Companion.

Pre-reading Activities

We began the read-aloud of Marie Curie by asking students if they'd ever heard about Marie Curie. Since most of them hadn't, we provided a brief overview of her life and career, which included receiving the Nobel Prize twice. After the discussion of her life, we introduced the cognates we felt were essential for comprehending the story: calculate/*calcular*, celebrate/*celebrar*, create/*crear*, fascinate/*fascinar*, graduate/*graduar*, excavate/*excavar*, exterminate/*exterminar*, and indicate/*indicar*.

Post-reading Activities

Table 9.1 lists the activities we used to meet our cognate and content area objectives. Once again, we used flashcards and sentence completion activities, and had the students create sentences using the vocabulary words in English and Spanish. For the assessment of the cognate suffix rule, we provided students with a list of infrequent English and Spanish words possessing the appropriate suffix, /-ate/ or /-ar/, and asked them to respond with the corresponding cognate word.

Cognate Orthography: The Double Consonant Rule

For the next lesson, we shifted our focus to introducing students to the orthographic rules for transforming English words containing double consonants to their Spanish cognates. For this lesson, we selected the picture book biography, Away with Words: The Daring Story of Isabella Bird (Mortensen, 2019). The book relates the life story of the British explorer, writer, photographer, and naturalist who wrote of her world travels and of the hospital she founded in India.

Pre-reading Activities

We activated students' interest in the book by discussing the role women were expected to play in Victorian England. After this discussion we introduced nine cognate words from the book that contained a double consonant: attention/*atención*, buffalo/*búfalo*, concession/*concesión*, finally/*finalmente*, mission/*misión*, possibility/*posibilidad*, suffer/*sufrir*, suggestion/*sugerencia*, and suppose/*suponer*.

Post-reading Activities

For the mini-lesson, we used the concept induction teaching strategy. To reinforce the lesson, we had the students cut out and study their flashcards, complete sentence completion exercises, and compose sentences in English and Spanish using the nine vocabulary words. To assess performance, we provided the students with a list of English words and had them transform them into their Spanish cognates. Since the double consonant rule does not work for the converse transformation of Spanish to English, we did not ask students to transform Spanish words to English words.

Cognate Orthography: Initial Sibilant Consonant Blends

On the following day, we taught the spelling rules for initial consonant sibilant blends including "sp"→«*esp*» and "st"→«*est*» and consonant digraphs such as "ph" and "th." We began with a read-aloud of the picture book, Someday Is Now: Clara Luper and the 1958 Sit-Ins (Rhuday-Perkovich, 2018). We provided background information about the civil rights pioneer, Clara Luper, who along with her young children and the NAACP youth council participated in a nonviolent sit-in of the Katz Drug Store in Oklahoma City protesting segregation, more than a year before the more famous Greensboro sit-ins by college students. This book contains five cognates: special/*especial*, spice/*especia*, spirit/*espíritu*, state/*estado*, and student/*estudiante*, which possess initial sibilant consonant blends.

> **LESSON PLAN**
>
> Someday Is Now: Clara Luper and the 1958 Sit-Ins (Rhuday-Perkovich, 2018)

Pre-reading Activities

Before beginning the read-aloud of Someday Is Now, we discussed the segregation practices that were prevalent in portions of the Southern states. Then we talked with the students about racism today. We introduced the spelling rules for the initial sibilant consonant blends found in the cognate vocabulary words: "sp"→«*esp*» and "st"→«*est*.» After the introduction, we performed the read-aloud. A discussion about the sit-in, its ramifications, and Clara Luper, a teacher–activist, followed.

We then gave the students a mini-lesson on the initial sibilant consonant blends as presented in the following vignette:

Authors: We have written the five vocabulary words we introduced earlier on the board. Look at the words carefully. Does anyone see a pattern in these words?

Ricardo: You told us they were cognates when you presented them.

Authors: Yes, we did. But there is still something else about them.

Marisela: Is it that they're spelled almost the same? The difference is that the English words begin with "s" and the Spanish words begin with «*es*». Am I right?

Authors: Yes, you are! Do you know why the Spanish words begin with «*es*»?

Class: Why?

Authors: The reason is that in Spanish you can't begin a word with consonant blends like "sp" and "st." You have to have an «*e*» before them. Because Spanish doesn't allow these

	blends beginning with [s], some Spanish speakers may say "estop" for "stop" and "Espanish" for "Spanish."
Luisa:	Okay, I get it now. So, when you want to spell an English word that begins with "st" or "sp," you have to add an «e» before it in Spanish.
Authors:	Yes, most of the time! And it also works for guessing English words if you know the Spanish words. What do you think the English word is for «*estampida*»? «*Estándar*»?
Adolfo:	Is «*estampida*» "stampede?"
Authors:	Yes, «*estampida*» is "stampede." But overall, it's a good rule to know. Anyway, can we think of a rule for the spelling of words beginning with a consonant blend beginning with "s"? We'll give you a few minutes to come up with one.
Oscar:	I'll try! When you have an English word that begins with a consonant blend starting with "s," you need to add an «e» before it to convert it to a Spanish word. For changing a Spanish word to an English word, you can usually just do the opposite.
Authors:	That was excellent, Oscar! So, let me write it out and you all write it down. "Whenever you have an English cognate that begins with a consonant blend that starts with 's,' you have to add an «e» to the beginning of the consonant blend to get its Spanish cognate. For changing a Spanish cognate beginning with an «es» consonant cluster, drop the «e» for its English cognate."

The mini-lesson went well. We taught the students the initial sibilant consonant rule and we gave them the reason that Spanish words require the «*e*» before the consonant blend. After the mini-lesson, we passed out the flashcards for the five vocabulary words and had the students cut them out and review the vocabulary. Then, we had the students do a short sentence completion activity from the vocabulary in <u>Someday is Now</u>, and had them write English and Spanish sentences with the vocabulary words.

Cognate Orthography: The Consonant Digraphs /ph/ and /th/

LESSON PLAN
<u>Odd Boy Out: Young</u> <u>Albert Einstein</u> (Brown, 2008)

The picture book, a biography of Albert Einstein, <u>Odd Boy Out: Young Albert Einstein</u> (Brown, 2008), was used to introduce the spelling rules for converting English words possessing the consonant digraphs "ph"→«*f*» and "th"→«*t*» to their Spanish cognates. <u>Odd Boy Out</u> contains the following cognates, which contain those particular consonant digraphs: method/*método*, theory/*teoría*, phenomenal/*fenomenal*, and photon/*fotón*.

Pre-reading Activities

We began our introduction to the read-aloud of <u>Odd Boy Out</u> by providing the students with background information on Albert Einstein and a discussion of his remarkable scientific career. We then introduced the four cognate vocabulary words containing the digraphs.

Post-reading Activities

After the read-aloud and a discussion of the book that followed, we presented students with a mini-lesson on the consonant digraphs, "ph" and "th" presented in the vignette below:

Authors:	Boys and girls, we've written the four cognate vocabulary words on the board. What can we say about them?
Herlinda:	I think that the English words are almost the same as the Spanish words, except that those that the English words have "ph" and "th" doesn't.
Authors:	Anything else?

Marilú: Instead of the "ph," the Spanish words have an «*f*», which makes the same sound as the "ph." The words in Spanish have a «*t*» in place of the "th."

Authors: You're right, Marilú! That's what we were looking for. Can anyone think of other words?

Joe: Telephone and thermos. In Spanish, "telephone" is «*teléfono*» and "thermos" is «*termo.*»

Sandra: "Photograph" and «*fotógrafo*». I can't think of one with "th"?

Authors: That's okay! It's hard to think of words sometimes. Another "th" word is "theater" and «*teatro*». Anyway, the important point is that there is a spelling rule for changing English words having "ph" and "th" to their Spanish cognates. Can anyone put that rule into words? We'll write it down as you say it.

Jovita: When you have English cognate words that have "ph" and "th," you can change the "ph" to «*f*» and the "th" to «*t*» to spell their Spanish cognates.

Authors: Thank you, Jovita! That was good.

To reinforce the rule, we had the students cut out and study their flashcards, complete sentence completion exercises, and compose sentences in English and Spanish using the four vocabulary words.

To assess student learning of both spelling rules, the initial consonant sibilant blends rule and the consonant digraph rule, we provided students with a list of English words for students to transform into Spanish. For the initial consonant sibilant blends, students also were given a list of Spanish words and asked to provide the English cognate for these words, which helps students with their spelling knowledge of cognates.

Unit Test for the Cognate Thematic Unit

At the end of the unit, we planned tests for the cognate vocabulary and morphological rules taught. To prepare, we reviewed for two days. We also had the students review their flashcards and went over the morphological and spelling cognate rules.

For the unit test, students worked on sentence completion exercises and wrote a sentence in English and Spanish with the selected cognate words. We also tested the morphological rules for prefixes and root words. We provided a list of definitions that the students had to match with the correct prefix or root word. For the suffix test, we presented students with a list of infrequent words in English and Spanish for which the students had to produce a cognate in Spanish or English. For the spelling rules, students were asked to produce the Spanish cognate of the listed English words.

We have found that this introductory unit on cognates works well for students in grades three and up. The cycle of lessons presented here helps students create a category for Spanish–English cognates in their memory. Upon completion of these lessons, the students had acquired a vocabulary—a metalanguage—they could use for discussing cognate morphology and orthography among themselves. Most important, students learned some of the strategies necessary to discover other cognate rules on their own while developing word consciousness (Manzo & Manzo, 2008).

SUMMARY

The cognate thematic unit was created as an introduction to the activities and Spanish–English rules teachers can use in their classrooms throughout the school year. By introducing the cognate unit at the beginning of the school year, students learned vocabulary terms they could use for discussing the cognates they will encounter in future readings and content-area lessons. As a result of the lessons in the unit test, students developed a sense of the ubiquity and importance of cognates. Additionally, students developed the ability for recognizing cognates and generating new ones through the valuable cognate morphology and cognate spelling rules.

Planning and implementing a cognate unit of study is facilitated through the use of the Cognate Companion. As with the grade-level units, teachers can select the cognate words and sequence their cognate morphology and spelling rules using award-winning picture books all found in the Cognate Companion. Teachers also have the choice of selecting and sequencing the ready-made lessons in the Cognate Companion to create their own unique cognate unit of study to meet the needs of their bilingual learners.

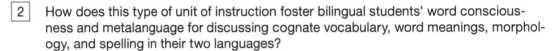

REFLECTION AND ACTION

1   What are the pros and cons of teaching an introductory cognate unit of instruction?

2   How does this type of unit of instruction foster bilingual students' word consciousness and metalanguage for discussing cognate vocabulary, word meanings, morphology, and spelling in their two languages?

References

Association for Library Service to Children (ALSC). (2016). *Pura Belpré Award.* http://www.ala.org/alsc/awardsgrants/bookmedia/belpremedal

Association for Library Service to Children (ALSC). (2016). *Theodor Seuss Geisel Award.* http://www.ala.org/alsc/awardsgrants/bookmedia/geiselaward/geiselabout

Baker, C. (2011). *Foundations of bilingual education and bilingualism.* Multilingual Matters.

Baugh, A., & Cable, T. (2012). *A history of the English language* (6th ed). Pearson.

Beck, I., & McKeown, M. G. (2007). Increasing young low-income children's oral vocabulary repertoires through rich and focused instruction. *The Elementary School Journal, 107,* 251–271.

Beck, I., McKeown, M. G., & Kucan, I. (2002). *Bringing words to life.* Guilford Press.

Beck, I., McKeown, M. G., & Kucan, I. (2008). *Creating robust vocabulary: Frequently asked questions and extended examples.* Guilford Press.

Beeman, K., & Urow, C. (2013). *Teaching for biliteracy: Strengthening bridges between languages.* Caslon.

Bialystok, E. (2001). Metalinguistic aspects of bilingual processing. *Annual Review of Applied Linguistics, 21,* 169–181.

Bialystok, E. (2007). Acquisition of literacy in bilingual children: A framework for research. *Language Learning, 57*(1), 44–77.

Biemiller, A. (2001). *Teaching vocabulary, early, direct, and sequential.* American Educator. http://www.aft.org/periodical/american-educator/spring-2001/teaching-vocabulary

Biemiller, A., & Boote, C. (2006). An effective method for building meaning vocabulary in primary grades. *Journal of Educational Psychology, 98,* 44–62.

Brinton, L., & Arnovick, L. (2006). *The English language: A linguistic history.* Oxford University Press.

Carver, C. (1991). *A history of English in its own words.* HarperCollins.

Consortium of Latin American Studies Programs (CLASP). (2016). *America's Book Award.* http://claspprograms.org/americasaward

Corson, D. (1997). The learning and use of academic English words. *Language Learning, 47,* 671–718.

Coxhead, A. (2000). A new academic word list. *TESOL Quarterly, 34*(2), 213–238.

Cummins, J. (1981). The role of primary language development in promoting educational success for language minority students. In *Schooling and language minority students: A framework* (pp. 16-60). California State Office of Education, Office of Bilingual Bicultural Education. Evaluation and Dissemination and Assessment Center, California State University.

Cummins, J. (2005). A proposal for action: Strategies for recognizing heritage language competence as a learning resource within the mainstream classroom. *The Modern Language Journal, 89,* 585–592.

De Groot, A. M. B., & Keijzer, R. (2000). What is hard to learn is easy to forget: The roles of word concreteness, cognate status, and word frequency in foreign language learning and forgetting. *Language Learning, 50*(1), 1–56.

De Groot, A. M. B., & Nas, G. L. J. (1991). Lexical representation of cognates and noncognates in compound bilinguals. *Journal of Memory and Language, 30,* 90–123.

Dickinson, D. K., & Smith, M. W. (1994). Long-term effects of preschool teachers' book readings on low-income children's vocabulary and story comprehension. *Reading Research Quarterly, 29,* 105–122.

Dutro S., & Moran, C. (2002). Rethinking English language instruction: An architectural approach. In Gilbert Garcia (Ed.), *English learners: Reaching the highest level of English literacy* (pp. 1-44). International Readers Association.

Elley, W. E. (1989). Vocabulary acquisition from listening to stories. *Reading Research Quarterly, 24,* 174–187.

Escamilla, K., Hopewell, S., Butvilofsky, S., Sparrow, W., Soltero-Gonzalez, L., Ruiz-Figueroa, O., & Escamilla, M. (2014). *Biliteracy from the Start: Literacy Squared in action.* Caslon/Brookes Publishing.

Fisher, D., Flood, J., Lapp, D., & Frey, N. (2004). Interactive read-alouds: Is there a common set of implementation practices? *Reading Teacher, 58*(1), 8–17.

Friess, S. (2014). The Jane Addams children's book awards: Toward a peace and justice curriculum. *The New Mexico Journal of Reading, 34*(1), 30–34.

Gómez de Silva, G. (1998). *Breve diccionario etimológico de la lengua española: 10,000 artículos, 1,300 familias de palabras* (2nd ed.). Fondo de Cultura Económica.

Helman, L. (2016). *Literacy development with English learners: Research-based instruction in grades K-6* (2nd ed.). Guilford.

Hernández, A. C. (2001). The expected and unexpected literacy outcomes of bilingual students. *Bilingual Research Journal, 25*(3), 251–276.

Hernández, A. C., & Montelongo, J. A. (2018). Word study with Spanish–English cognates. In Kathy Ganske (Ed.), *Word sorts and more: Sound, pattern, and meaning explorations K-3* (pp. 81–93). Guilford.

Hernández, A. C., Montelongo, J. A., Delgado, R., Holguin, R., & Carmona, L. (2014). Strengthening vocabulary instruction for Latino English learners: Cognate word walls and anchor charts. *New Mexico Journal of Reading, 34*(2), 36–40.

Hernández, A. C., Montelongo, J. A., & Herter, R. J. (2016). Crossing linguistic borders in the classroom: Moving beyond English-only to tap rich linguistic resources. In B. Couture & P. Wojahn (Eds.), *Crossing borders, drawing boundaries: The rhetoric of lines across America* (pp. 93–110). University Utah Press.

Hernández, A. C., Montelongo, J. A., Minjarez, P., & Oblack, A. (2011). English-Spanish cognate phenomena in a fourth-grade classroom. *The New Mexico Journal of Reading, 32*, 7–11.

Hickey, P. J., & Lewis, T. (2013). The common core, English learners, and morphology 101: Unpacking LS.4 for ELLs. *The Language and Literacy Spectrum, 23*, 69–84.

Holmes, J., & Guerra Ramos, R. (1995). False friends and reckless guessers: Observing cognate recognition strategies. In T. Huskins, M. Haunes, J. Coady (Eds.), *Second language reading and vocabulary learning* (pp. 86–108). Ablex.

Hopkins, M. (2012). Arizona's teacher policies and their relationship with English learner instructional practice. *Language Policy, 11*(1), 81–99.

Jane Addams Peace Association. (2016). *Jane Addams children's book award.* http://www.janeaddamspeace .org/jacba/

Jiménez, R. T. (1997). The strategic reading abilities of five low-literacy Latino readers in middle school. *Reading Research Quarterly, 32*, 224–243.

Jiménez, R. T., & Gámez, A. (1996). Literature-based cognitive strategy instruction for middle school Latino students. *Journal of Adolescent and Adult Literacy, 40*, 84–91.

Johnston, M. C. (1941). Spanish-English cognates of high frequency. *Modern Language Journal, 25*, 405–417.

Kindle, K. J. (2009). Vocabulary development during read-alouds: Primary practices. *The Reading Teacher, 63*, 202–211.

Kucan, L. (2012). What is most important to know about vocabulary? *The Reading Teacher, 65*(6), 360–366.

Library of Congress. (n.d.) *WorldCat.* www.worldcat.org

Lubliner, S., & Hiebert, E. H. (2011). An analysis of English-Spanish cognates as a source of general academic language. *Bilingual Research Journal, 34*, 76–93.

Means, T. (2003). *Instant Spanish Vocabulary Builder.* Hippocrene Books.

Moll, L. C., Amanti, C., Neff, D., & Gonzalez, N. (1992). Funds of knowledge for teaching: Using a qualitative approach to connect homes and classrooms. *Theory into Practice, 31*(2), 132–141.

Montelongo, J. A. (2002). *Concept learning and memory for Spanish-English cognates* [Unpublished doctoral dissertation]. New Mexico State University.

Montelongo, J. A. (2010). Library instruction and Spanish-English cognate recognition. *Teacher Librarian, 38*, 32–36.

Montelongo, J. A. (2012). Spanish-English cognates and the Dewey Decimal System. *The California Reader, 45*, 11–16.

Montelongo, J. A. (2013). Online cognate databases for picture book read-alouds to Latino ELLs. *School Library Monthly, 30*, 35–37.

Montelongo, J. A. (2013). The Tomas Rivera Book Award and a cognate database. *The New Mexico Journal of Reading, 34*(1), 35–40.

Montelongo, J. A., Durán, R., & Hernández, A. C. (2013). English-Spanish cognates in picture books: Toward a vocabulary curriculum for Latino ELLs. *Bilingual Research Journal, 36*(2), 244–259.

Montelongo, J. A., Freiss, S., Hernández, A. C., & Herter, R. (2015). Reading the word and the world: Cognates and the Jane Addams Award picture books: Social justice for Latino ELLs. *Learning and Teaching, 8*(1), 5–17.

Montelongo, J. A., & Hernández, A. C. (2007). Reinforcing expository reading and writing skills: A more versatile sentence completion task. *The Reading Teacher, 60*(6), 538–546.

Montelongo, J. A., & Hernández, A. C. (2013). The Teachers' Choices cognate database for K-3 teachers of Latino ELLs. *The Reading Teacher, 67*(3), 187–192.

Montelongo, J. A., Hernández, A. C., Esquivel, J., Serrano-Wall, F., & Goenaga Ruiz de Zuasu, A. (2018). Teaching English-Spanish cognate-recognition strategies through the Américas Book Award-winners and honor picture books. *Journal of Latinos and Education, 17*(4), 300–313. http://dx.doi.org/10.1080/15348431.2017.1348299

Montelongo, J. A., Hernández, A. C., Goenaga, A., Esquivel, J., Serrano-Wall, F., Plaza, M., Madrid, I., & Campos, I., (2015). The cognates in the Beck, McKeown, and Kucan tier two word lists. *New Mexico Journal of Reading, 35*(3), 21–25.

Montelongo, J. A., Hernández, A. C., & Herter, R. J. (2011). Identifying Spanish-English cognates to scaffold instruction for Latino ELs. *The Reading Teacher, 65,* 161–164.

Montelongo, J. A., Hernández, A. C., & Herter, R. J. (2013). A database of the English-Spanish cognates in the California Young Reader Medal Books. *The California Reader, 47*(1), 32–36.

Montelongo, J. A., Hernández, A. C., & Herter, R. J. (2014). English-Spanish cognates and the Pura Belpré children's award books: Reading the word and the world. *Multicultural Perspectives, 16*(3), 170–177.

Montelongo, J. A., Hernández, A. C., Herter, R. J., & Cuello, J. (2011). Using cognates to scaffold context clue strategies for Latino ELs. *The Reading Teacher, 64,* 429–434.

Morgan, H. (2009). Picture book biographies for young children: A way to teach multiple perspectives. *Early Childhood Education Journal, 37,* 219–227.

Nagy, W. E., García, G. E., Durgunogulu, A. Y., & Hancin-Bhatt, B. (1993). Spanish-English bilingual students' use of cognates in English reading. *Journal of Reading Behavior, 25,* 241–258.

Nash, R. (1997). *NTCs dictionary of Spanish cognates thematically organized.* McGraw Hill.

National Council for the Social Studies (NCSS). (2016). *Notable social studies trade books for young people.* http://www.socialstudies.org/notable

National Governors Association Center for Best Practices, Council of Chief State School Officers (2010). *Common core state standards: English language arts.* National Governors Association Center for Best Practices, Council of Chief State School Officers.

National Science Teachers Association of America (NSTA). (2016). *Outstanding science trade books for students K–12.* http://www.nsta.org/publications/ostb/ostb2016.aspx

Real Academia Española. (2002). *Diccionario de la lengua Española de la Real Academia.* Real Academia Española.

Renaissance Learning. (2016). *AR bookfinder.* http://www.arbookfind.com/default.aspx

Side, R. (1990). Phrasal verbs: Sorting them out. *English Language Teaching Journal, 44*(2), 144–152.

Templeton, S. (2012). Teaching and learning morphology: A reflection on generative vocabulary instruction. *Journal of Education, 192*(2/3), 101–107.

Templeton, S., Bear, D., Johnson, F., & Invernizzi, M. (2010). *Vocabulary their way: Word study with middle and secondary students.* Pearson.

Valencia, R. (2010). *Dismantling contemporary deficit thinking: Educational thought practice.* Routledge.

Vozza, H. C. (2018). *Vocabulary strategies and cognate literacy instruction for secondary students: An experimental Spanish-English cognate intervention study* (Order No. 10983806). Available from Dissertations & Theses @ New Mexico State University; ProQuest Dissertations & Theses A&I. (2101486080).

WordReference.com. (n.d.). *Oxford Spanish dictionary.* http://www.wordreference.com/english_spanish_dictionary.asp

Wright, W. (2019). *Foundations for teaching English language learners: Research, policy, and practice.* Caslon.

Children's Literature References

Ahmed, R. (2018). *Mae among the stars*. HarperCollins.

Alarcón, F. (2008). *In animal poems of the iguazú/Animalario de iguazú*. Children's Book Press.

Alarcón, F. (2011). *Poems to dream together*. Lee & Low Books.

Anderson, B. (2020). *Lizzy demands a seat: Elizabeth Jennings fights for streetcar rights*. Calkins Creek.

Aston, D. (2014). *A seed is sleepy*. Chronicle Books.

Aston, D. (2015). *A butterfly is patient*. Chronicle Books.

Bardoe, C. (2015). *Gregor Mendel: The friar who grew peas*. Abrams Books for Young Readers.

Bardoe, C. (2018). *Nothing stopped Sophie: The story of the unshakable mathematician Sophie Germain*. Little, Brown Books for Young Readers.

Barnes, D. (2017). *Crown: An ode to the fresh cut*. Agate Bolden.

Berne, J. (2013). *On a Beam of Light: A Story of Albert Einstein*. Chronicle Books.

Bishop, N. (2009). *Nic Bishop: Butterflies and moths*. Scholastic Nonfiction.

Brown, D. (2008). *Odd boy out: Young Albert Einstein*. Clarion Books.

Brown, M. (2010). *Side by side: The story of Dolores Huerta and César Chávez/Lado a lado: La historia de Dolores Huerta y César Chávez*. HarperCollins Español.

Browne, M. (2020). *Woke: A young poet's call to justice*. Roaring Brook Press.

Cherry, L. (2003). *How groundhog's garden grew*. Blue Sky Press.

Chin-Lee, C. & de la Peña, T. (1999). *A is for the Américas*. Orchard Books.

Christensen, B. (2012). *I, Galileo*. Knopf Books for Young Readers.

Clinton, C. (2017). *She persisted: 13 American women who changed the world*. Philomel Books.

Davies, N. (2016). *Tiny creatures: The world of microbes*. Candlewick.

Davies, N. (2020). *Grow: Secrets of our DNA*. Candlewick.

Demi. (2018). *Marie Curie*. Henry Holt and Co.

Denise, A. (2019). *Planting stories: The life of librarian and storyteller Pura Belpre*. HarperCollins.

Dobell, D. (2020). *The world of whales: Get to know the giants of the ocean*. Little Gestalten.

Drummond, A. (2017). *Pedal power: How one community became the bicycle capital of the world*. Farrar, Straus and Giroux.

Eggers, D. (2017). *Her right foot*. Chronicle Books.

English, K. (2005). *Speak English for us Marisol*. Albert Whitman & Co.

Ernst, L. (2006). *The gingerbread girl*. Dutton Books for Young Readers.

Ferris, J. (2015). *Noah Webster and his words*. Clarion Books.

Flint, K. (2019). *The Butterfly House*. Frances Lincoln Children's Books.

Franklin, A. (2019). *Not quite Snow White*. HarperCollins.

Galbraith, K. (2015). *Planting the wild garden*. Peachtree Publishing Company.

Goodman, S. (2016). *The first step: How one girl put segregation on trial*. Bloomsbury USA Childrens.

Heling, K. (2019). *Clothesline clues to the first day of school*. Charlesbridge.

Henkes, K. (2006). *Lily's purple plastic purse*. Greenwillow Books.

Herrera, L. (2010). *La tortilla corredora*. Ediciones Ekaré.

Jenkins, S., & Page, R. (2015). *How to swallow a pig*. HMH Books for Young Readers.

Jiménez, F. (2000). *The Christmas gift/ El regalo de Navidad*. HMH Books for Young Readers.

Kelly, I. (2007). *It's a butterfly's life*. Scholastic Inc.

Kimmel, E. (2016). *The runaway tortilla*. WestWinds Press.

Koontz, R. (2007). *What's the difference between a butterfly and a moth?* Picture Window Books.

Kraft, B. (2015). *The fantastic Ferris wheel: The story of inventor George Ferris*. Henry Holt and Co.

Krull, K. (2003). *Harvesting hope: The story of César Chávez*. HMH Books for Young Readers.

Krull, K. (2014). *The story of Philo Farnsworth*. Dragonfly Books.

Krull, K. (2021). *No truth without Ruth: The life of Ruth Bader Ginsburg*. Quill Tree Book.

Lactman, O. D. (1995). *Pepita speaks twice*. Arte Publico Press.

Lasky, K. (1994). *The librarian who measured the earth*. Little Brown Books.

Lawlor, L. (2014). *Rachel Carson and her book that changed the world.* Holiday House.

Lerner, C. (2002). *Butterflies in the garden.* HarperCollins.

Levinson, C. (2017). *The youngest marcher: The story of Audrey Faye Hendricks, a young civil rights activist.* Atheneum Books for Young Readers.

Lomas-Garza, C. (1999). *Magic windows/Ventanas mágicas.* Children's Book Press.

Lukoff, K. (2019). *When Aidan became a brother.* Lee & Low Books.

Luna, J. (2010). *The runaway piggie/El cochinito fugitivo.* Piñata Books.

Maillard, K. N. (2019). *Fry Bread: A Native American family story.* Roaring Book Press.

McCully, E. (2007). *The escape of Oney Judge: Martha Washington's slave finds freedom.* Farrar.

Messner, K. (2017). *Up in the garden and down in the dirt.* Chronicle Books.

Miller, D. (2003). *Are trees alive?* Bloomsbury USA Childrens.

Miller, P. (2016). *The hole story of the doughnut.* Clarion Books.

Mortensen, L. (2019). *Away with words: The daring story of Isabella Bird.* Peachtree Publishing Company.

Most, B. (2003). *The cat that went oink.* HMH Books for Young Readers.

Muñoz Ryan, P. (1996). *The Crayon counting book.* Charlesbridge.

Muñoz Ryan, P. (2002). *When Marian sang: The true recital of Marian Anderson.* Scholastic.

Murray, L. (2011). *The Gingerbread Man on the loose in the school.* G.P. Putnam's Sons Books for Young Readers.

Myers, W. (2021). *Frederick Douglas: The lion who wrote history.* Quill Tree Books.

Nivola, C. (2012). *Life in the ocean: The story of oceanographer Sylvia Earle.* Farrar.

Pattison, D. (2019). *Darwin's 130-year predication.* Mims House.

Pérez, A. (2009). *My diary from here to there/Mi diario de aquí hasta allá.* Children's Book Press.

Pinkney, A. (2010). *Sit-in: How four friends stood up by sitting down.* Little, Brown Books for Young Readers.

Rappaport, D. (2020). *Ruth objects: The life of Ruth Bader Ginsburg.* Little, Brown Books for Young Readers.

Rhuday-Perkovich, O. (2018). *Someday is now: Clara Luper and the 1958 sit-ins.* Seagrass Press.

Robinson, F. (2016). *Ada's ideas: The story of the first computer programmer.* Abrams Books for Young Readers.

Robinson, F. (2019). *The bluest of blues: Anna Atkins and the first book of photography.* Abrams Books for Young Readers.

Rockwell, A. (2015). *Bugs are insects.* HarperCollins.

Roth, S., & Trumbore, C. (2018). *The mangrove tree: Planting trees to feed families.* Lee & Low Books.

Roy, K. (2017). *How to be an elephant.* David Macaulay Studio.

Rusch, E. (2019). *Mario and the hole in the sky: How a chemist saved our planet.* Charlesbridge.

Salas, L. (2019). *Lion of the sky: Haiku for all seasons.* Millbrook Press.

Schories, P. (1996). *Over under in the garden.* Farrar Straus & Giroux.

Seluk, N. (2018). *The sun is kind of a big deal.* Orchard Books.

Shetterly, M., & Freeman, L. (2018). *Hidden figures: The true story of four black women and the space race.* HarperCollins.

Siy, A. (2011). *Bug shots: The good, the bad, and the bugly.* Holiday House.

Skármeta, A. (2003). *The composition.* Groundwood Books.

Squires, J. (2006). *The gingerbread cowboy.* Scholastic.

Steig, W. (1969). *Sylvester and the magic pebble.* Simon & Schuster Books for Young Reader.

Tonatiuh, D. (2013). *Pancho rabbit and the coyote: A migrant's tale.* Harry N. Abrams.

Tonatiuh, D. (2017). *Danza!: Amalia Hernández and El Ballet Folklórico de México.* Harry N. Abrams.

Warren, S. (2012). *Dolores Huerta: A hero to migrant workers.* Two Lions.

Winter, J. (2019) *Thurgood.* Anne Schwartz Books.

Yaccarino, D. (2012). *The fantastic undersea life of Jacques Cousteau.* Dragonfly Books.

Zoehfeld, K. (2012). *Secrets of the garden: Food chains and the food web in our backyard.* Dragonfly Books.

Glossary

Academic vocabulary. Words used in academic subjects and in formal school contexts, which include teacher dialogues in classrooms, and sophisticated Tier 2 and Tier 3 vocabulary found in content area textbooks.

Bilingual, bilingualism. Knowledge of two languages, which can include listening and speaking, but can also refer to an individual's reading and writing skills in two languages. There are varying degrees of bilingualism.

Bilingual learners. Students who use two languages in their everyday lives and draw on both of those languages for learning in English-medium and bilingual contexts. This includes students from Spanish-speaking homes who are learning English as a new language at school, simultaneous bilinguals who have used both languages since early childhood, and students from English-speaking homes who are learning Spanish in dual language programs.

Biliteracy. The ability to read and write in two languages.

Concept induction. A form of indirect learning by using a guided approach to teaching, such as the use of questions to facilitate a student to acquire a new skill, concept, or process.

Cognates. Words in two languages that: 1) share the same meaning, 2) have identical or similar spelling, and 3) share the same etymology.

Cognate recognition skills. Ability to perceive cognate vocabulary while listening, speaking, reading, and writing.

Cognate generation skills. Ability to guess at the meaning of an unfamiliar word and produce its cognate in speaking or writing.

Context clues. In reading, hints about the meaning of an unknown word from surrounding text.

Context clues strategies. Skill or plan to problem-solve the meaning of an unknown word by using familiar words near the unknown words as clues. Context clue strategies include the use of synonyms, antonyms, personal experiences, appositive words or phrases, punctuation clues (parentheses) or boldface type, and definitions of terms mediated by the different forms of the verb *to be* (is, was, were . . .).

Dual language classrooms. Classrooms that use two languages for official purposes across content areas where the goal is bilingualism and biliteracy. There are various models of dual language classrooms. There are classrooms that start with 90% Spanish and 10% English and by fourth grade move to 50% Spanish and 50% English. There are 50–50 dual language classrooms, which maintain 50% Spanish and 50% English throughout the grade levels. Some programs use other primary languages such as Mandarin, Japanese, or Portuguese.

English learners (ELs) or English language learners (ELLs). Official designation for students who are acquiring English as a new (second or third, additional) language.

English–Spanish cognates.   Words that are spelled identically or similarly in English and Spanish and possess the same or nearly the same meanings in both languages as a result of a shared **etymology**—the origin of a word and the historical development of its meaning.

ESL.   The acronym for English as a second language, used to identify programs, classes, and teachers for students who are officially designated as in need of learning to speak, read, and write English.

Etymology.   The study of word origins and its changes in meaning throughout its history. Dictionaries contain the etymology or origin of the word. Many academic English words originated from the Latin and Greek languages. Spanish is a Latinate language, which means many of its words originated from Latin.

Home–school connection.   An activity or task that involves the child and family meaningfully and collaboratively in the child's education. In some cases, the child consults with the family to find out about funds of knowledge, or sources of linguistic and cultural knowledge found in home and community practices that can be used for school learning.

Heuristic.   An approach to problem solving, to figure out how to learn on one's own or how to use a model to learn a new concept or process.

Metalinguistic awareness.   Ability to think about language and its patterns (Bialystok, 2001).

Morphology.   In linguistics, it is the study of the structure and meaning of words and word parts. Prefixes, root words, and suffixes are parts of words or morphemes that carry meaning and combine to make new words.

Opportunity gap.   Recognition that not all individuals are born with the same resources and opportunities and hence a discrepancy in life chances and school achievement are evident. See Carter and Welner (2013).

Prefix.   In linguistics, a word part found in front of a root word and that carries meaning. For example, "bi-" means two, in such words as "bicycle" and "bilingual" in English. There are a number of cognate prefixes, such as /bi-/ in English is also /bi-/ in Spanish, in such cognate pairs as bicycle/*bicicleta*, and bilingual/*bilingüe*.

Root word.   In linguistics, it is the basic part of a word that carries meaning. A root word has no affixes (prefixes or suffixes). For example, the root word "-ceed-," which means to move forward in English, is the same as «-*ceder*-» in Spanish, as in the cognate pair proceed/*proceder*.

Scope and sequence.   In textbooks, the scope is the organization of the concepts, topics, and skills. The sequence is the order in which those concepts, topics, and skills are presented.

Snap-on cognate lesson plan.   A brief cognate lesson plan to accompany an award-winning picture book that can be integrated into content-area instruction. Each snap-on lesson plan includes cognate objectives, activities, and assessments.

Suffix.   In linguistics, a word part attached to the end of root words and that carries meaning. For example, "ly-" forms adverbs from adjectives, such as "finally," "regularly," and "absolutely." There are a large number of cognate suffixes using /-ly/ in English is /-mente/ in Spanish in such words as finally/*finalmente*; regularly/*regularmente*; and absolutely/*absolutamente*.

TESOL.   The acronym for Teaching English to Students of Other Languages. The acronym is used to identify the international organization as well as types of programs for students who are learning English.

Tier One words.   High-frequency words such as "book," "red," and "apple" in English that rarely require teacher instruction as to their meanings. The majority of these most frequent words are Old English in origin and are usually not English–Spanish cognates.

Tier Two words.   Vocabulary words that 1) are not ordinarily used or heard in everyday language; 2) appear across a variety of content areas; 3) are important for understanding content-area textbooks; and 4) allow for rich representations and connections to other words (Kucan, 2012). Most of these Tier 2 words are cognates derived from Latin, as in the cognate pairs analyze/ *analizar* and factor/*factor*. The Coxhead Academic Words are Tier 2 and many are also cognates.

Tier Three words.   Vocabulary words that are used for particular topics in specific disciplines: "oligarchy" (social studies), "pollen" (biology), and "rhomboid" (geometry). Tier 3 words can be explicitly taught when their meanings are necessary for understanding a particular discipline-specific text. Most Tier 3 words are Spanish–English cognates, as in the cognate pairs oligarchy/ *oligarquía*, pollen/*polen*, and rhomboid/*rhomboidal*.

Index

Page numbers followed by *f* and *t* indicate figures and tables, respectively.